30-Minute
Watercolor Animals

Create Beautiful Beginner-Friendly
Paintings in No Time at All

Kiley Busko

Creator of Painted Wing

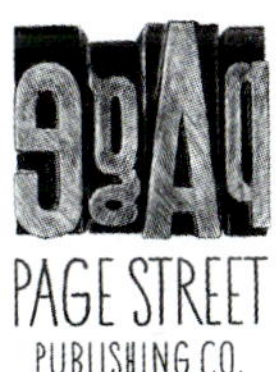

PAGE STREET
PUBLISHING CO.

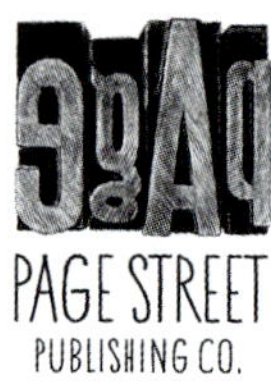

PAGE STREET
PUBLISHING CO.

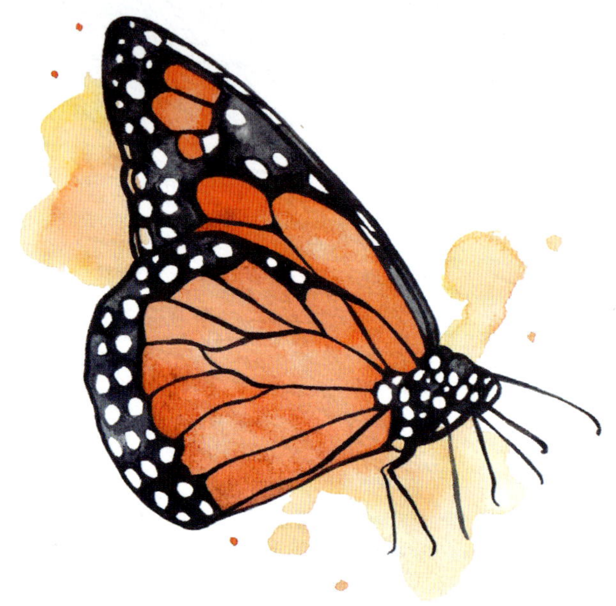

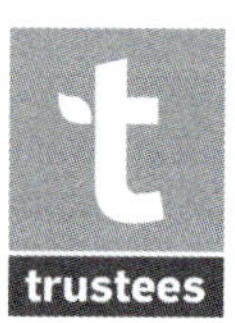

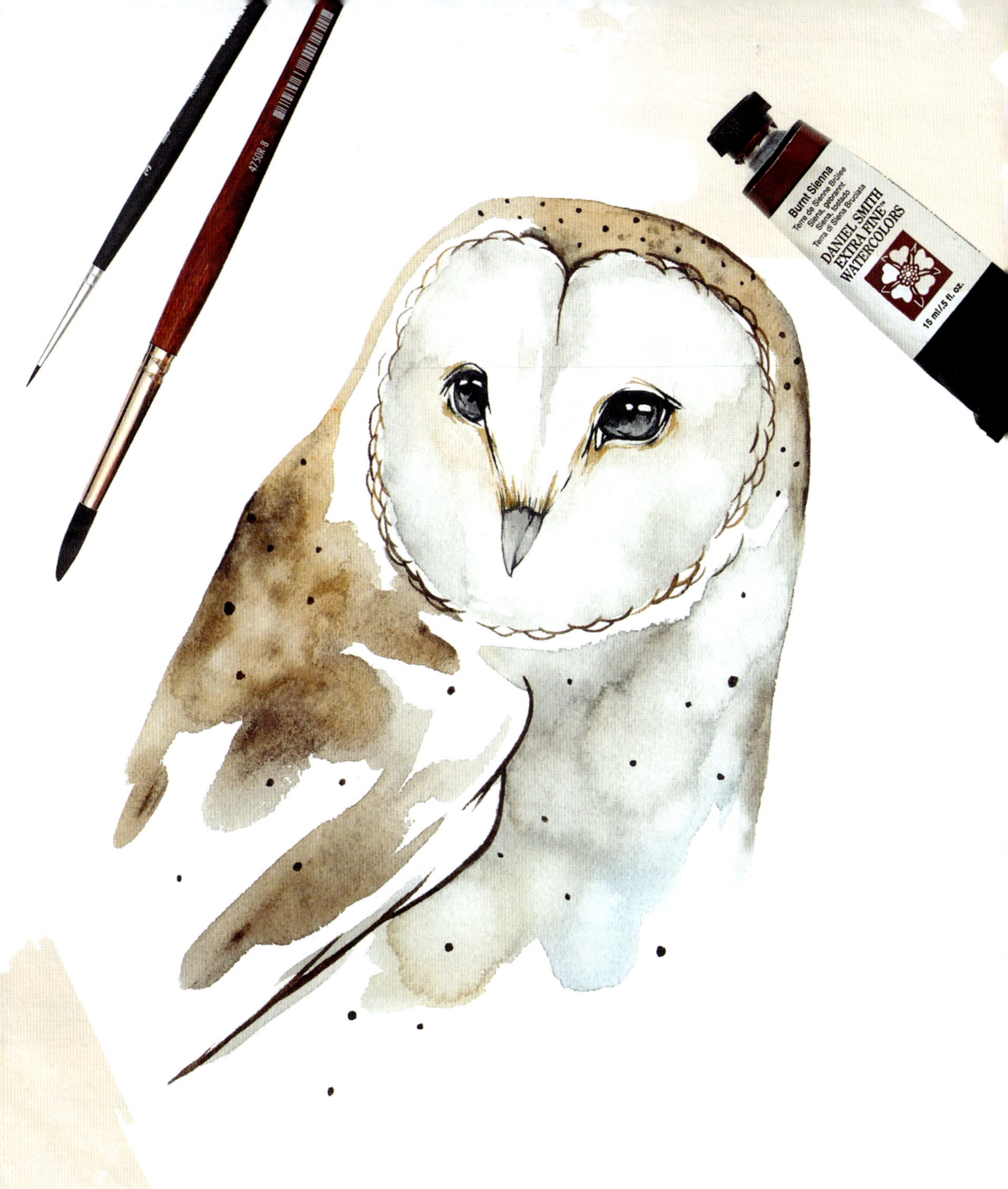

To the creative souls longing for their next adventure

Contents

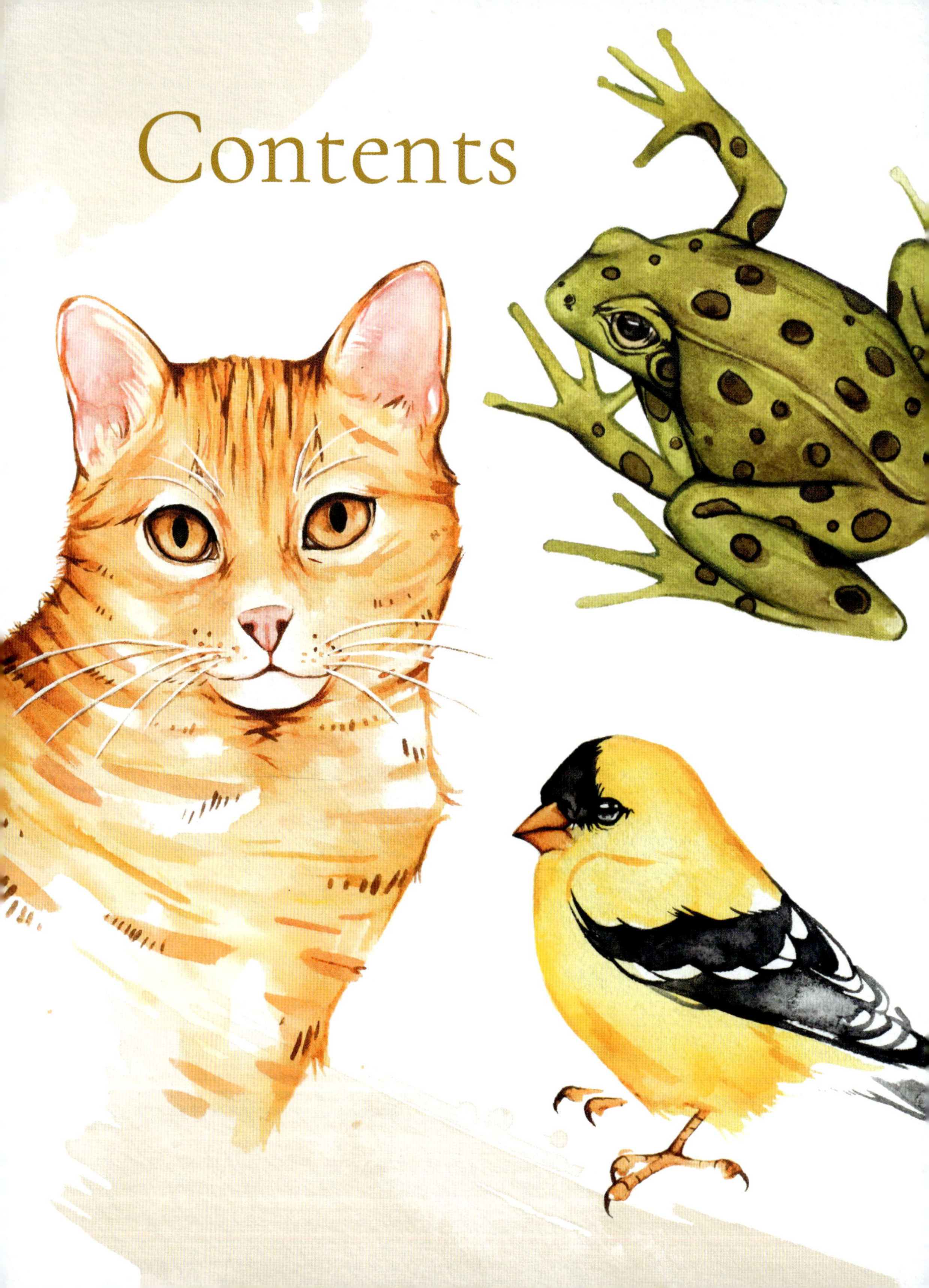

Introduction

I originally discovered my love of watercolor painting in high school art classes. I became sort of obsessed; I remember squeezing in painting sessions after school before heading off to my part-time cleaning job. While dusting cubicles and mopping bathrooms, I would often daydream about being a full-time artist someday. But after graduating college and working my first full-time job, I struggled to fit creativity into my daily schedule, and the longer I went without making art, the more difficult it was to start again.

Then one day, I decided to take a walk around my new neighborhood. I had been living in an industrial area of the city, surrounded by concrete, warehouses and noisy machinery, so what I stumbled upon surprised me. Behind a nearby baseball field next to the river, a bunch of pterodactyl-looking creatures were high up in their nests. They had long, slender necks and expansive wings: great blue herons. While watching them collect sticks for their nests and feed their begging young, I began to wonder how many other species of birds lived in my neighborhood without me ever noticing.

Shortly after this experience, I started spending more time out in nature going for hikes. As I was learning how to identify birds by their calls and colorations, I had the sudden desire to paint them. I hadn't picked up a paint brush in a few years, but I couldn't wait to get started again. I dusted off some unopened watercolor supplies and my new journey began.

I am excited to share my love of animals and of painting with watercolors with you, whether you are completely new to painting or just looking to try out a different approach. This book will guide you on how to create unique animal portraits in as little as 30 minutes, so that no matter how busy your schedule may be, you can carve out a little bit of time to paint. The projects are meant to be completed fairly quickly. By limiting the time it takes to complete each project, it will prevent you from over-working your watercolors and help you to let go and allow the paints to work their magic.

This book is perfect if you are a beginner because each project comes with a drawing template, so you can focus on jumping right in and exploring the possibilities of watercolors. If you want to challenge yourself or add your own twist to the project, feel free to forgo the templates or add on to them. In the first section of this book, you will learn watercolor basics by painting smaller, more detailed paintings, and then as you learn skills and gain confidence, the projects will become looser and more impressionistic.

I am happy you picked up this book and hope you are ready to get started. By setting aside just 30 minutes of your day, you will learn many different techniques on how to create expressive and beautiful animal paintings. I hope you will not only learn to appreciate the unpredictable yet fascinating nature of watercolors but also gain a greater appreciation for animals like the ones found in this book.

Getting Started

Gather Your Supplies

Before you get started painting, you will want to make sure you have all the right supplies. Remember these supplies are just recommendations and if you don't have the exact materials I have, that is okay! You do not need the most expensive materials or a whole bunch of them in order to start painting. When I first started painting with watercolors, I only used two brushes and a basic set of watercolor paints.

Paints

Most of the paints I am using for this book are by the brand Daniel Smith Inc., but there are many other options out there. I prefer using paints that come in a tube, but you can also use pans if you like. For this book, you will be using a pretty limited color palette, mostly made up of earth tones and some blues and greens. Below are swatches of every color used in this book. If you don't have the exact paint color, you can find something similar or mix your own color.

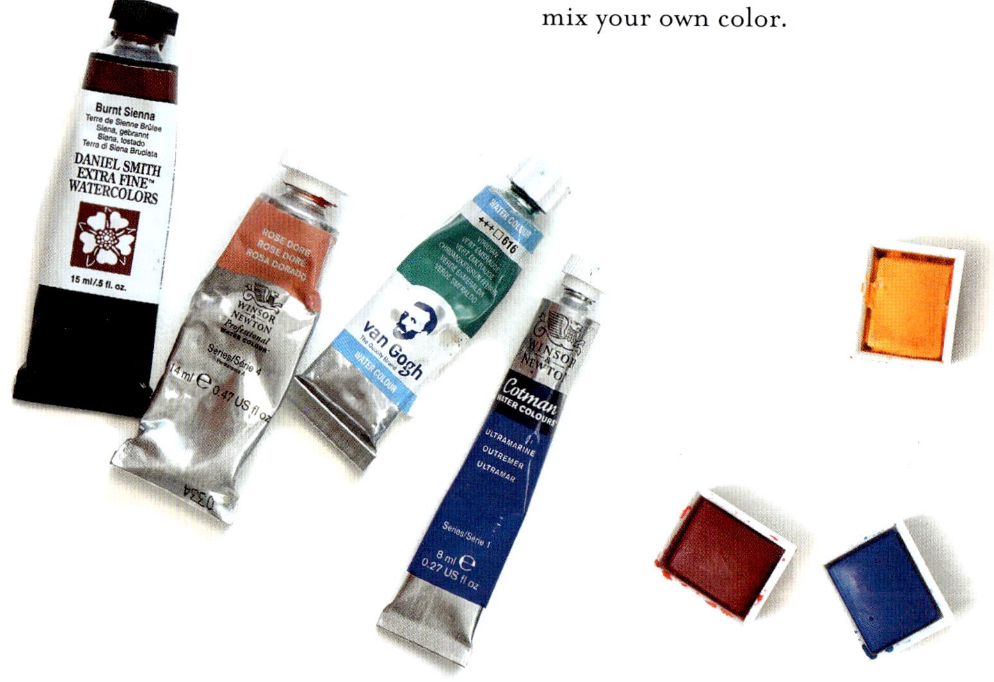

Below are all of the paint colors used in this book: Raw Umber, Burnt Umber, Burnt Sienna, Yellow Ochre, Cadmium Yellow Medium Hue, Payne's Gray, Prussian Blue, Cobalt Blue, Cascade Green, Olive Green, Cadmium Orange Hue, Cadmium Red Medium Hue, Rose Doré.

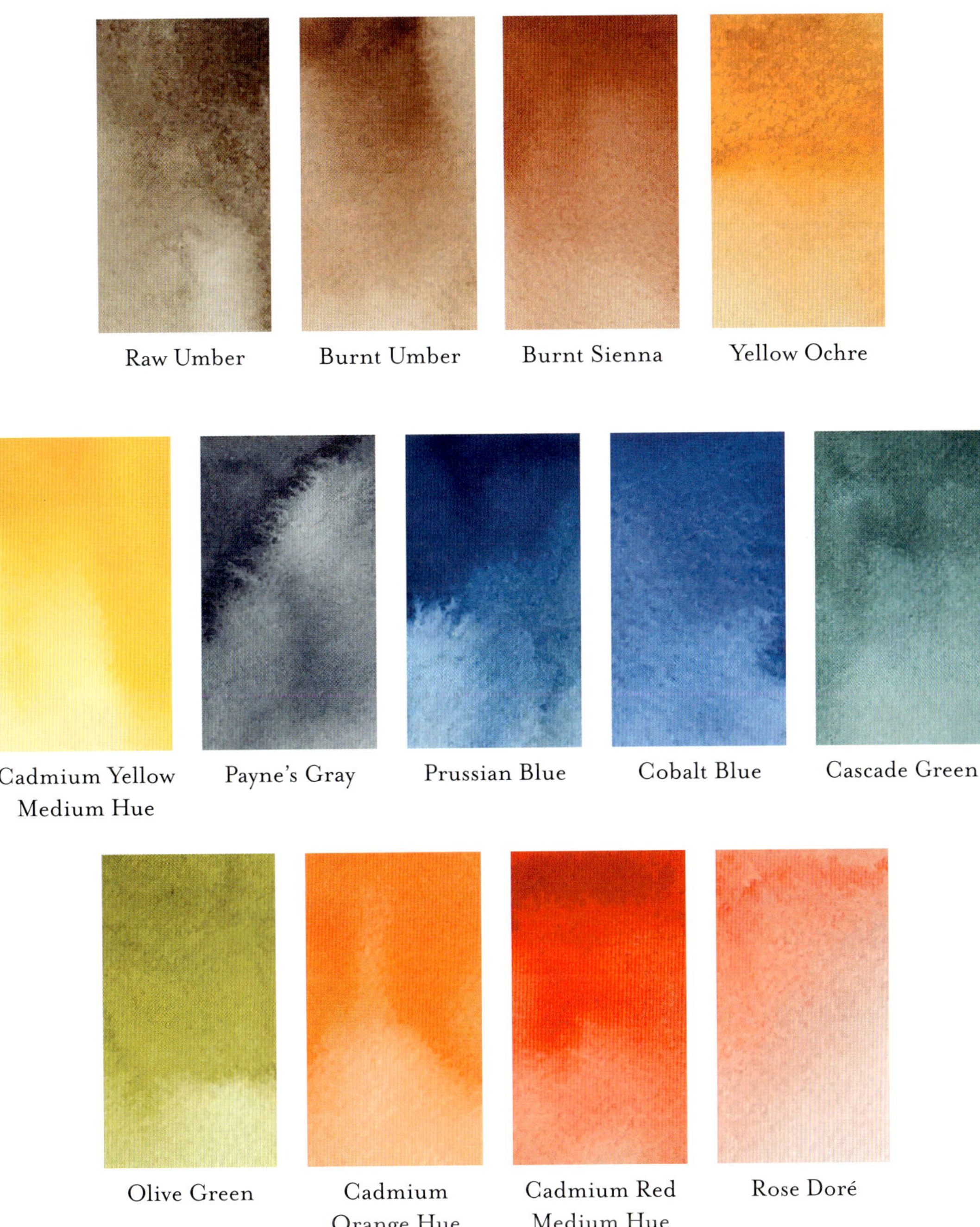

Raw Umber   Burnt Umber   Burnt Sienna   Yellow Ochre

Cadmium Yellow Medium Hue   Payne's Gray   Prussian Blue   Cobalt Blue   Cascade Green

Olive Green   Cadmium Orange Hue   Cadmium Red Medium Hue   Rose Doré

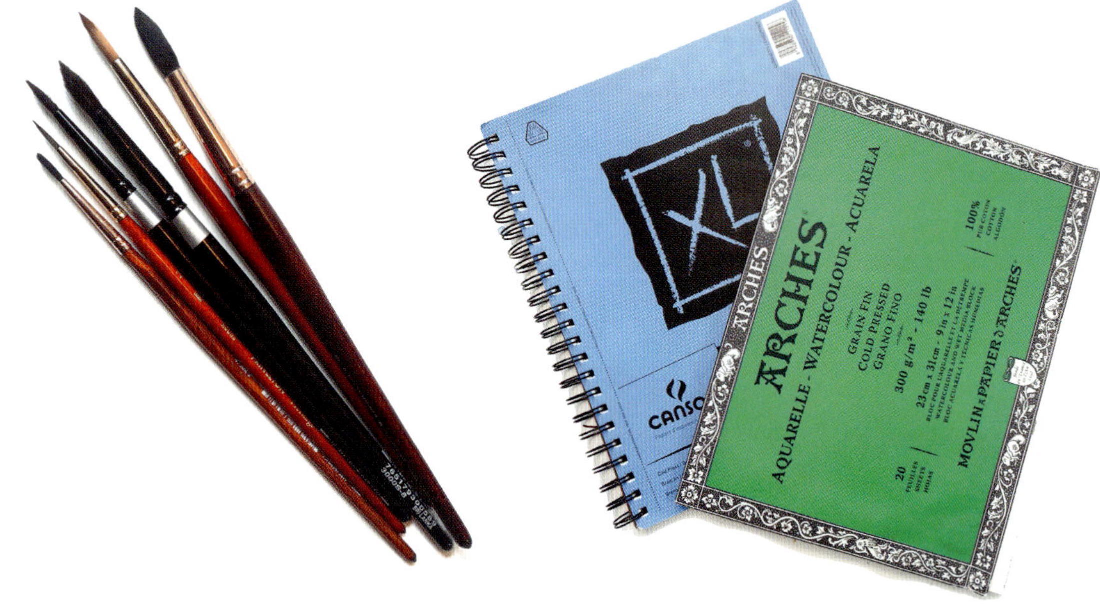

Brushes

For this book, you will need a small round brush and a medium round brush.

For a small watercolor round brush, I recommend using a round brush between the sizes #0 to #4. A small brush will help you create fine details.

For a medium-sized round brush, I would recommend using a size between #6 and #8.

My favorite round brushes are by a brand called the Princeton Artist Brush™ Company, but there are many great options for different budgets.

Paper

The main three types of watercolor paper are hot-pressed, cold-pressed and rough paper. Hot-pressed paper is a smooth paper with very little texture to it, cold-pressed paper has a mid-grain texture and rough paper is, well, rough.

For the projects in the book, I would recommend using cold-pressed paper, as it is generally the easiest to work with, and using either 8 x 10–inch (20 x 25–cm) or 9 x 12–inch (23 x 31–cm) sheets.

My favorite brand of watercolor paper is ARCHES®, but I understand that it might not be within everyone's budget. For full disclosure, I represent this company as a brand ambassador and stand by their products. Some more affordable papers to start with are Canson® XL® Watercolor and Strathmore® 400 series.

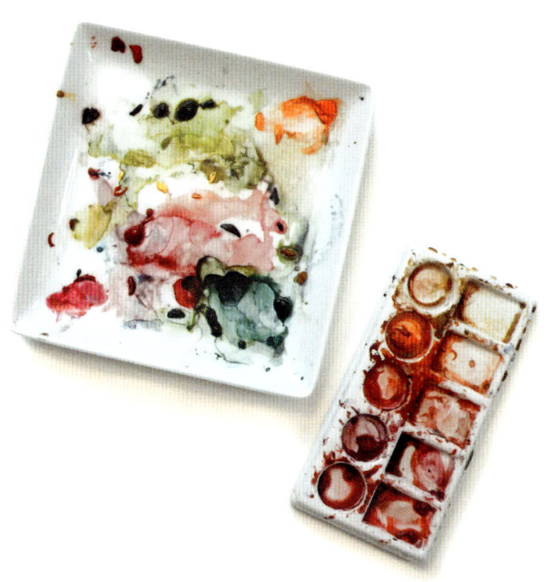

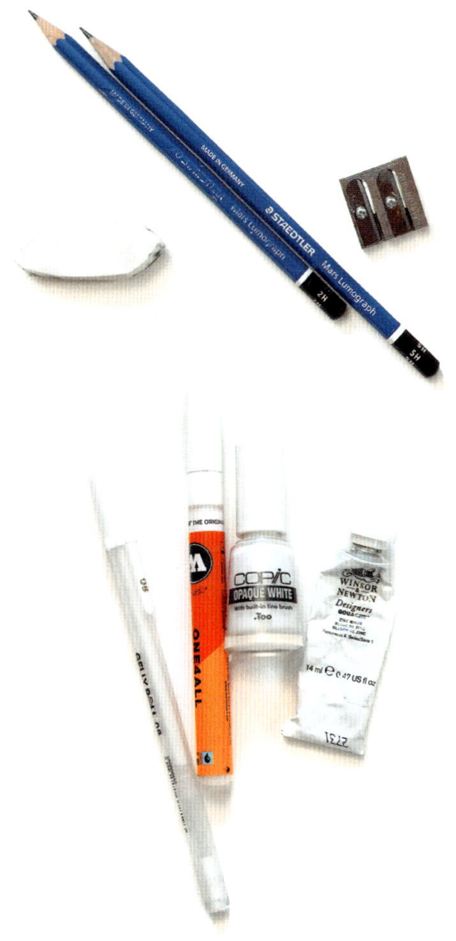

Palette

For a paint palette, you can purchase one
from an art supply store, or you can use
something as simple as a white plate or the
lid from a container of yogurt. How you
use and set up your palette is personal to
each painter; I have multiple that have color
themes and I tend to never clean mine,
while others prefer very neat palettes.

Pencils and Eraser

I would recommend using a hard or H pencil
for your sketches. These pencils are great for
creating thin, light lines that can be easily
erased. When using hard pencils, try to use
a small amount of pressure to keep the lines
light, since applying too much pressure can
leave an imprint on the paper. Make sure
you have an eraser for your drawing process.
I just use a simple white plastic eraser.

White Ink or Paint

For some of the paintings, you will need
to use white for whiskers. There are a few
different options for this. You can use a
white gel pen, opaque ink or paint. For
paint, I would recommend using either
acrylic or gouache; just make sure you
have a separate fine-tipped brush for your
highlights. I usually use a small round
brush with opaque white ink by the
brand Copic© (optional).

Pen

This is optional, but if you have a hard time painting small, black details, a fine-tipped black pen might be a good idea. I recommend using a micron pen or something similar that is water-resistant.

Hair Dryer (optional)

I often use a hair dryer while painting in order to speed up the drying time of my paintings and control the drying process. You by no means need to use one, but I would recommend it if you are short on time or are simply impatient like me. An inexpensive hair dryer is all you need; just make sure you use one that has a low setting and isn't too powerful, as a really powerful one could spread the water too much. I would recommend having your painting lie down flat on the table for the drying process and hold your hair dryer a few inches above the painting without an angle in order to not spread the water around too much.

Water Cup

Some artists like to use two water cups as they paint, one for clean water and one for dirty water. The clean water is great for making sure you don't contaminate your colors. For example, if you were to dip your brush into gray, dirty paint water and then dip it into yellow paint, it might tint the yellow gray.

Towel

In order to wipe excess paint off of your paint brush, you may need a paper towel or an old rag. You can also use them to lift color or water if you accidentally add too much. Just carefully dab a clean towel into the water or paint to absorb it.

Template Supplies

Some supplies you might need for the drawing templates are: artist's tape, scissors, graphite paper, tracing paper and a light pad.

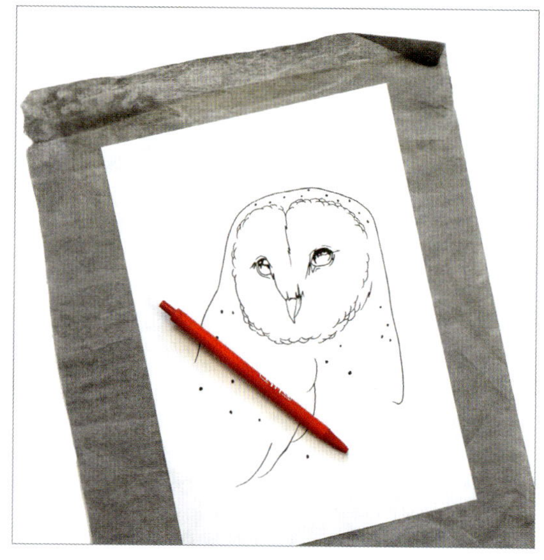

How to Use the Templates

In the back of the book, there will be drawing templates that you can trace to create your paintings. Using a drawing template instead of creating your own sketch will help take some of the pressure off of the painting process. With a drawing template, you can easily re-create your sketch if you are not happy with your painting results. If you would prefer to draw out each sketch without the template, that is also completely fine! In order to use the templates, begin by cutting them out with scissors. If you don't want to cut the images out of the book, you can use tracing paper to copy the images to use as templates.

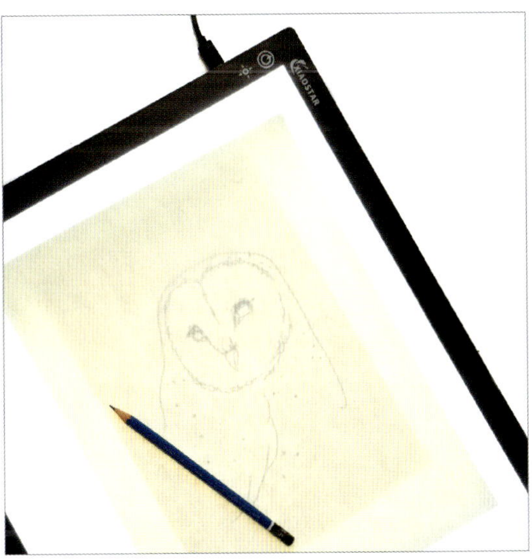

For the drawing templates, there are a few different ways to transfer the images onto paper. The three main methods are graphite paper, a light pad or using a window. I use graphite paper because I paint on watercolor blocks which don't allow light to travel through; if you use graphite paper, I would recommend using a paper towel to wipe off some of the excess graphite on the paper before you begin. If you don't, it can cause your paper to get really messy. In order to transfer the image, place the graphite paper graphite side down onto your watercolor paper and then put your drawing template on top of the graphite. Then, using a ball-point pen, trace over the lines. You may need to tape down your paper with artist's tape if you find it moves while you trace.

The other two methods involve using light. Using a window is an affordable way to trace an image; you just have to make sure that it is bright enough outside. For this method, you will place your drawing against the window or light pad and then place your watercolor paper on top of the template. Most watercolor paper that is 140lb (300gsm) or less should allow light to penetrate through. Again, use artist's tape if you have problems with the image moving while you trace.

Watercolor Techniques and Exercises

The Importance of Paint Consistency and Value

With watercolors, your value will be determined by how much water you add to your paints. The more water you add, the lighter your value will be and vice versa. Another thing to take into consideration is that watercolors dry lighter than they appear on paper while things are still wet.

What is Value?

Value is the lightness or darkness of a color or hue. Light values are diluted with water and appear pale and transparent, while dark values are saturated with pigment and will be rich and opaque. Value is important for creating a painting that doesn't look flat. For some of these paintings, you will be using a limited color palette, so you will instead focus on value to create dimension and life.

In this book, you will be using three main values: light, medium and dark. Light value is a water to paint ratio of about 80 percent water, 20 percent paint. Medium value is about 50:50 and dark value about 20 percent water, 80 percent paint. On the next page, I have some examples of different paint colors with different paint consistencies. Throughout the book I will often refer to dark value paint as saturated and light value paint as diluted. I would recommend testing out some of your colors with different values if you are new to watercolors. Don't worry if your values are slightly different than the ones in the book; what makes painting with watercolors so exciting is the unpredictable nature of the material.

Payne's Gray

Dark Value   Medium Value   Light Value

Prussian Blue

Dark Value   Medium Value   Light Value

Burnt Sienna

Dark Value   Medium Value   Light Value

Exploring Different Types of Washes

Washes

Washes are an essential watercolor technique. Washes are when you use a brush to apply paint over a larger area of a painting to either paint a background or to fill in a shape. There are four main types of washes: flat, graded, variegated and wet-on-wet. I would recommend testing out and experimenting with these washes if you are new to watercolors.

The Four Main Types of Washes

Flat Wash

This wash is a solid, flat color that doesn't have much variation. You can create this wash using a wet-on-dry technique, meaning you add wet paint to dry paper, or by adding a layer of clean water to the paper first to create a wet-on-wet flat wash. I prefer using a wet-on-dry method as it is easier to control and I don't often fill in large shapes with a solid, flat wash. For this wash, I would recommend using a medium round brush and an even amount of water. The larger your brush, the more water and pigment it can hold, making it easier to create a consistent flat wash.

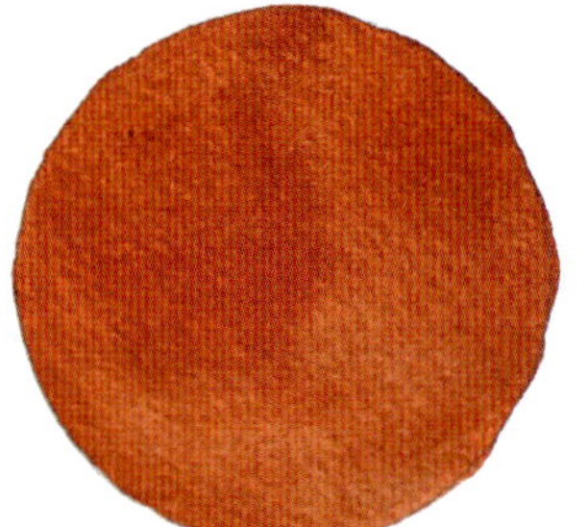

Flat Wash

Graded Wash

Variegated Wash

Graded Wash

A graded wash is where the value of a color goes from a dark value to a light value. I would recommend testing this wash out in order to get comfortable with value shifts. To create this wash using a wet-on-dry technique, first add a saturated amount of paint to your paper and then slowly dilute your paint as you work your way across the shape you are filling in. By the end of your wash, you might only be using clean water to spread out the color.

Variegated Wash

With this wash, you will be transitioning to different colors to create a gradient. There are a few different ways to create this type of wash. I like to add one color to one end of the shape and then the second color to the opposite end of the shape, and then after cleaning my brush off and loading it up with water, I will blend the two colors together.

Wet-on-Wet Technique

With this wash, you will start by applying either clean water or a flat wash of color on paper. Then, while the wash or water is still wet, you will dab paint into it. Using a wet-on-wet technique creates a beautiful, soft effect while painting, but it can be harder to control. I like to use wet-on-wet washes to create loose, abstract washes in my paintings. I also like using this technique to mix colors directly on my watercolor paper instead of pre-mixing them on my paint palette.

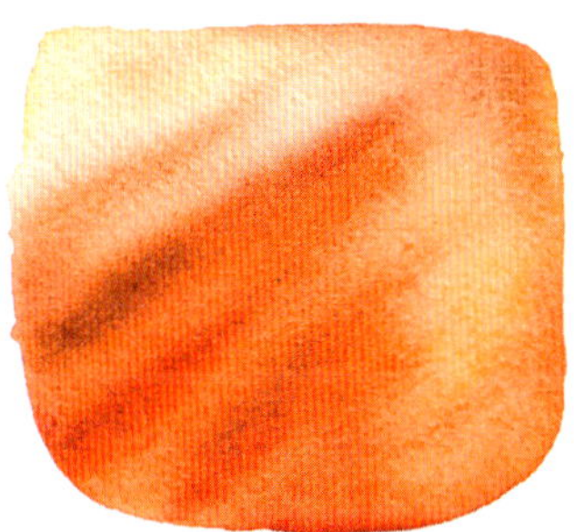

Wet-on-wet technique used
to create soft stripes

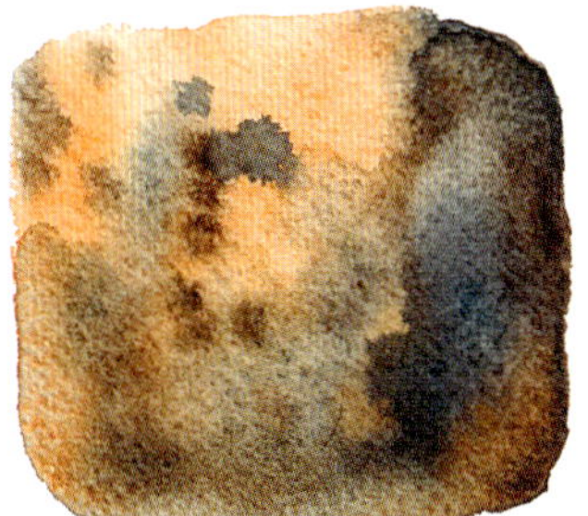

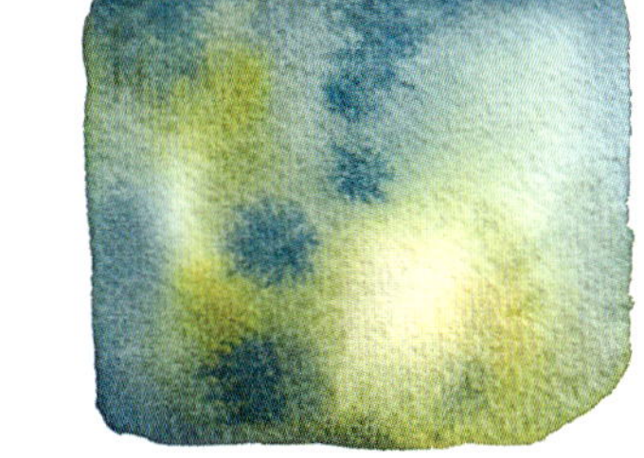

Examples of wet-on-wet washes

Wet-on-Dry Technique

Throughout this book you will be using a wet-on-dry technique quite often, as it is an essential watercolor technique for adding layers. *Wet-on-dry* simply means adding wet paint or water on top of dry paper or paint. This technique is used a lot for adding fine details as it is easier to control versus the wet-on-wet technique, and the lines will appear sharper.

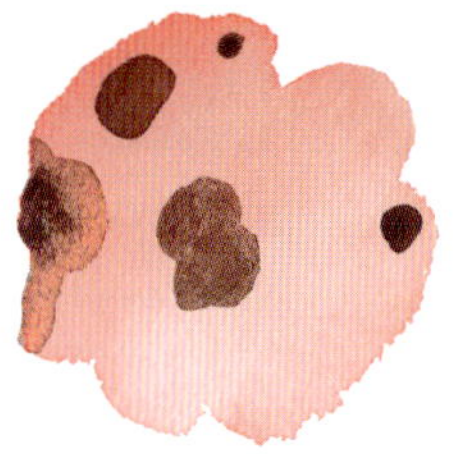

Wet-on-dry technique to create a spotted pattern

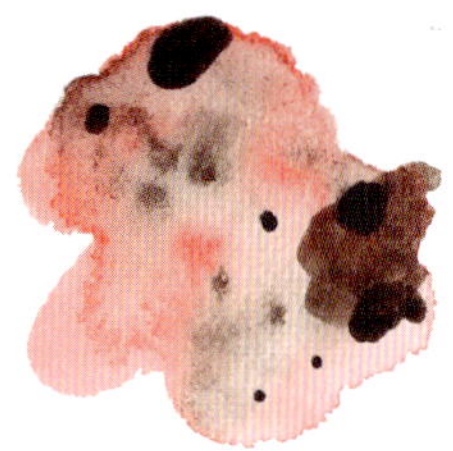

Wet-on-dry spots layered on top of a wet-on-wet wash

Creating Expressive Paintings— Texture and Mark-Making

Blooms

Blooms, also called back-runs, blossoms and cauliflowers, are some of my favorite ways to create visual texture on a watercolor painting. Blooms form when additional water or pigment is added to a damp, drying wash. After adding a drop of water, it spreads out the pigment on your paper, leaving a lighter, new area with a dark, organic ring around the outside. This is a great technique for giving the illusion of fur or texture without painting every single hair on an animal. It is also important to know how to avoid them. To avoid accidentally creating them, keep an eye on the moisture levels of your wash.

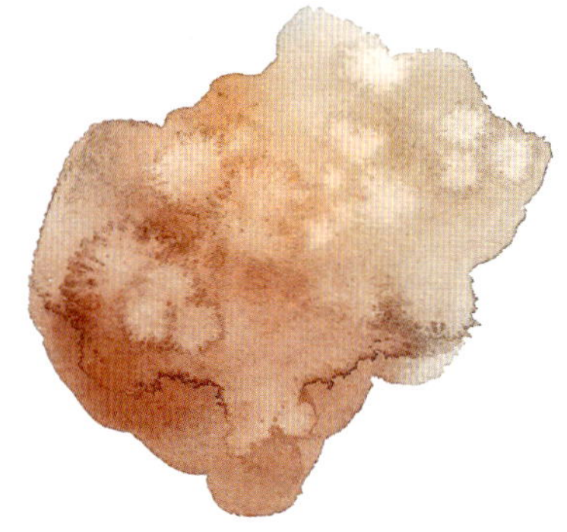

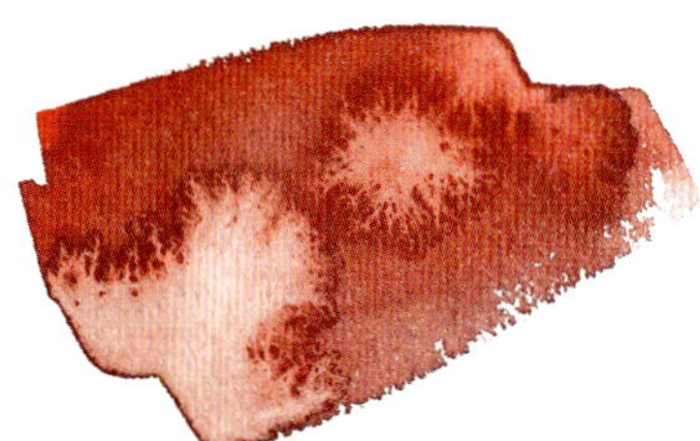

Salt

You can use salt to create texture on a wash of watercolor paint. When salt sits on wet paint it absorbs the moisture and leaves a pattern after things dry. The size and shape of your salt will change the effects, and I often use table salt as my salt of choice. When using salt, sprinkle it onto a wet wash and allow the wash to fully dry without disturbing it. The effects will change depending on how wet your wash was when applying the salt, so you might have to practice a few times to get the timing right. After the wash dries, carefully wipe the salt away with your dry, clean hand.

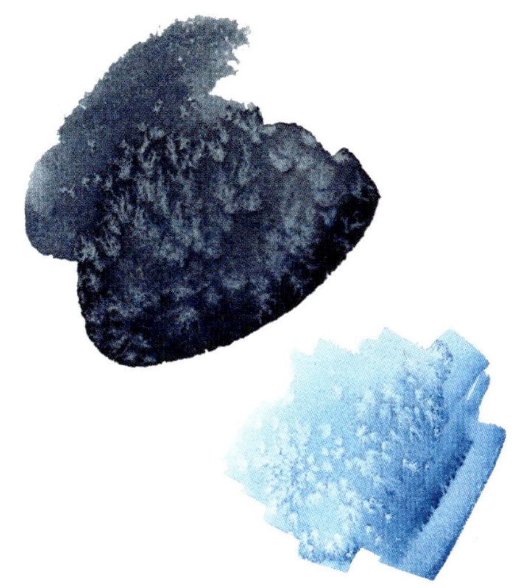

Mark-Making

Mark-making is the term that describes the different types of textures, patterns, dots and lines you can create in art using a utensil. Marks can be either smooth and controlled or energetic and gestural. They can also vary in weight from very thin, light lines to dark, bold marks that are created by using a lot of pressure. I often use different mark-making techniques to help convey different textures and patterns found on animals.

Dry Brush Technique

Get the brush wet, but not excessively wet, and move your brush quickly without too much pressure so it doesn't stay on the paper for too long. The dry brush effect is created because watercolor paper has a texture of high and low spots, and the paint will only sit on the high spots, thus creating texture. You will be practicing this technique on a few different projects, such as when you paint the fluffy hair on a chipmunk's tail and on a fox's coat.

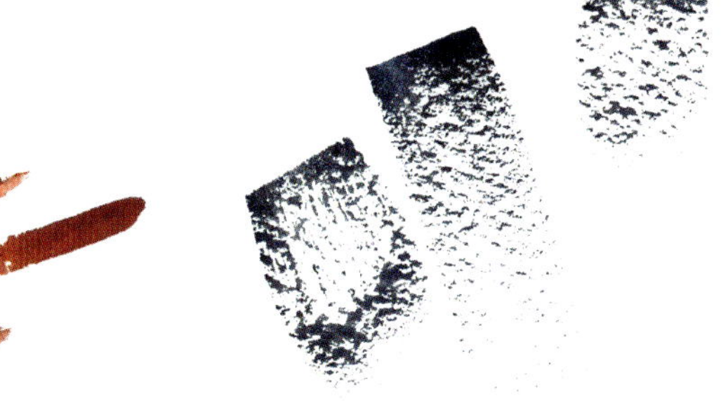

Splatters

Load up your brush with paint and water, and using your finger, tap or flick the brush over the paper to create splatters. You can also pull back your paint bristles to create splatters or use a toothbrush.

Practice Making Marks

On a test piece of paper, play around with the different types of marks you can create using your brush. Use different amounts of water and change up the speed and direction you move your brush. Here are some examples to get you started.

Loose and Tight Watercolors

Some watercolor artists prefer to create very gestural paintings while others prefer rendering things with tight, controlled details. In this book, you will get to practice both types of techniques, starting using mostly wet-on-dry techniques and slowly loosening up and introducing more water as you make your way through the projects. The projects are arranged this way because watercolor can be a difficult medium to work with due to the unpredictable nature of water. I personally like combining both styles of painting within my work depending on what I am trying to convey and in order to create a sense of balance.

When painting loosely, try not to paint every detail on the subject and instead try to paint the essence of the subject, and move in a more intuitive manner. You can also try using larger paint brushes and more water, positioning your hand farther up the brush and moving more quickly, or not focusing on one area for too long. It can take confidence and practice to work this way, which is why I will be easing you into using these techniques. Keep in mind your results may look very different than the examples in the book because you will be letting go of control and embracing the unpredictable nature of watercolors. I would also encourage you to take risks and to experiment when painting in a loose style to discover what you like and don't like.

In contrast to painting loosely, painting in a tight and controlled way often requires using smaller brushes and less water, and positioning your hand closer to the tip of your brush as though you are using a pencil and using slower, more focused movements. I often paint this way to draw attention to a certain area, which is why I often use tight details when working on the facial features of my subjects.

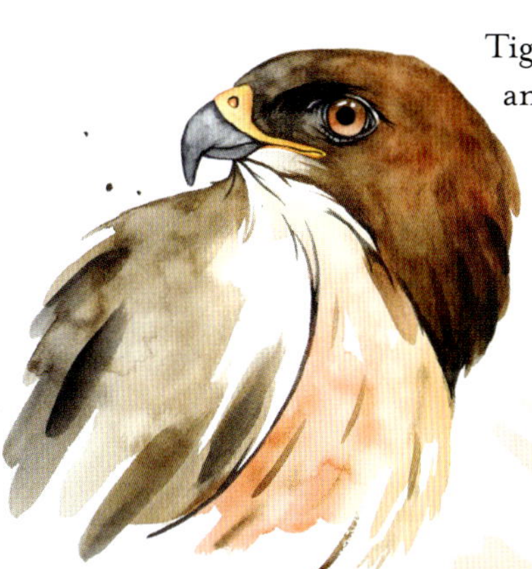

Tight details on the eye and beak of the hawk

Loose expressive washes and mark-making on its body

Practice Painting Animal Features

Before we get started, let's practice painting some different features you might find on animals, such as eyes, wings and different patterns! These exercises will help break down these complex forms into a few easy steps.

I would recommend practicing some of these before getting started or coming back to these if you need help during one of your projects. So, grab a pencil, brush and some paints, and let's get started!

How to Paint an Animal Eye

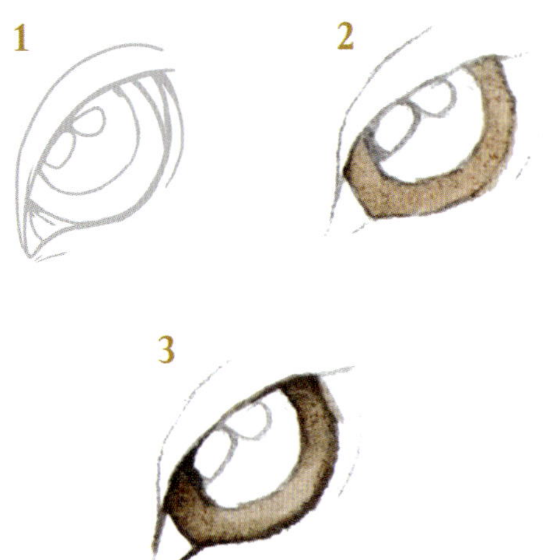

The eyes of an animal are one of the most important features and they bring life to the subject. In this example, I am using Raw Umber to paint an eye of a deer, but you can paint it whatever color you like.

Step 1
Draw an eye of an animal using a hard pencil in order to keep the lines light.

Step 2
After drawing the eye, start by filling in the iris with a layer of paint. This eye in the example is painted with Raw Umber.

Step 3
Add a saturated amount of Raw Umber to the top portion of the iris below the eyelid and around the outside diameter of the iris.

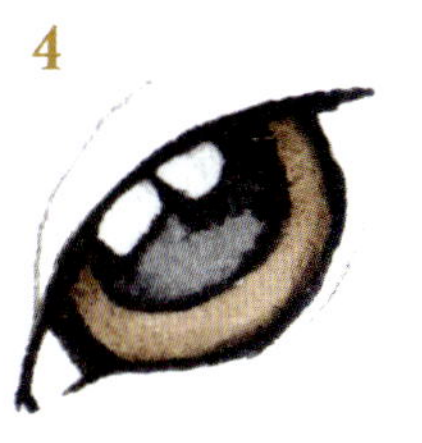

Step 4

After everything dries, outline the eye with a saturated Payne's Gray, and then fill in the pupil as well, making sure to leave the two highlights white. While filling in the pupil with paint, make sure to concentrate the pigment towards the top portion of the pupil. This will represent a shadow below the eyelid.

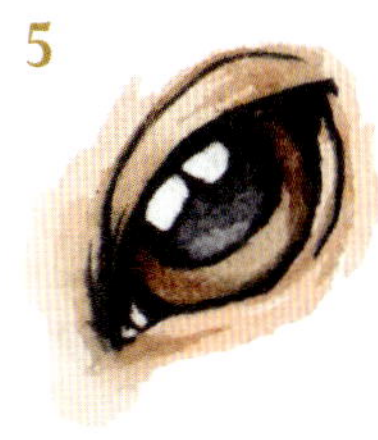

Step 5

Paint the outside of the eye with the color of the animal's fur. Use a darker color to paint out the upper and lower eyelid details. Add a little extra Raw Umber to increase the contrast in the eye.

How to Paint a Beak

Here is a short exercise on how to paint the hooked beak of a hawk. Beaks on birds come in all sorts of different shapes and sizes depending on what they eat. Despite this, the process of how to paint the shapes is pretty similar.

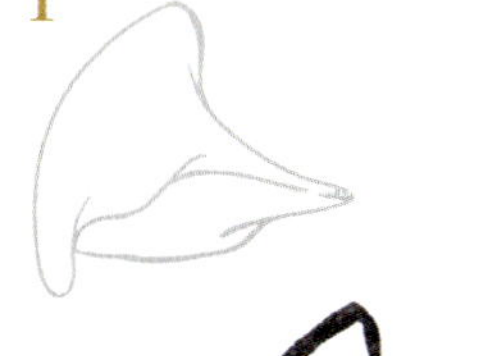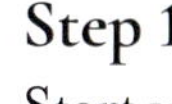

Step 1

Start with a light drawing of the bird's beak.

Step 2

Outline the shape of the beak with a saturated amount of Payne's Gray using a small round brush.

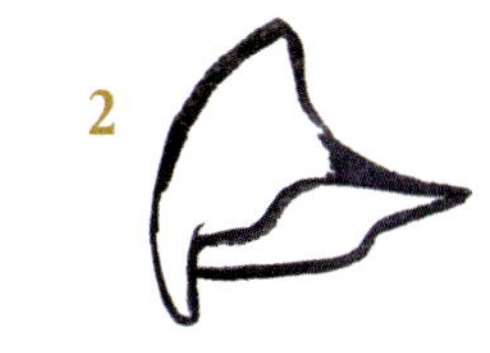

Step 3

While step two is still wet, dip a medium-sized round brush into water and blend out the paint until it fills in the entire beak.

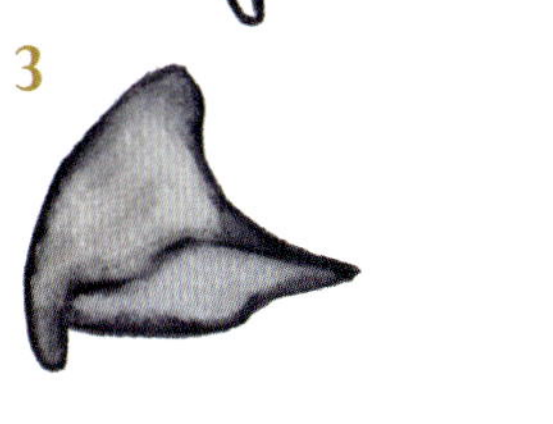

Step 4

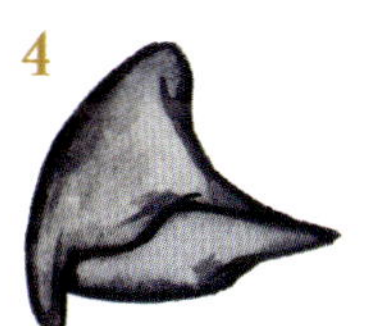

Your lines might have lost definition from the last step, so now you will be repainting them. After everything is dry, use a wet-on-dry technique and a saturated amount of gray paint to add details to the beak.

How to Paint Fur

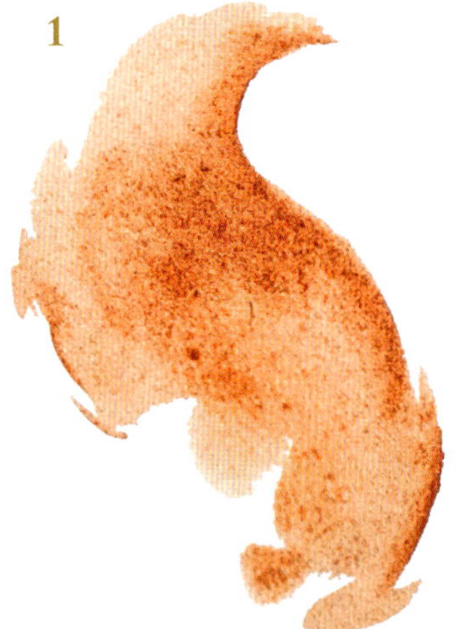

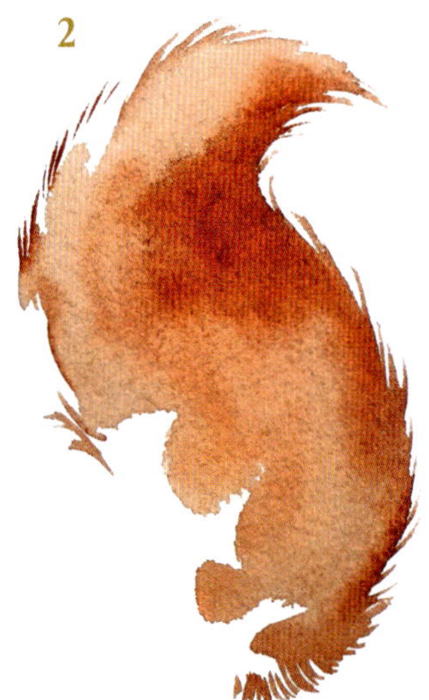

One of my favorite techniques to paint animal fur is to first create a wash and then use a smaller brush with a fine tip to pull out small hairs. This is a perfect way to convey the sense of soft fur without having to paint out every little hair mark. For this small exercise, you will be painting the curved, fluffy tail of a squirrel.

Step 1

To practice this technique, start off by creating a wash using any color you would like in the loose shape of a tail.

Step 2

While the wash is still wet, using either a small round brush or a fine-tipped brush, drag out some hairs. It is easiest to pull the hairs out toward yourself, so if you need to rotate your paper as you go, that is perfectly fine. Make sure to pay attention to the direction the hair goes on the animal you are painting, since you will want to create these marks in that direction.

Simple Wing Technique

You will be using this technique in multiple bird projects through this book. With this method, you will quickly create beautiful, airy, flying wings. Practice this technique before you get started or come back to this page for reference.

1

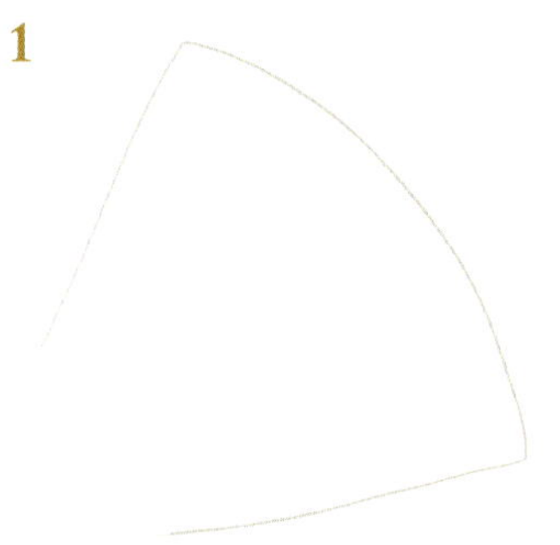

Step 1

Lightly draw out the general shape of a flying bird wing. You do not need to draw out each individual feather because you will use the shape of your paint brush to create them.

2

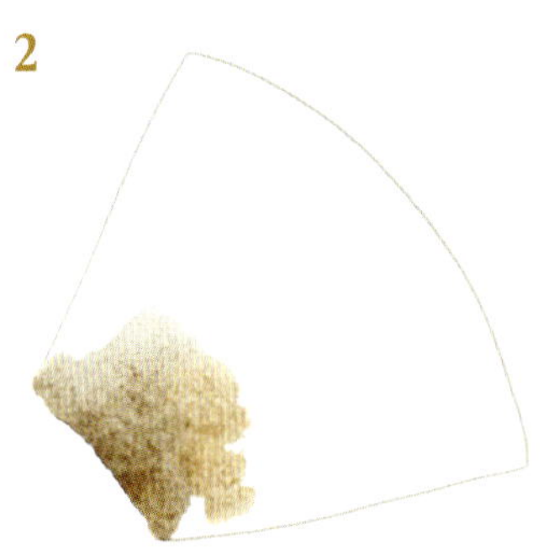

Step 2

Next, add a diluted wash of paint near where the wing connects to the body of the bird using a medium round brush. For this example, I used Raw Umber, but you can use whatever color you would like.

3

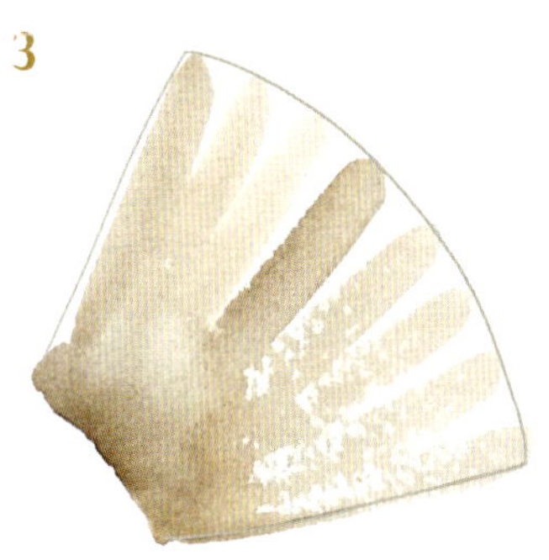

Step 3

While the wash from step two is still wet, dip your brush into the paint and start with the tip of your brush at the curved line you drew. Drag the brush inward until it meets the wash. Repeat this step as you create each feather mark. The shape of your brush's tip will affect how your feather shapes appear. I like to use the Princeton Neptune™ Series round brushes, as they have a little bit more of a rounded shape while other round brushes have more pointed, angular tips.

Creating a Spot Pattern

This is a technique that can be used to paint spots on different animals such as frogs, snakes and lizards. You can use whatever colors you would like; the colors for the example are based on the colors of a leopard frog. If you want to paint the entire frog, go to page 33!

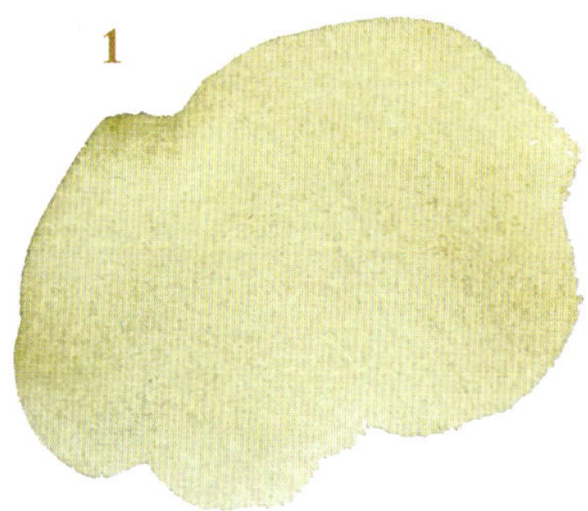

Step 1

Start out with a diluted wash of paint, about an 80:20 water-to-paint ratio with a medium-sized round brush. You can use any color you like as long as it is light in value. For this example, Olive Green was used.

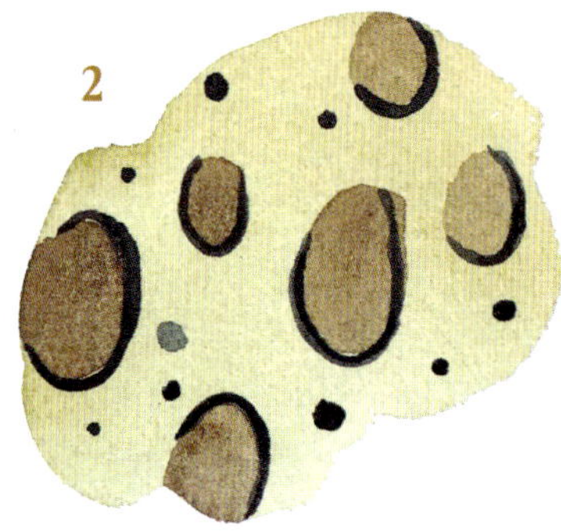

Step 2

After it dries, add spots in a variety of sizes. For the example, larger, diluted Raw Umber spots were added with a medium round brush. After those dried, rings were created around the spots with a medium round brush and using a saturated amount of Payne's Gray paint. Then, using the same brush, small dots were added by gently poking the paper with pigment.

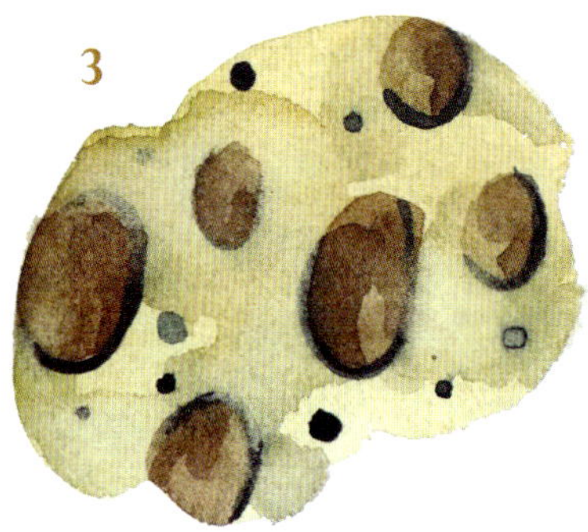

Step 3

This step is optional, and if you like the crisp edges from step two, leave things as they are. If you want a more painterly effect, soften the edges of the spots by dipping a medium-sized round brush into clean water and gently adding a thin layer of water over the dried paint.

Painting a Stripe Pattern

Many different animals have stripes on them, from furry ones like tabby cats to reptiles like turtles. To paint layered stripes, start with a diluted base wash for your first layer and then increase the value for each layer.

Step 1

Start with the base color of your stripes. This should be the lightest color you use. For this example, a diluted wash of Cadmium Yellow Medium Hue is used.

Step 2

Add stripes using a diluted amount of paint. For this example, I am using Payne's Gray and a medium-sized round brush. You can create stripes that are all one uniform size, or you can add them in a variety of line thicknesses.

Step 3

After step two is fully dry, add more stripes, this time increasing the saturation of your paint. You can use the same color as before or a different one. For this example, a saturated amount of Payne's Gray was used. Create lines on top of your previous stripes, making sure they are thinner so the previous stripes still show.

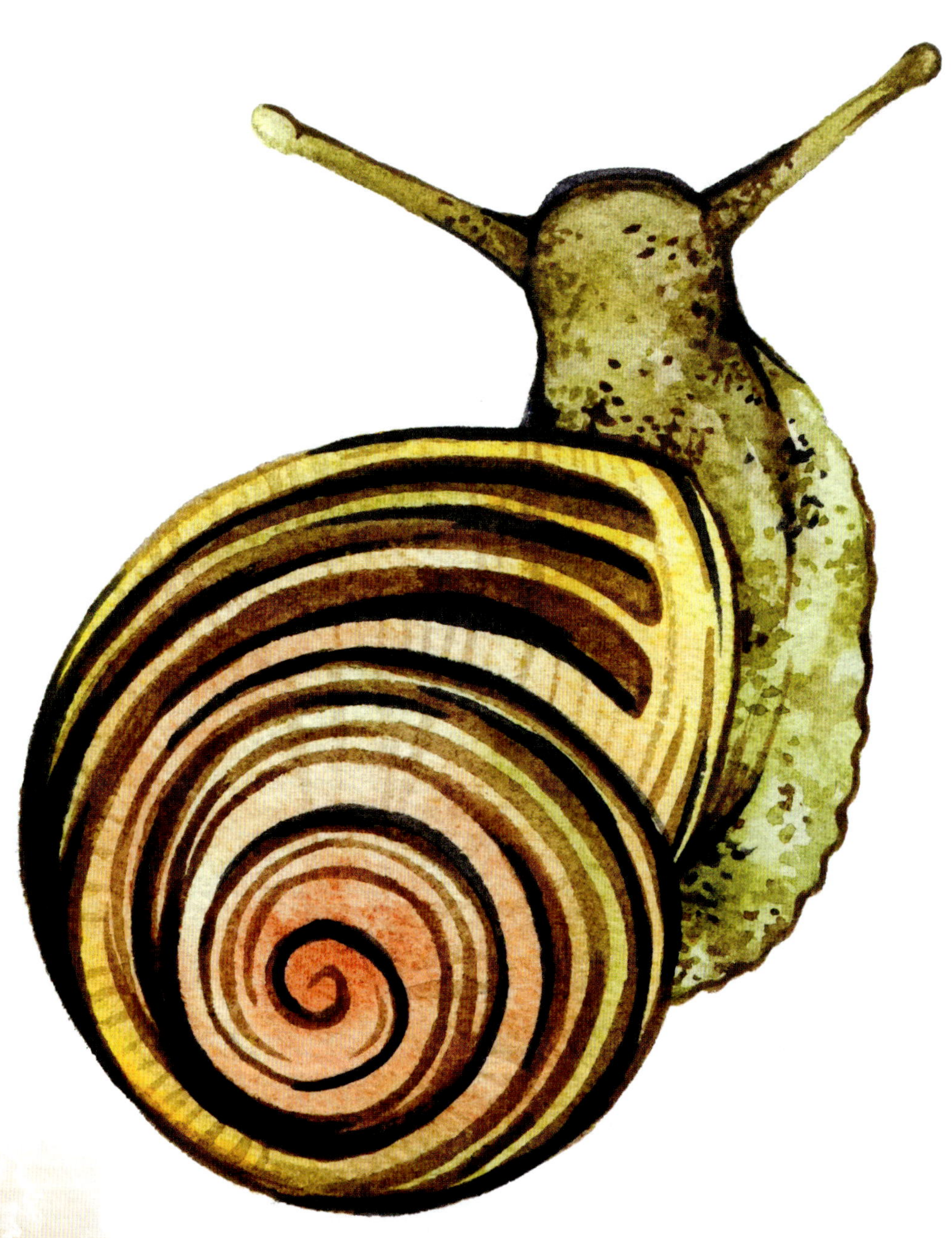

Little Critters

In this chapter, we will be starting off with some small critters to help ease you into your watercolor adventure. Some of these little friends might be found in your backyard if you just look close enough, from fuzzy bumblebees going from one flower to the next to dragonflies darting through the air.

Many small critters, such as insects and reptiles, are known for their vibrant colors and patterns that we will be showcasing in this chapter. You will practice a variety of watercolor techniques, such as how to paint transparent wings, how to soften hard edges and how to create a stippling pattern. You will start by using small washes that are easier to control to help you understand how much water to use. You will also practice how to use layers to create depth in your painting and to practice some looser watercolor techniques, such as creating paint splatters and splotchy backgrounds.

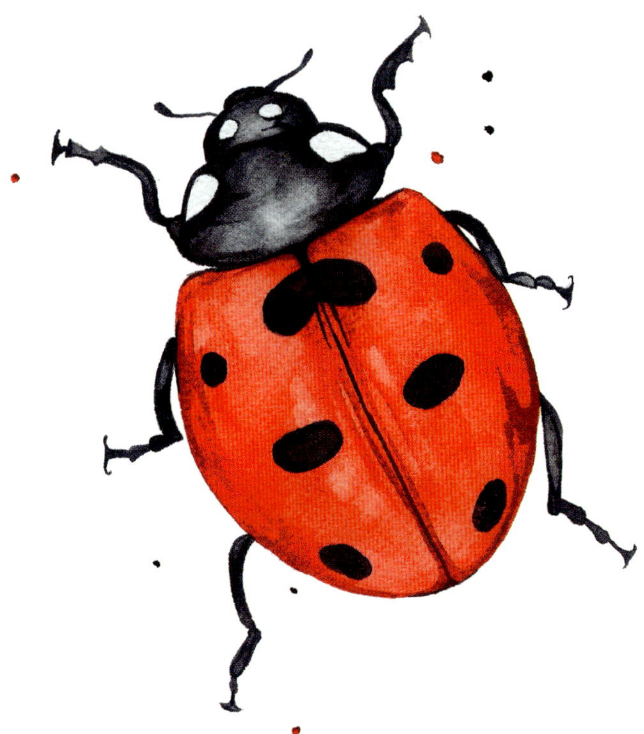

Ladybug

Ladybugs, also known as lady beetles or ladybirds, are a symbol of good luck. Their bright red color is meant to ward off predators by communicating that they taste nasty. The ladybugs commonly found in North America have seven spots, but different species will have different patterns and spots. In this tutorial, you will practice creating value and dimension using only two paint colors by layering washes of paint. You will then be using saturated paint to create the bold black spots on a ladybug's body.

Lesson

Painting using only two colors

Colors

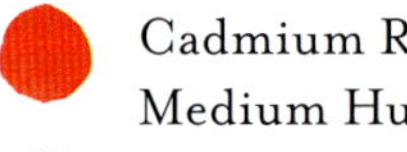 Cadmium Red Medium Hue

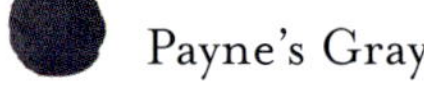 Payne's Gray

Brushes

Medium Round Brush

Small Round Brush

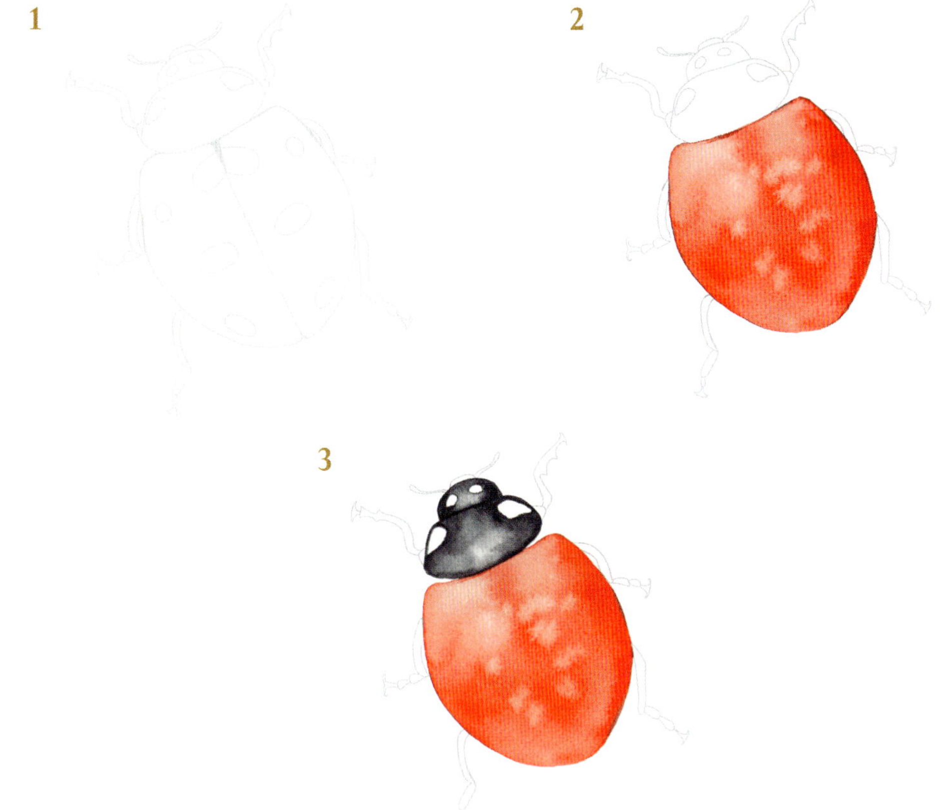

Step 1

Trace the drawing template of the ladybug on page 151 using your preferred method. Try to keep your sketch light. If you need to lightly erase any lines to lighten them, do so.

Step 2

Fill in the body of the ladybug with your Cadmium Red Medium Hue paint, using about a 50:50 ratio of water to paint for a medium-value consistency. Apply your wet paint to dry paper. Don't worry if your wash isn't perfectly even, as we will be adding another layer of red on top of this one later. Allow this step to fully dry before moving on to the next step.

Step 3

Carefully create an outline around the black portion of the ladybug's body by tracing your pencil lines with a saturated amount of Payne's Gray paint and a small round brush. By creating an outline first, it will help make sure you do not go outside of your lines when you fill it in. After outlining the shapes with Payne's Gray, use a medium-sized round brush to fill in the rest of the shape with the same color.

Step 4

In this step, we will be adding another layer of red to the body of the ladybug. In order to create some contrast between the layers of red, use a more saturated red paint, about a 20:80 water-to-paint ratio. You will also be using a wet-on-dry technique for this process, so make sure your first layer of red paint is completely dry. Using a small round brush, add details to the outer edges of the body and where the ladybug's wings would be.

Lastly, blend out your red paint with your medium round brush by dipping it into water and gently pulling the saturated paint into a gradient.

Step 5

In this step, we will be adding the ladybug's legs and antennae. Use your small round brush dipped into a saturated amount of Payne's Gray and carefully paint over your outline.

Step 6

For this step, use your small round brush dipped into Payne's Gray and carefully paint out the line that defines the ladybug's wings. Next, paint out the shapes of the spots on the ladybug's back. After creating the outline of the shapes, fill them in with Payne's Gray. Make sure that the paint is saturated enough that it appears almost black. Lastly, if you like the look of paint splatters, add a few using your red and black paints.

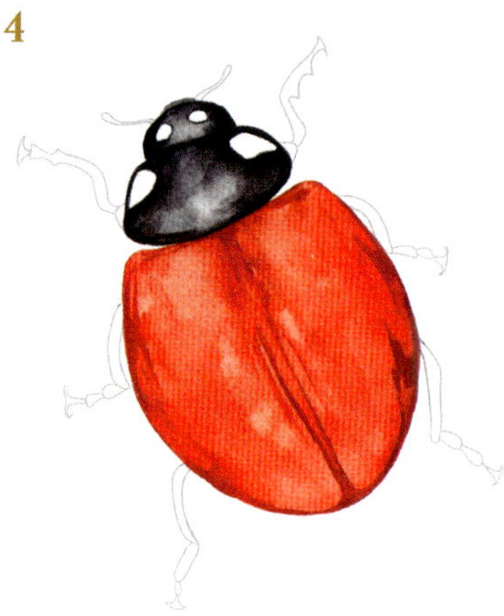

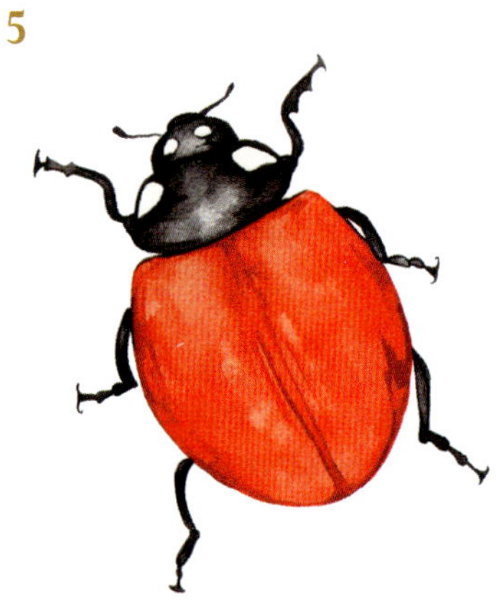

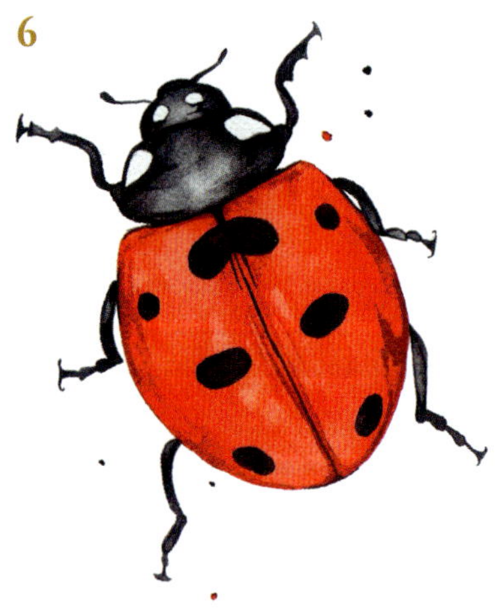

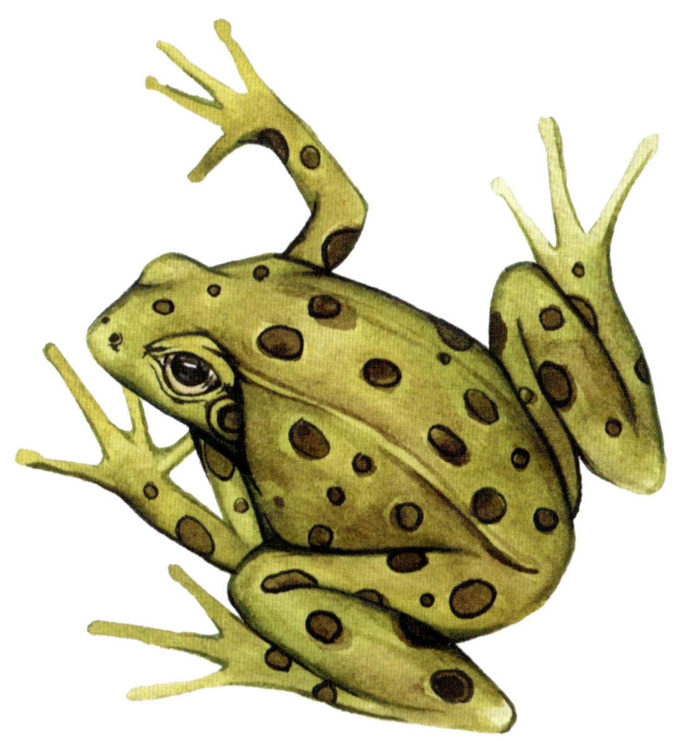

Leopard Frog

There are many different leopard frog species, but what they all have in common is their green-brown color and spotted pattern. This frog uses this pattern to camouflage into its surroundings, so you have to look carefully to see it on the forest floor or swimming in the shallows. In this project, you will get to practice layering ovular shapes to create this frog's leopard-like pattern and blending colors together with a light wash.

Step 1

Trace the drawing template on page 151. You can draw each dot in the pattern if you would like, otherwise you can free-hand paint the spots later. Make sure your drawing stays light.

Step 2

The first step of this painting is to use a medium-sized round brush to apply a light layer of Olive Green paint to your frog's body. After you fill in the center of its body, paint out the legs and feet of the frog as well. You may need to switch to using a small round brush for the tighter areas to help you stay in control and not paint outside of the lines.

Step 3

After your layer in step two dries, use a more saturated consistency of Olive Green paint and small round brush to carefully trace around the shape of your frog's body. This will help define the shape of the frog and add some contrast. Afterward, add a thin, transparent layer of Olive Green paint to create more depth and richness to the frog. Add this thin layer of green paint to the sides of the frog's abdomen and along the legs and head. Make sure this layer doesn't fully cover the first layer of green.

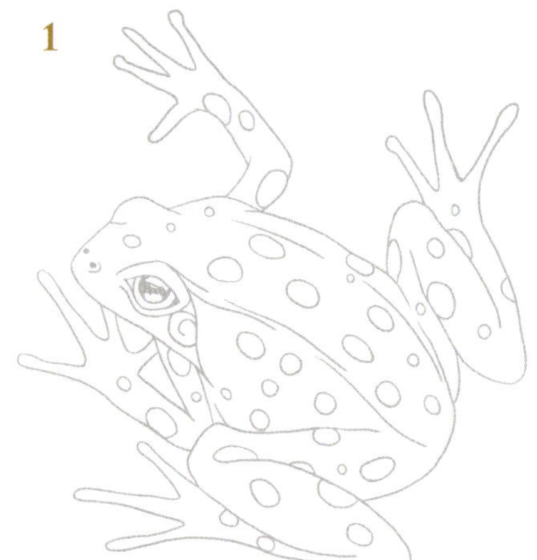

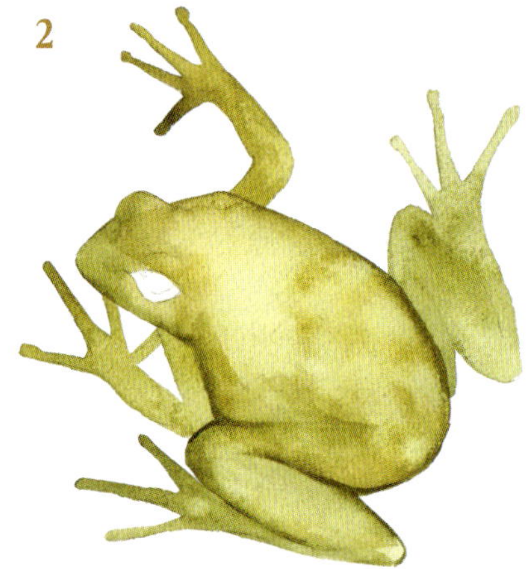

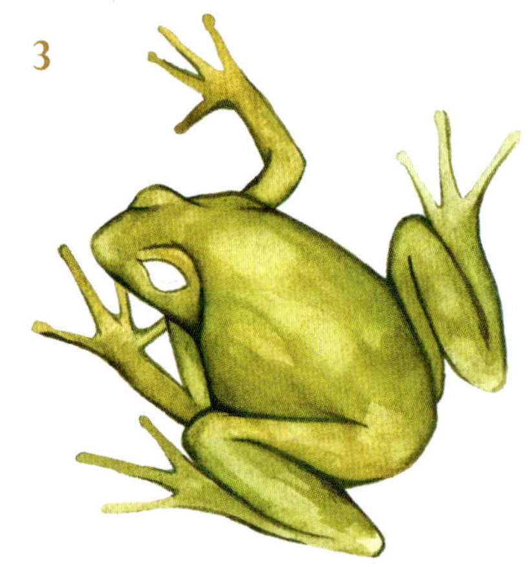

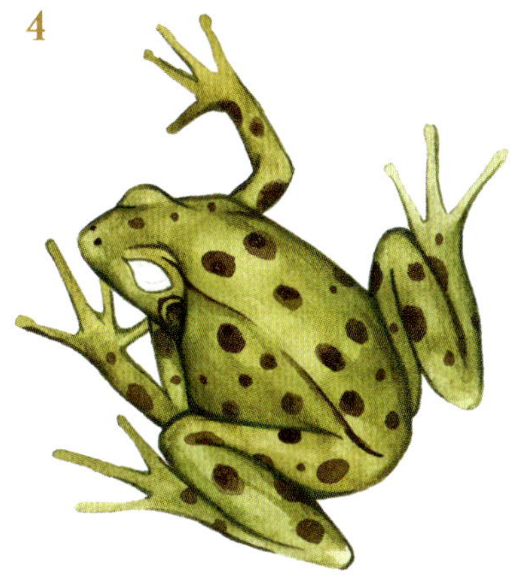

Step 4

Add spots using Raw Umber paint after your previous layer is dry. You may use either a small- or medium-sized round brush depending on how large or small you want the spots to be.

Step 5

In this step, you will begin by painting the eye of the frog. Add a light layer of Cadmium Yellow Medium Hue to the eye using a small round brush. While the yellow paint is drying, add thin lines of Payne's Gray paint along the head and upper legs to increase the contrast. Then, once the yellow of the eye is dry, trace around the shape of the eye and create a pupil using the gray paint and a small round brush.

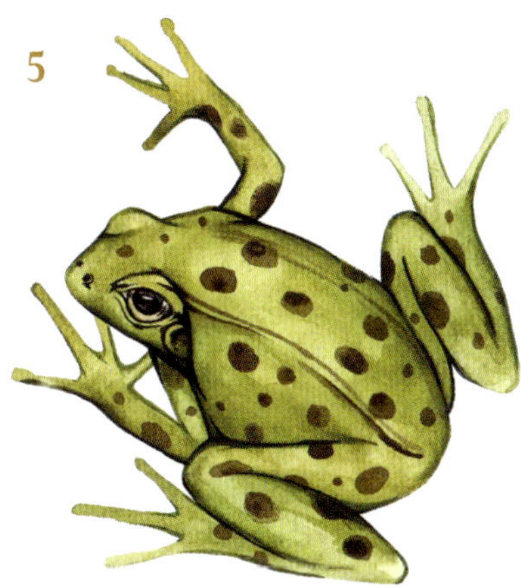

Step 6

Next, add a light layer of Raw Umber to the back of the frog, avoiding the frog's spots. This will add a brownish hue to your green frog. Next, add dark Payne's Gray rings around the brown spots on the frog's back using your small round brush.

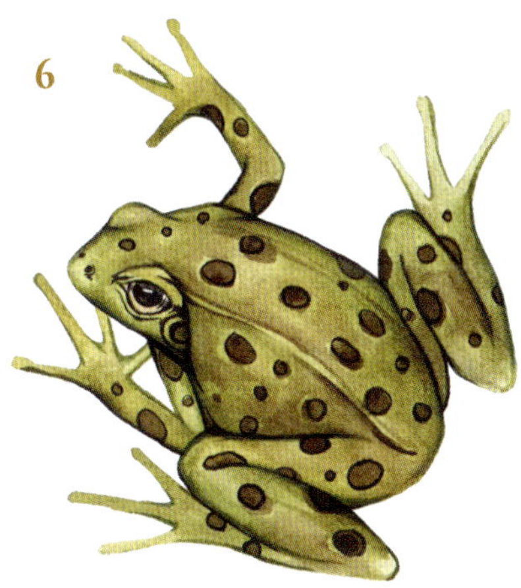

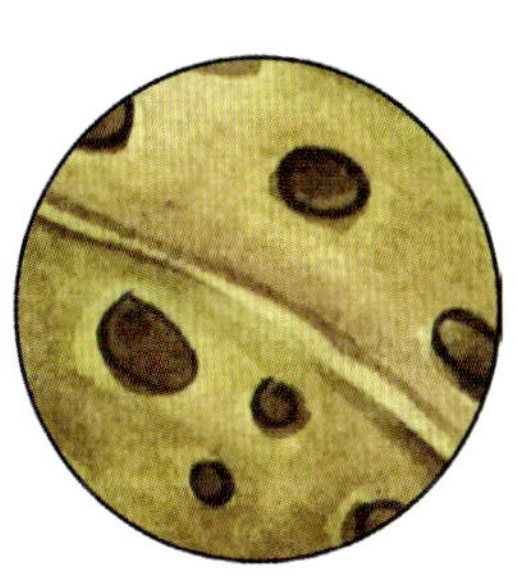

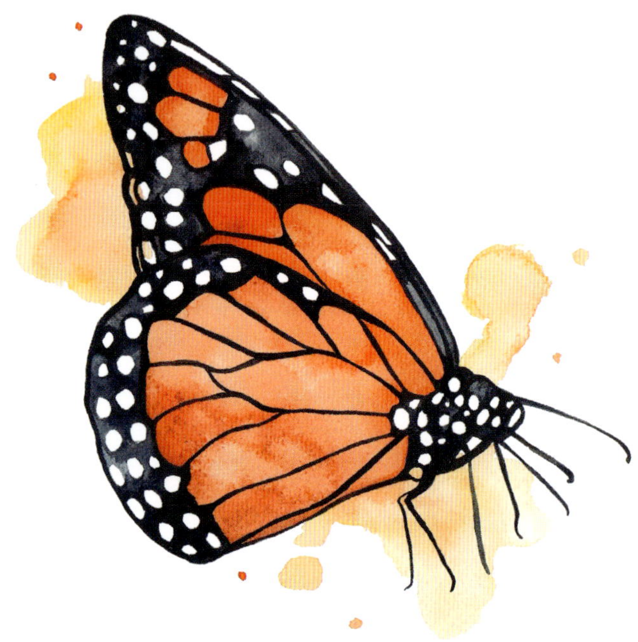

Monarch Butterfly

The monarch butterfly is one of the most recognizable
butterflies in North America, with its distinctive orange-
and-black wing pattern. Each year monarch butterflies
migrate three thousand miles, and they are the only
butterflies that make such a long journey. In this painting, you will create a splash of bold watercolor for the
background to contrast against the sharp, inky edges of
the butterfly. You will also be using a small round brush
to carefully paint the spots and fine lines that make up
the butterfly's wings.

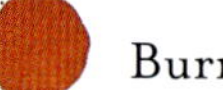

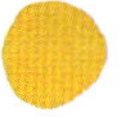

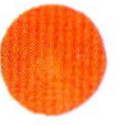

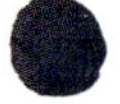

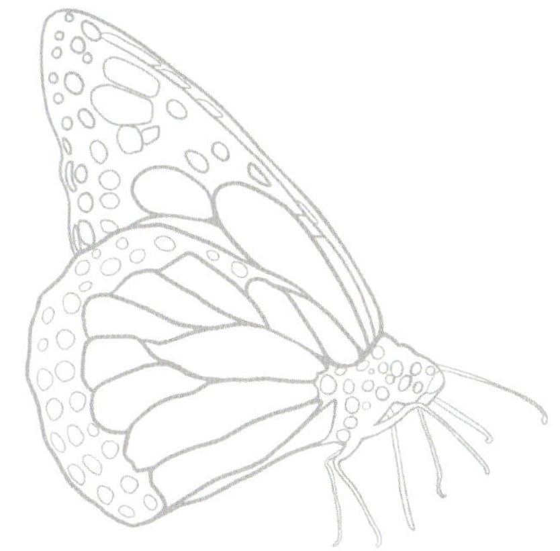

Step 1

Trace the template on page 151. You can trace the entire drawing if you would like. Otherwise, you can leave out the small dots if you would prefer to freehand paint them.

Step 2

Add Burnt Sienna paint to the wings of the butterfly using your medium round brush. Don't worry if you paint outside the lines a little, as you will be painting over this area later using a darker color.

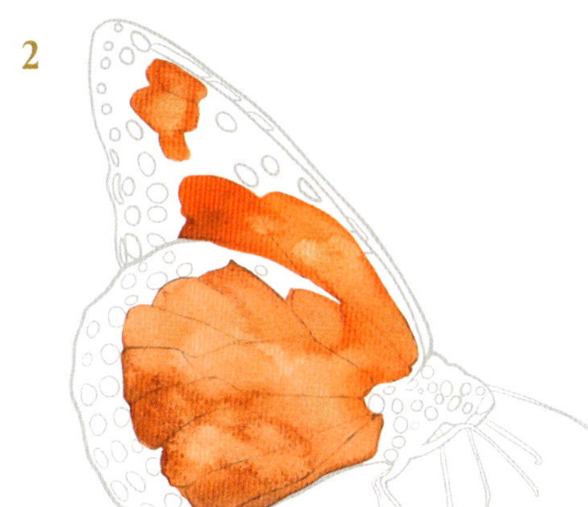

Step 3

In this step, we will be adding a few water-color splotches around the outside of the butterfly. Mix together your Cadmium Yellow Medium Hue and Cadmium Orange Hue paints, using about a 50:50 paint mixture of both colors. After mixing the two colors together, add some water to create a medium value, warm yellow color. Add the wash around the outside of the butterfly. You can even create some paint splatters as well. If you want to mix things up a little, you can use a different color for your paint splotches for the background, such as green or blue!

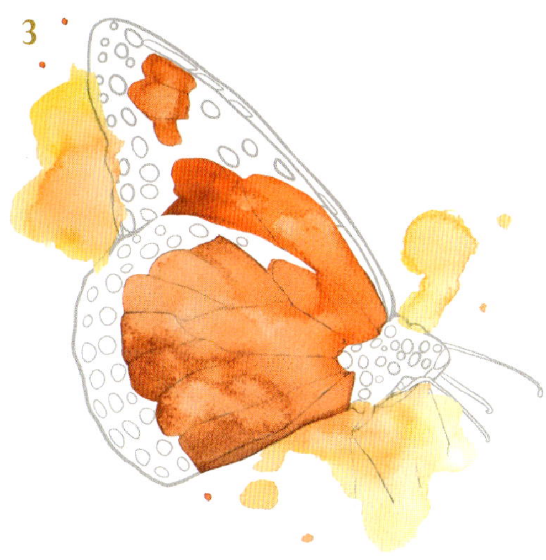

Step 4

Make sure your paint from the last step
is fully dry! The paper should no longer
be shiny if it is dry, and you can even
touch the paint lightly to check. For this
step, you will be adding dark details to
the butterfly's body and wings. Using
your small round brush dipped into a
saturated amount of Payne's Gray paint,
start outlining the circles you drew. After
you outline the pencil lines, fill things in
using a little more water with your paint
so it isn't so saturated. Next, paint out the
legs, antennae and proboscis with more
saturated Payne's Gray paint.

Step 5

In this layer, you will start to define your
subject from the background you added
earlier. To begin, fill out the wings of the
butterfly using your Payne's Gray paint
and a small round brush. Make sure to
leave the white of the paper showing for
the spots.

Step 6

Similarly to step five, start filling out the
rest of the butterfly's wings using Payne's
Gray. For the tight areas I would recommend using a small round brush, but
you can switch to using a medium round
brush to fill in some of the larger areas.

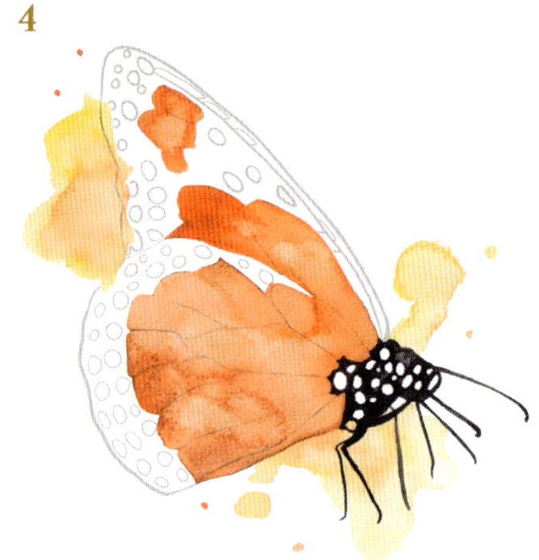

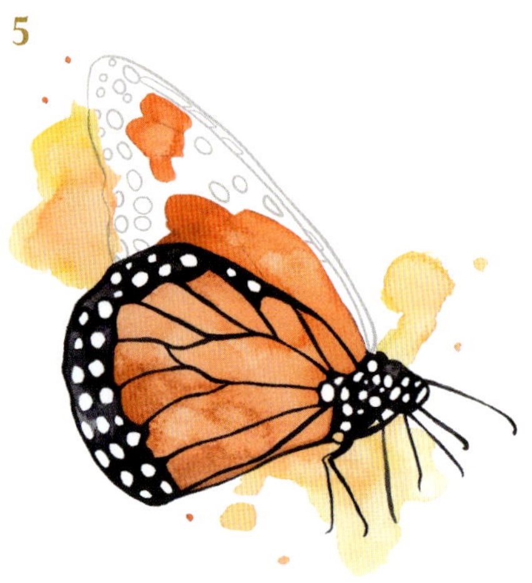

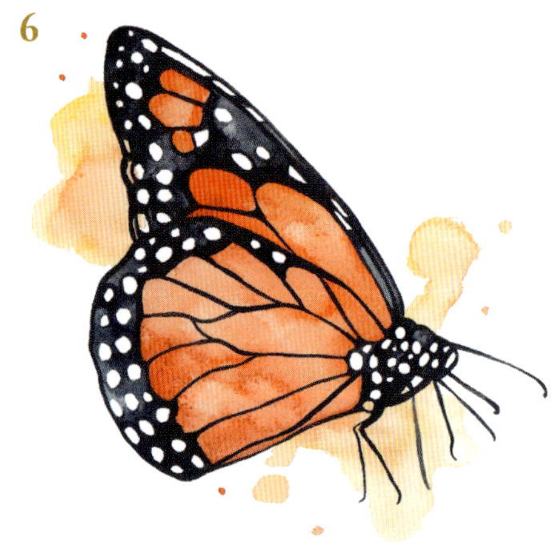

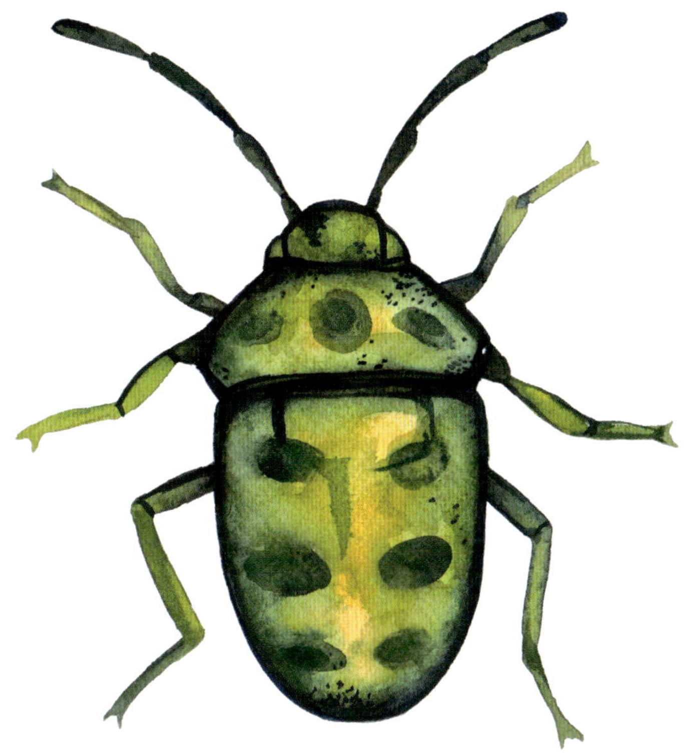

Green Beetle

Beetles can be found almost everywhere on the planet. They come in many different shapes, sizes and colors, have front wings and a hard exoskeleton. The beetle you will be painting will be made up of a variegated wash with a spotted pattern on its shell-like body. Creating a wash that goes from yellow to a deep blue-green will give the impression that its body is iridescent and almost glowing right on your paper!

Lesson
Creating a wet-on-dry variegated wash

Colors
Cadmium Yellow Medium Hue

Cascade Green

Prussian Blue

Payne's Gray

Brushes
Medium Round Brush
Small Round Brush

Step 1

Create your drawing of your beetle by using the template on page 151. Make sure your pencil lines are not too dark so your paint will cover them. You can always lightly erase your lines if they appear too dark.

Step 2

For this painting you will start off by creating a variegated wash. Start by applying Cadmium Yellow Medium Hue paint to the center of the beetle's body. Use your medium round brush to load up your paint and apply it to dry paper. Make sure this step doesn't fully dry before moving on to the next.

Step 3

While your yellow paint from the previous step is still wet, add Cascade Green paint to the outer edge of your yellow paint, allowing the two colors to mix. I would recommend using a small round brush for this process and a saturated amount of Cascade Green paint. If your two colors aren't mixing very well, add a little extra water to encourage them to do so. If you want to add a little texture to the wash, you can dab little green dots into the yellow as well.

Next, paint the head of the beetle by first applying Cadmium Yellow Medium Hue to your paper and then Cascade Green to the outside edge of the yellow while things are still wet so that they lightly blend together.

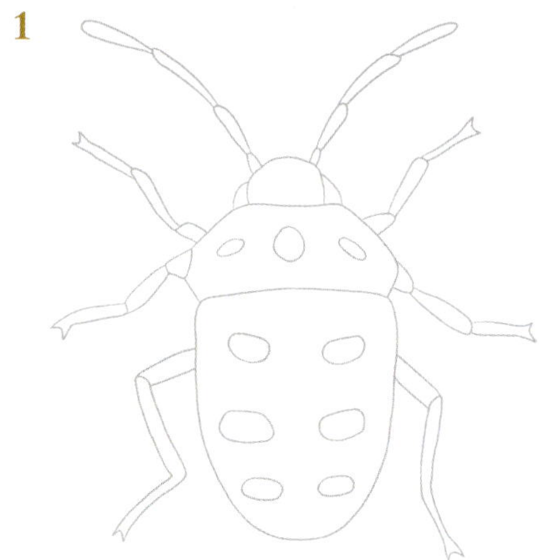

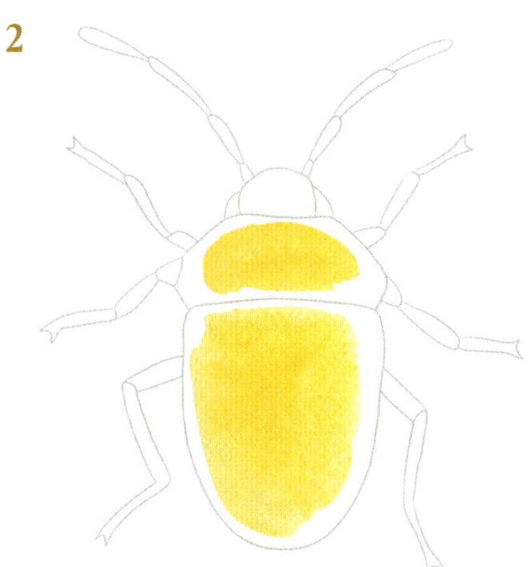

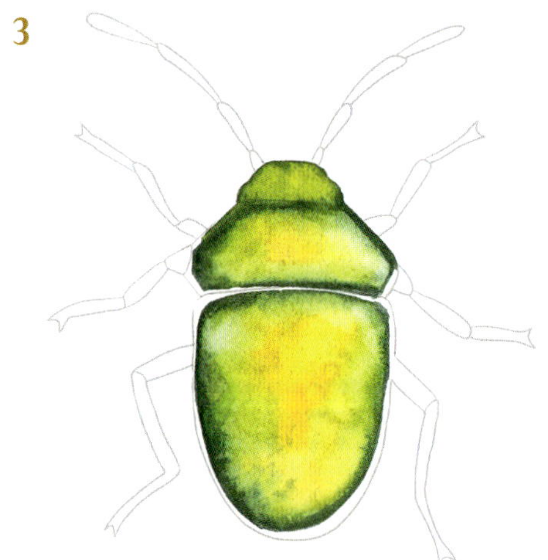

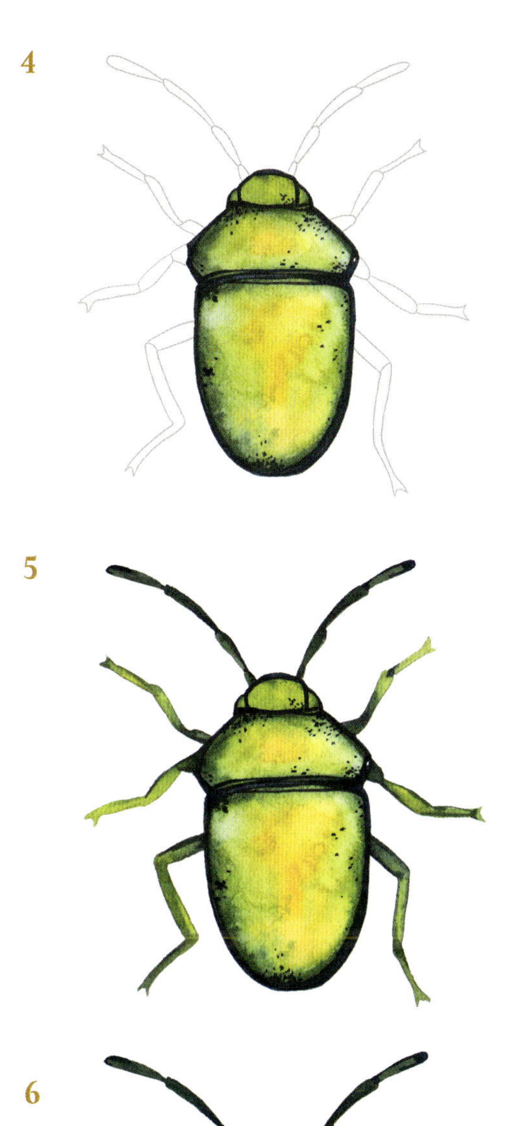

Step 4

After your wash from step three is completely dry, combine together a 50:50 mixture of Prussian Blue and Cascade Green to create a deep blue-green color. Don't use too much water because you want the colors to appear very dark. Then load up your small round brush with the paint you just mixed and outline the outer edges of the beetle's head and body. Next, using the same brush and paint mixture, add some small spots on its body and head.

Step 5

In this step, you will be painting out the legs and antennae on the beetle. Paint out the legs using a mixture of Cascade Green and Cadmium Yellow Medium Hue with a small round brush. Add extra Cascade Green to the area of the legs that comes out of the beetle's body to create shadows.

Step 6

Using your medium round brush, add a medium value wash of Cascade Green to create spots and other details on the back of the beetle. After adding the spots, add a light layer of diluted Cascade Green to the head and body of the beetle to soften any harsh lines.

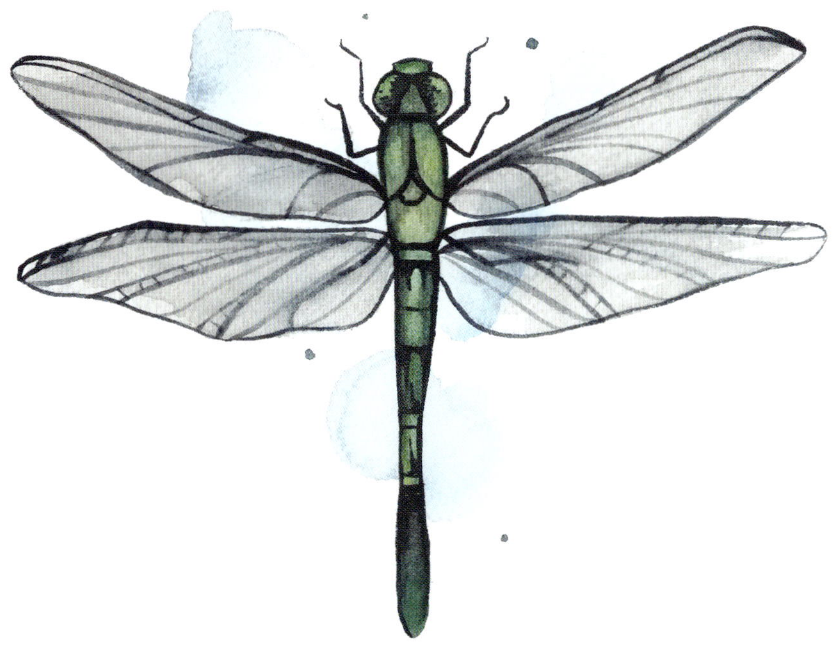

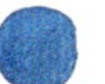

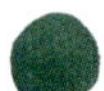

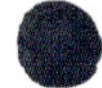

Dragonfly

Dragonflies are often found zooming around freshwater
areas. They are said to be one of the first insects, and
they have been around for 300 million years. In this
project, you start off by creating an abstract background
for your dragonfly. This background will help highlight
the dragonfly's most distinct feature, its transparent yet
detailed wings! This relaxing project will help you
practice creating fine lines that bring a lifelike quality
to your work.

Creating transparent wings
layered with fine details

Prussian Blue

Cascade Green

Payne's Gray

Medium Round Brush
Small Round Brush

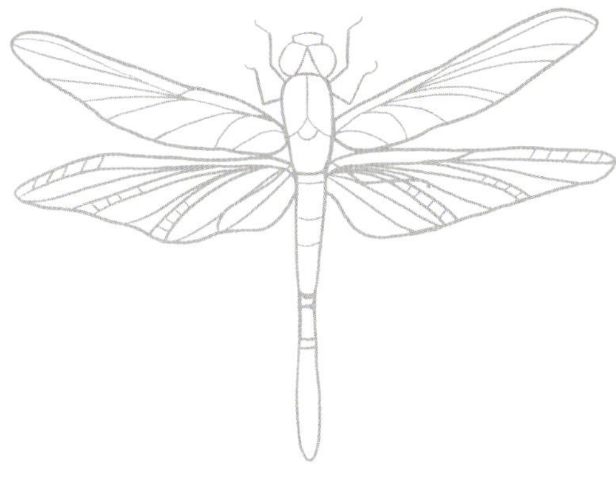

Step 1

Trace the drawing template provided on page 153. Make sure to draw out the entire shape of the dragonfly and trace the details on the wings of the dragonfly unless you prefer to freehand paint the pattern.

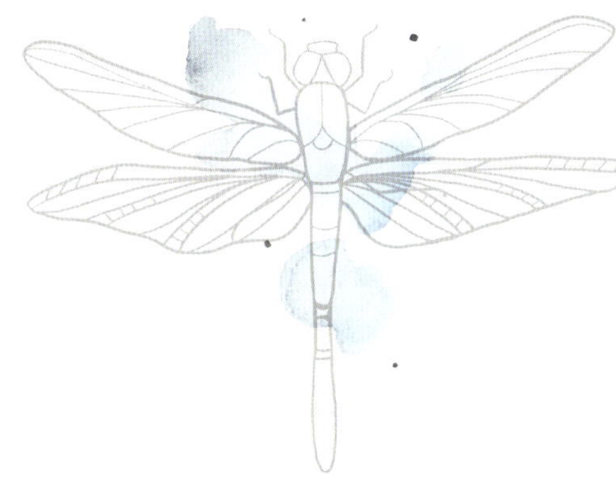

Step 2

For this painting, you will start off with a simple paint-splotch background. Using your medium-sized round brush, add a diluted amount of Prussian Blue paint around the drawing of your dragonfly. You can add your splotches to look like the ones in the book or feel free to play around with your background. The most important thing is to make sure that your paint doesn't get too dark because you will be layering transparent paint over it.

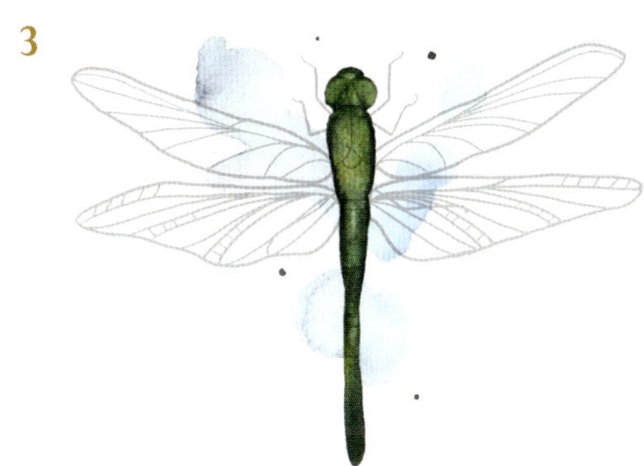

Step 3

To dry the wash from the previous step, you can either allow it to air-dry or use a hair dryer to speed up the process. Next, apply Cascade Green paint to the dragonfly's body using a medium-sized round brush. Have the value of the paint be lighter in the center of the dragonfly's body and darker along the outer edges.

Step 4

In this step, you will be using your medium-sized round brush and Payne's Gray paint to create the wings of the dragonfly. You want the wings to appear translucent and for the background layer to show through them. In order to make them look translucent, make sure to add plenty of water to your Payne's Gray paint, about an 80:20 water-to-paint ratio. You can always test your paint mixture out on a separate sheet of watercolor paper to see how things look. After your mixture looks good, apply it to the wings.

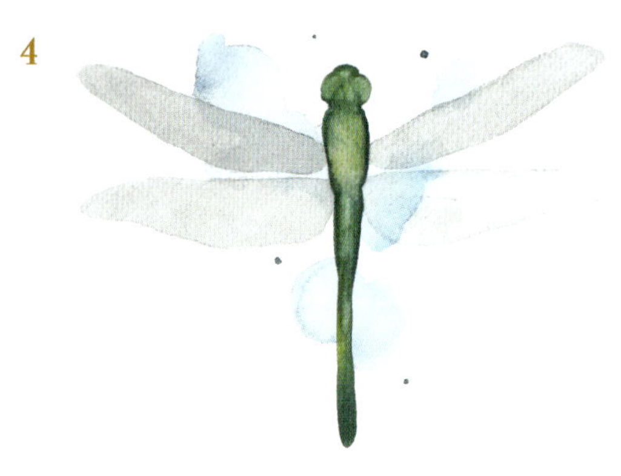

Step 5

Using your small round brush and Payne's Gray paint, add fine lines to create the pattern on its body and face. You will want your Payne's Gray paint to be saturated enough that it appears almost black when applied to paper. After creating the details on the body, paint out the legs.

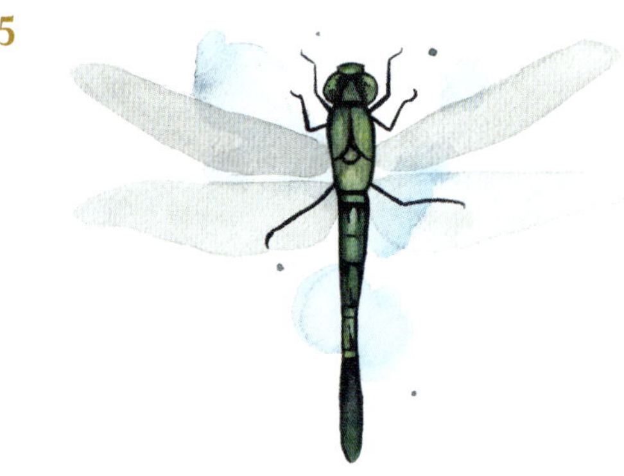

Step 6

In this step, you will be adding details to the dragonfly's wings. If you can no longer see your original pencil lines you can redraw them onto the wings before painting; just make sure that your paper is fully dry. Again, use your small round brush with Payne's Gray paint to create the fine lines. The value of the paint can range from medium to dark gray. If you want the pattern to appear softer, you can apply a light wash of water to the wings after things dry.

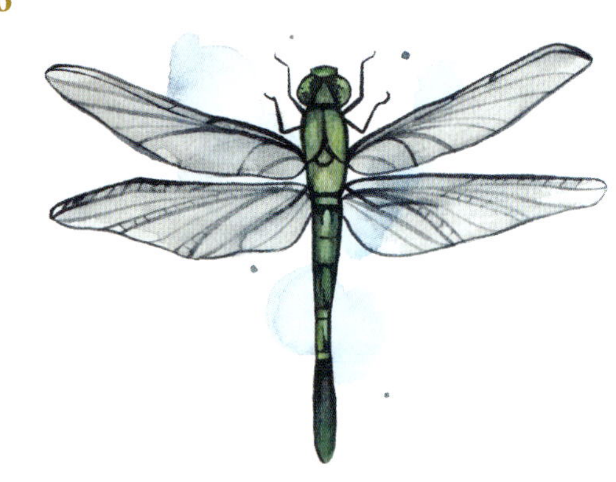

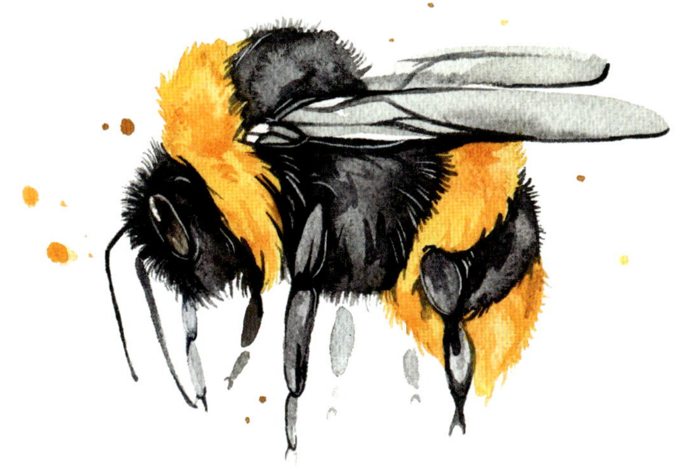

Bumblebee

These fluffy little bees are one of my favorite insects. You can find them bouncing from one flower to the next gathering nectar and pollen, making them an important pollinator for wild flowering plants. Their small bodies are covered in soft hairs, giving them a fluffy appearance. In this tutorial, you will combine some of the skills you learned in previous lessons, such as painting detailed, transparent wings and painting a mostly two-colored subject like the ladybug. Additionally, you will be adding small, white hair details to your bee to create a soft, fuzzy appearance.

Lesson
Adding white details

Colors

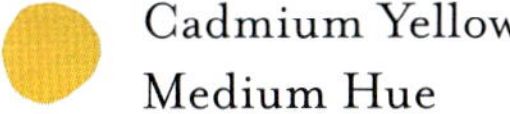 Cadmium Yellow Medium Hue

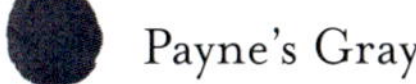 Payne's Gray

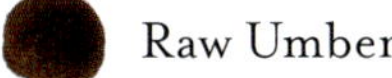 Raw Umber

Yellow Ochre

Brushes
Medium Round Brush
Small Round Brush

Extra Supplies
White ink or gel pen

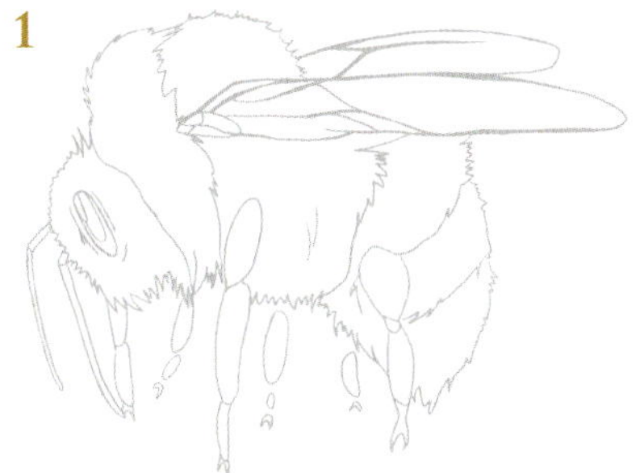

Step 1
Copy the drawing template provided on page 153 onto watercolor paper, making sure to keep the lines light, especially around the yellow areas of the bee. If your pencil lines appear too dark, gently erase them until they appear just faintly.

Step 2

You will begin by painting the yellow
sections of the bumblebee's stripes. Apply
Cadmium Yellow Medium Hue paint to
the sections of the bee using a wet-on-dry
technique with a medium-sized round
brush. After applying a wash of yellow
paint that fills in the striped shapes, use
your small round brush to paint out small
hair marks.

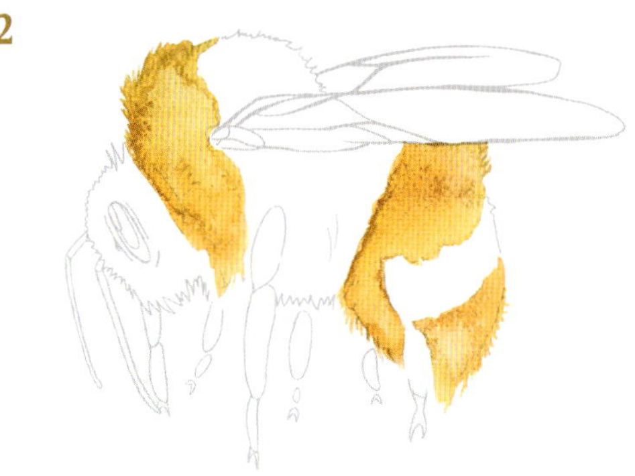

Step 3

After your Cadmium Yellow Medium
Hue paint in step two is fully dry, you
will begin painting in the black parts
of the bee. Start by filling in the black
sections of the bee using a medium value
of Payne's Gray paint then add a saturated
amount of Payne's Gray to the wash to
create the shadows on the back of its head
and around its wing. While the gray wash
is still wet, paint out small little hair
marks like you did in step two using a
small round brush.

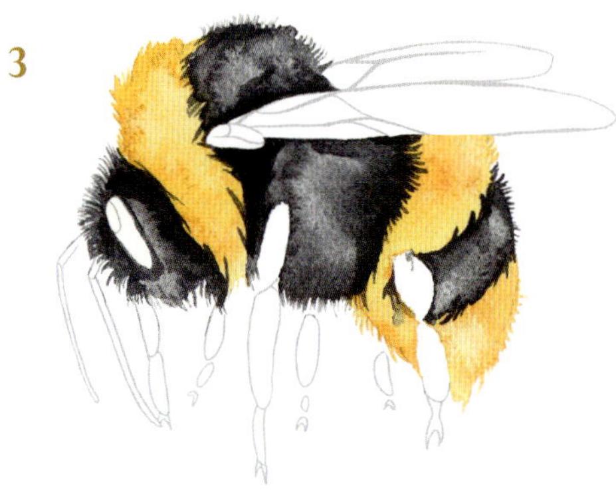

Step 4

Paint the wings of the bumblebee with a
medium-sized round brush and a diluted
consistency of Payne's Gray paint, about
an 80:20 water-to-paint ratio. Paint the
bumblebee's legs with the diluted Payne's
Gray as well, and for the tiny feet you may
need to switch to a small round brush
since they are so little. Allow this layer to
air-dry or use a hair dryer to save time.

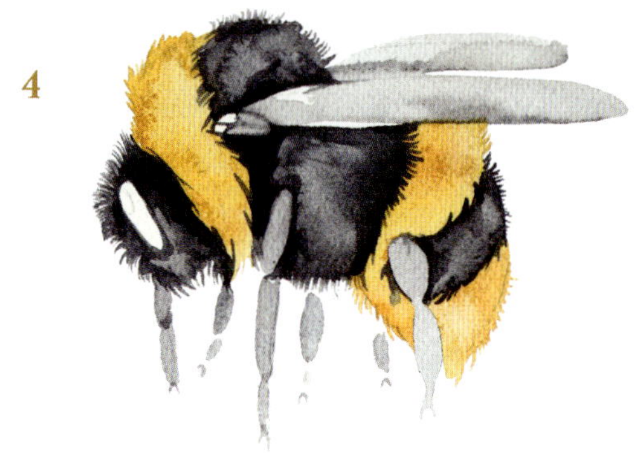

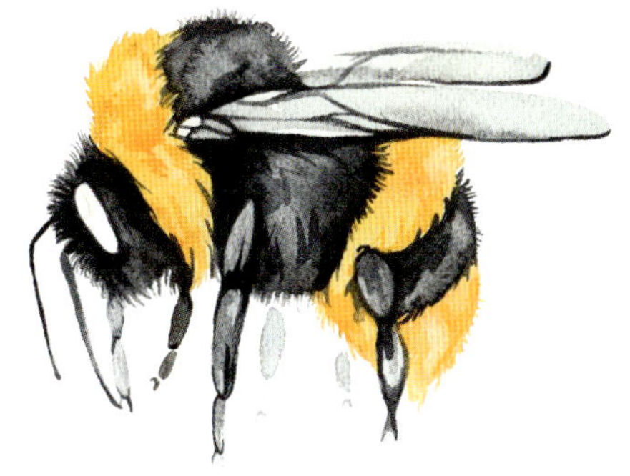

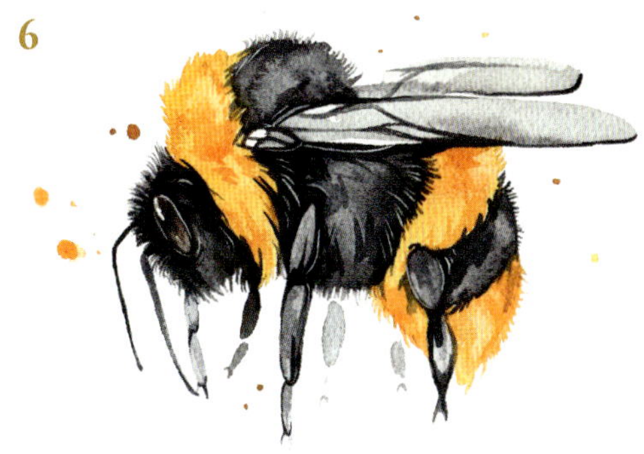

Step 5

After your bee's wings and legs are dry,
use a small round brush and a saturated
consistency of Payne's Gray paint and start
adding thin lines on the bee's wings and
hair marks on the bee's body. Do not use
a lot of water for this step in order to stay
in control.

Next, add a touch of Payne's Gray to the
legs to create some shadows. This will also
help create a sense of perspective by keeping
the back legs lighter and less detailed than
the front legs. Finally, paint the antennae
on the front of the bee's head using a small
round brush and Payne's Gray paint.

Step 6

Begin this step by filling in the eye with
Raw Umber paint, making sure to leave a
white oval unpainted in the bee's eye for
a highlight. While that paint dries, add
details on the bee's body using either a
white gel pen or ink to create little hair
marks. On the yellow parts of the bee's
body, add hair marks using a saturated
amount of Yellow Ochre paint and small
round brush. After the eye is dry, you can
outline the eye with white ink as well.

Optional

If you like the look of paint splatters, you
may add some splatters of yellow paint
to the outside of the bee. You can either
paint them out or gently flick your paint
brush at the paper after loading it up with
yellow paint.

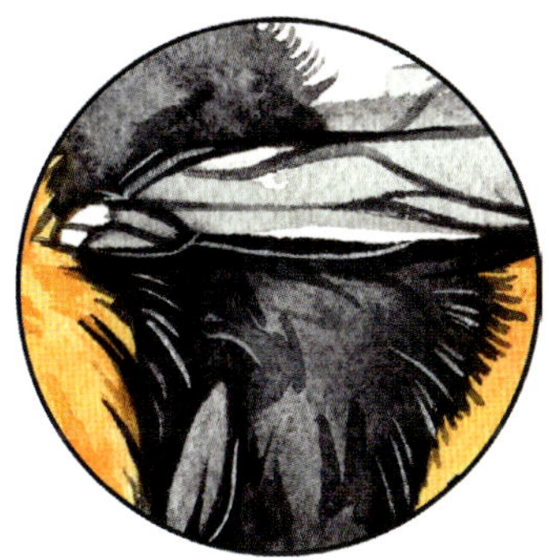

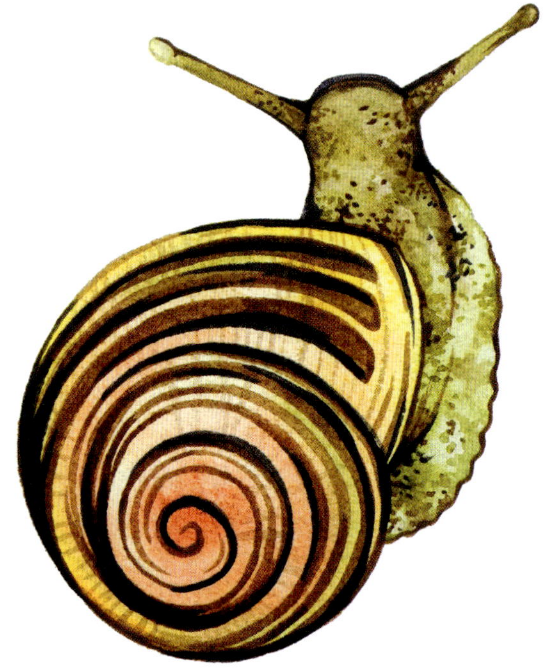

White-Lipped Snail

Snails are soft-bodied animals that are part of the mollusk family. Snails have coiled shells that help protect their body. Did you know most snail shells coil in a clockwise direction? These shells are called *dextral shells*. The type of snail you will be painting is a white-lipped snail, and in this lesson, you will practice using a stippling technique—which is when you use dots to create value—on the snail's body.

Lesson
Using a stippling technique

Colors
Olive Green
Raw Umber
Cadmium Yellow Medium Hue
Burnt Sienna
Payne's Gray

Brushes
Medium Round Brush
Small Round Brush

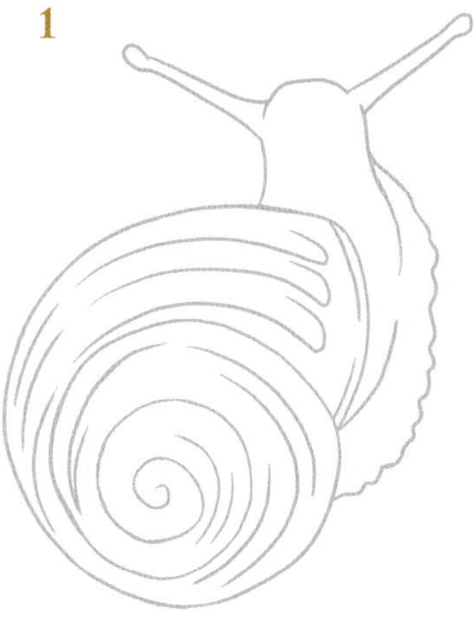

Step 1

Draw your snail using the drawing template provided on page 153 or by freehand sketching it out onto watercolor paper. Make sure your sketch is light by not applying too much pressure as you draw. You can draw out the entire spiral pattern on its shell if you want, or you can leave them out if you would rather freehand paint the design.

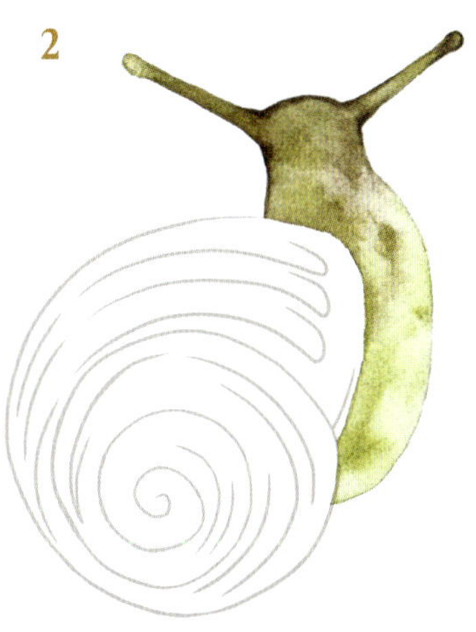

Step 2

Paint the body of the snail with a wet-on-wet technique, using Olive Green and Raw Umber paint and a medium-sized round brush. Start by adding a layer of Olive Green, concentrating more of the color on the head of the snail. While the wash is still wet, dab in Raw Umber into the wash. For the eyestalks, you might have to use your small round brush to accurately fill them in.

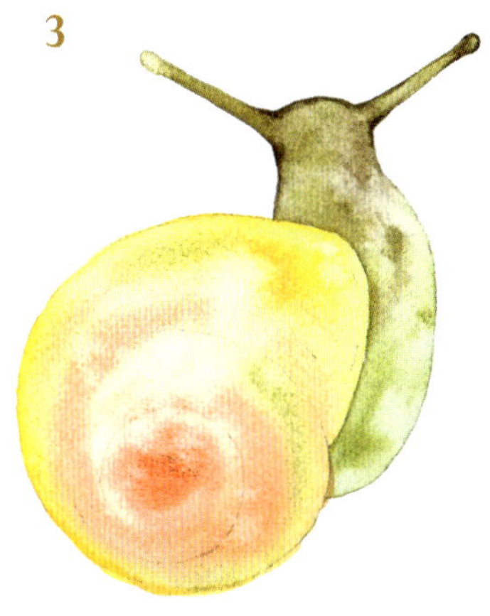

Step 3

For the shell of the snail, start with a light wash of Cadmium Yellow Medium Hue paint to fill it in, and while the wash is still wet, dab in some Olive Green. Once the wash is just lightly damp, use your medium-sized round brush and some Burnt Sienna to paint out a spiral shape into the wash. By using a wet-on-wet technique, the shape should have soft edges.

Step 4

Make sure everything from the previous step is dry before starting this one. Next, you will be using a stippling technique to create a dotted texture on the snail's body. To create this stippling effect, dip a small round brush into your Olive Green paint and dot it around the contours of the snail's body. After adding a layer of Olive Green dots, use the same brush but with Payne's Gray paint to create additional dots and to define the snail's body.

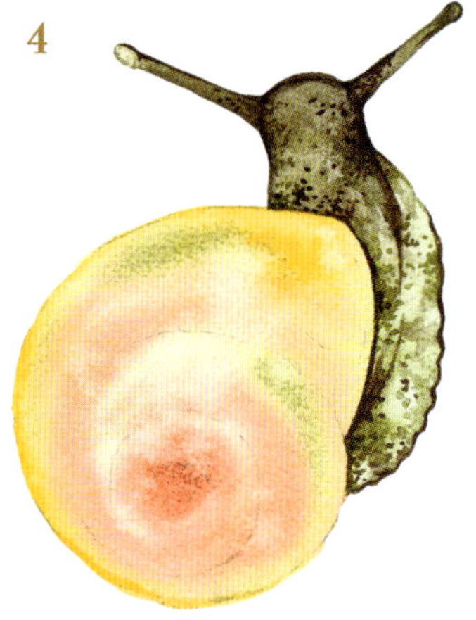

Step 5

In this step, you will be creating stripes on the back of the snail's shell using a wet-on-dry technique. To create the thicker stripes, use a medium-sized round brush and Raw Umber paint. When you get to the tighter areas and to the thinner stripes, switch to using a small round brush with Raw Umber paint. Try to not use too much water for this process in order to stay in control and keep the paint color saturated.

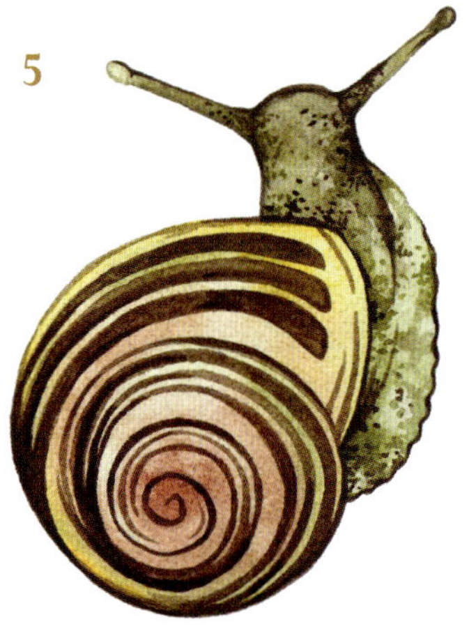

Step 6

After creating the stripe pattern on the last step, you will create the thin light lines going the opposite direction on the shell using a diluted amount of Raw Umber paint and your small round brush. Next, to add some extra contrast to the snail, add saturated Payne's Gray details to the shell and body of the snail.

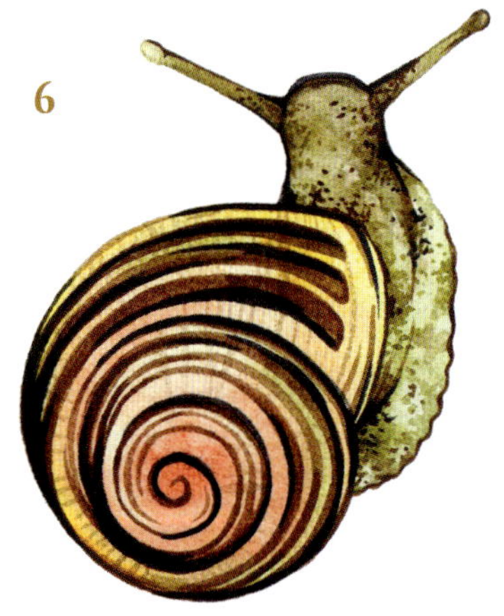

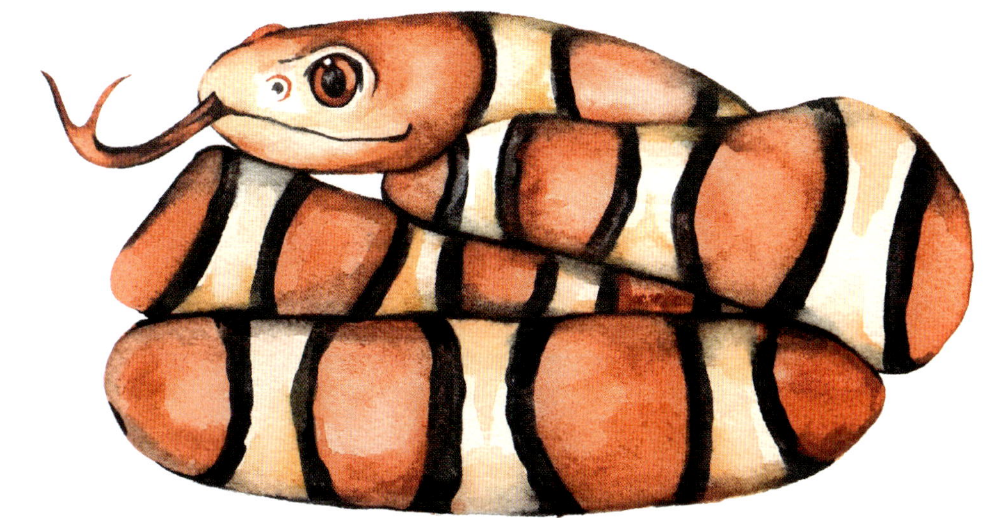

Milk Snake

This brightly colored striped snake is harmless to humans but is often mistaken for the extremely venomous coral snake. By painting this sneaky snake, you will practice painting a contrasting striped pattern. After creating the stripe pattern, you will then soften the edges to give the snake a more realistic look.

Lesson
Softening hard edges to create contours

Colors
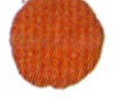 Burnt Sienna

 Yellow Ochre

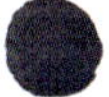 Payne's Gray

Brushes
Medium Round Brush
Small Round Brush

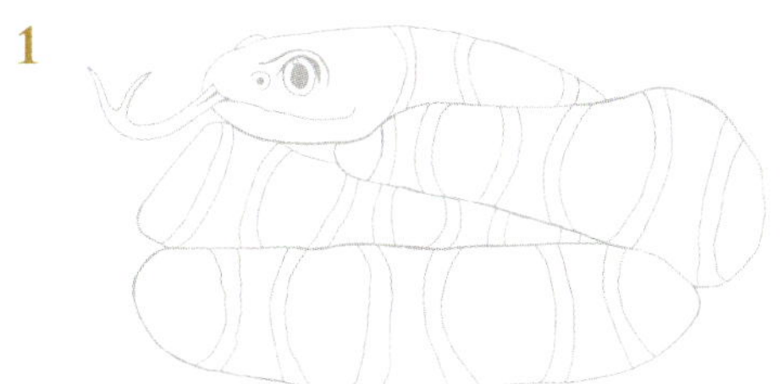

Step 1
Trace the outline on page 153. Make sure to trace lightly so the pencil marks don't show through your painting.

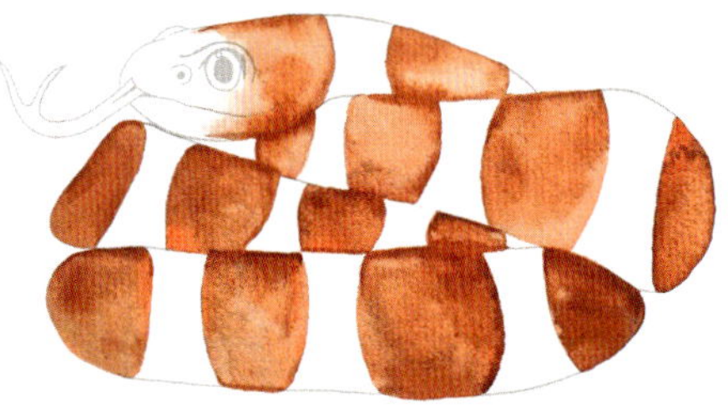

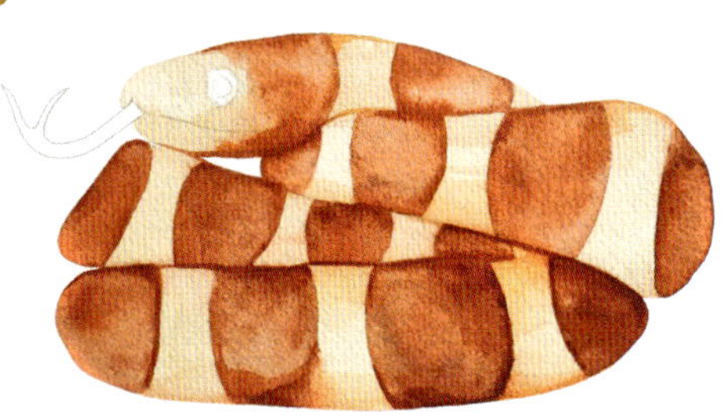

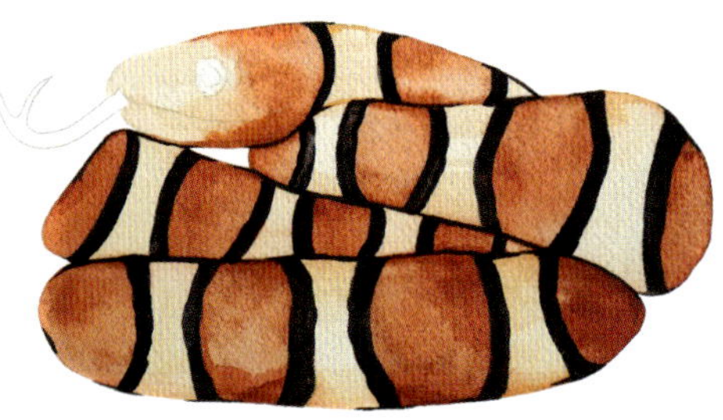

Step 2

Using your medium-sized round brush and Burnt Sienna paint, start filling in the striped pattern on the snake. Be careful to fill in the correct parts of the pattern. If it helps, you can draw a light X on the spots that you will be leaving white in this step; just remember to erase the Xs in the next step.

Step 3

Add a light diluted wash of Yellow Ochre to the stripes on the snake after the first layer is dry. If you want to dry things faster, you can use a hair dryer on its lowest setting. It is okay if you paint outside the lines a little as you will be adding more stripes on top of things in the next step.

Add some Yellow Ochre to the head of the snake, making sure to leave the eye white for now.

Step 4

In this step, add thin horizontal lines of Payne's Gray paint using a small round brush to separate the coiled layers that make up the snake's body. Make sure your paint is saturated for this part by using about a 20:80 water-to-paint ratio.

Next, paint on the dark gray stripe pattern using your medium round brush and Payne's Gray paint. Try to keep the pattern uniform as you paint it. You will want to use a wet-on-dry technique for this process, so make sure that the paper is dry when you add each stripe.

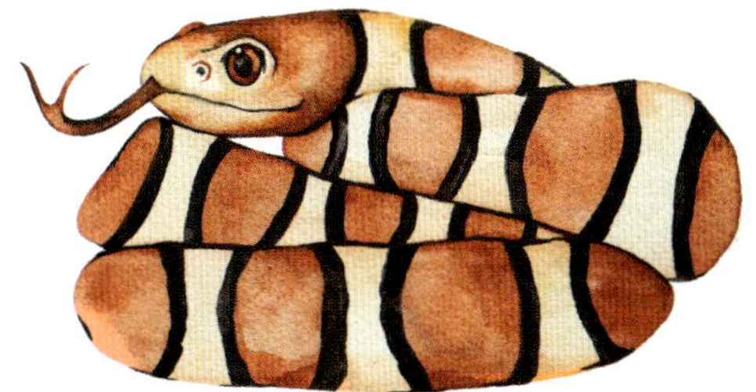

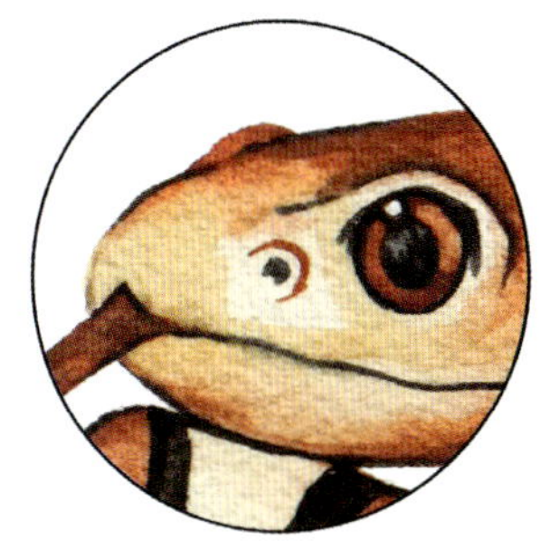

Step 5

In this step, we will be adding the facial details to the snake. I would recommend using a small round brush to really get those fine lines. For the eye of the snake, start with a layer of Burnt Sienna, making sure to leave a white dot for the highlight of the eye. After that layer of Burnt Sienna is dry, outline the entire shape with Payne's Gray and fill in the pupil. For the tongue, you will be using the same two colors, starting with Burnt Sienna. After adding the Burnt Sienna, add in the shadows with Payne's Gray, making sure to blend things into a soft gradient. Next, paint out the rest of the facial details and add a light layer of Yellow Ochre around the features to blend everything together.

Step 6

For this final step, you will be softening the harsh edges of the snake's shape to make it appear more realistic. Doing this is pretty simple. Dip your medium-sized round brush into clean water and apply it to the edges of the snake's body, making sure to stay within the lines. You do not need to add a lot of water for this process. Just use a light layer and gently move your brush horizontally in the direction of the snake's body. This contouring technique will make its rounded body appear more three-dimensional.

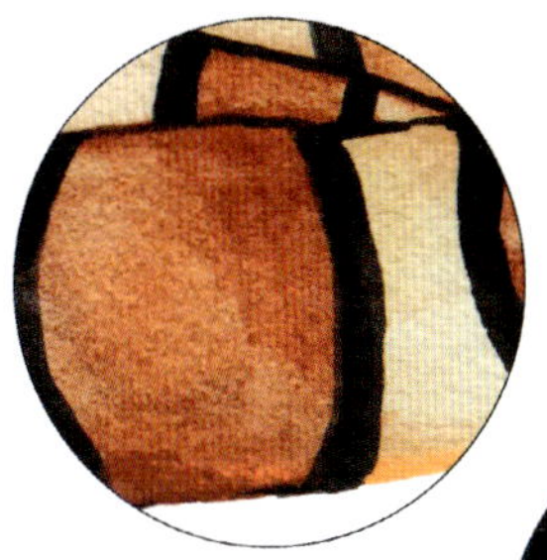

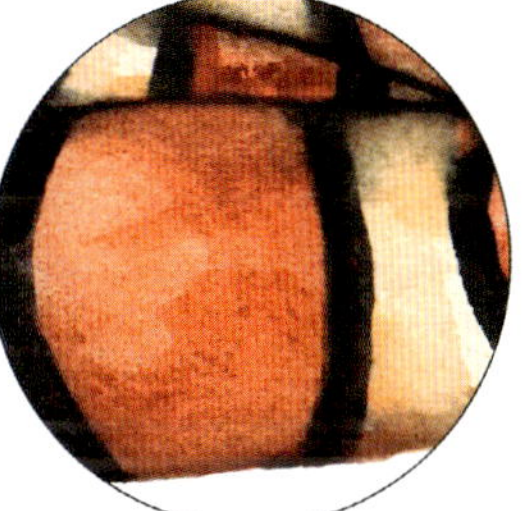

Before and after adding water

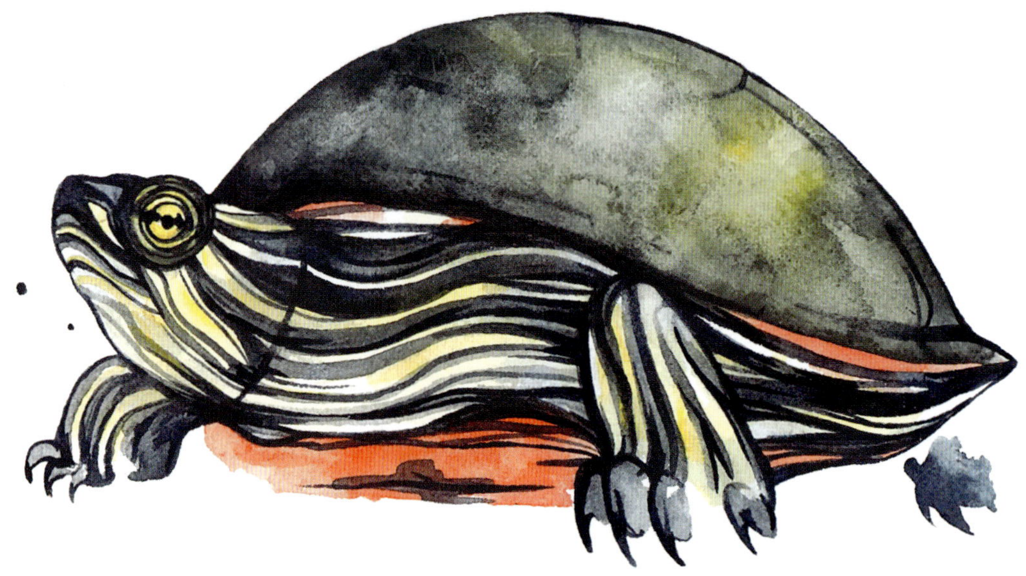

Painted Turtle

The painted turtle is one of the most common turtles in North America. You can often find them sunning themselves on logs and rocks near water. They are pretty easy to identify because they have a striking striped pattern with yellow and red markings. The bold colors on their bodies are contrasted by a murky, green shell. In this project, you will practice how to paint the intricate striped pattern found on their bodies by breaking it down into layers of different line weights.

Lesson

Creating an intricate stripe pattern using different line weights

Colors

Cadmium Yellow Medium Hue

Burnt Sienna

Payne's Gray

Brushes

Medium Round Brush

Small Round Brush

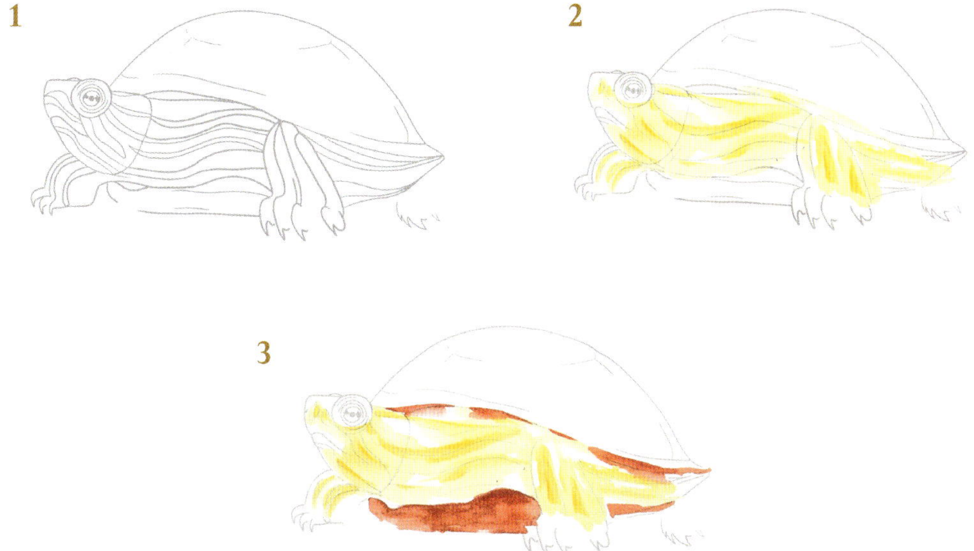

Step 1

Either trace the template on page 155 or freehand sketch the turtle using a light pencil. The turtle has a lot of fine details on it, especially the stripes on its body and its eye. For these parts of the drawing, I would recommend applying more pressure with your pencil so your lines appear a little darker and don't disappear when adding your first layer of paint.

Step 2

In this step, you will apply two layers of Cadmium Yellow Medium Hue paint to the body of the turtle using a medium-sized round brush. For the first layer, dilute the yellow into a light wash, about an 80:20 water-to-paint ratio, and apply it to the turtle's head and body. It is okay to leave some white of the paper showing through your wash as it will add some variation to the painting. Next, using a wet-on-wet technique, add more yellow stripes on top of your previous stripes, but this time use about a 50:50 water-to-paint ratio so they appear darker than the first wash.

Step 3

In this step, you are still creating the initial layers of the turtle, so things might appear a little strange. Apply some Burnt Sienna to the bottom of the turtle's shell and around the rim of the top of its shell. It is okay if the paint bleeds into the yellow from the previous step. Make sure this step fully dries before moving to the next step; use a hair dryer or allow it to air-dry.

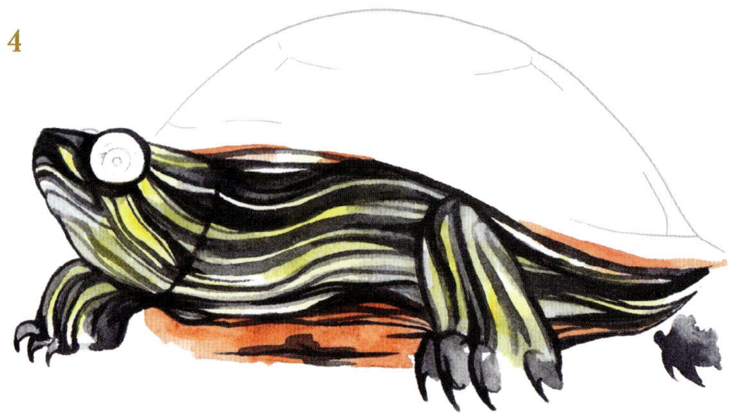

Step 4

This step might look intimidating, but you can do it! Using a diluted amount of Payne's Gray paint and your medium round brush, create the thicker lines of the stripe pattern first. After you create the thicker lines, switch to using a small round brush and apply a saturated amount of Payne's Gray to paint out the fine lines on the turtle. Next, create the stripes on the legs and feet of the turtle as well, and use your small round brush to paint out its sharp claws. To soften the lines after creating them, add clean water to the body with your medium round brush.

Stripe Steps

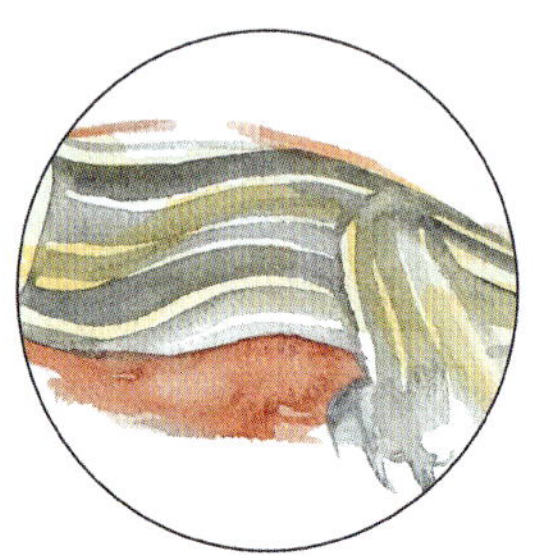

Light Payne's
Gray stripes

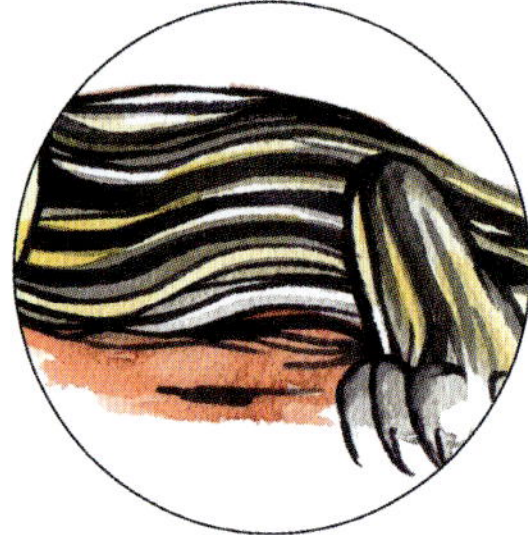

Saturated Payne's
Gray stripes

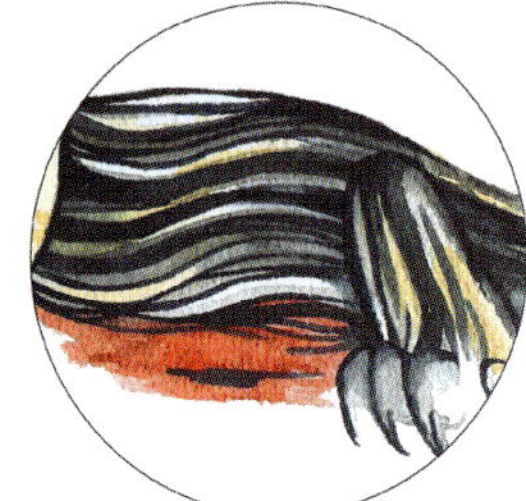

Soften hard lines
with water

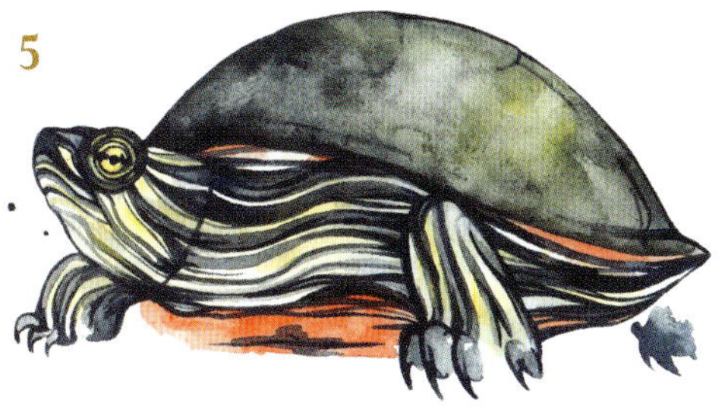

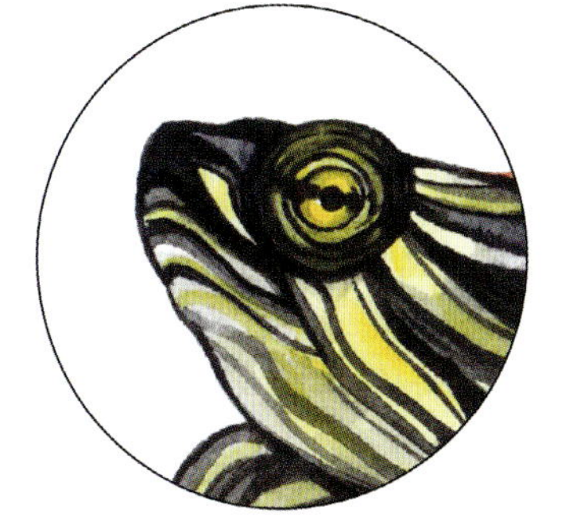

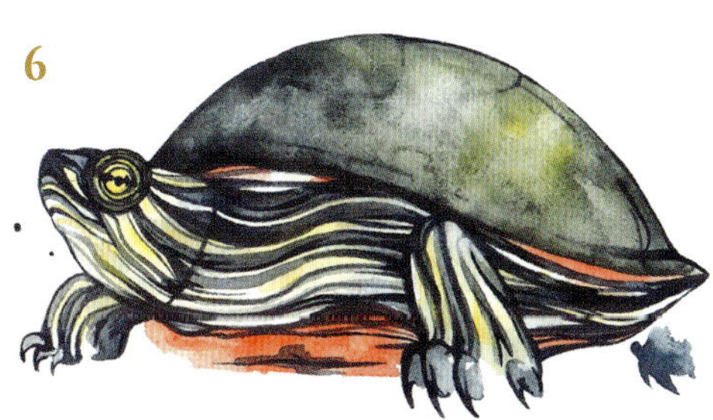

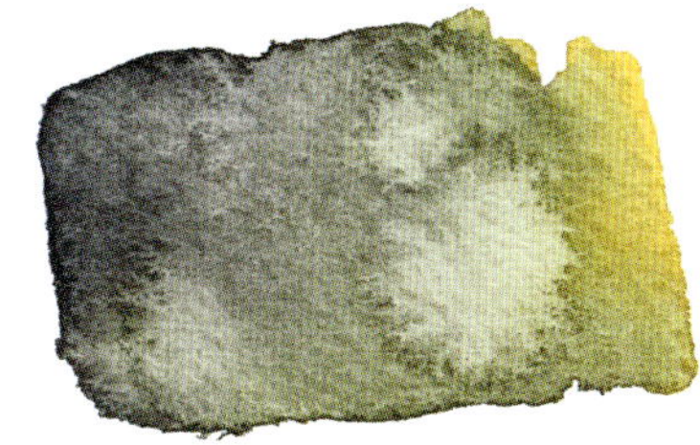

Wash created with Cadmium Yellow
Medium Hue and Payne's Gray paint
for the turtle's shell

Step 5

In this step, you will be painting the eye of the turtle. Start by adding Cadmium Yellow Medium Hue to the center of the eye using a small round brush. After the yellow paint dries, add rings around the outside of the eye using Payne's Gray paint. Then, using the same brush and paint, paint out a small pupil in the center of the eye and the lines leading out from it on either side.

Step 6

For the shell of the turtle, you will be using a wet-on-wet technique and your Cadmium Yellow Medium Hue paint and Payne's Gray. Start by applying clean water to the center of the shell, and then apply your yellow paint to the water. After adding the yellow paint, add some Payne's Gray as well; your yellow and gray paint will mix on the paper to create a murky, greenish color. Fill out the entire shell using this technique, and when you get to the edges of the shell, use only Payne's Gray paint and less water to stay in control. A darker edge to the shell helps to define its shape and make it appear more three-dimensional.

Lastly, while the shell is just lightly damp, add small lines using your small round brush and Payne's Gray paint to show the turtle shell facets or *scutes*.

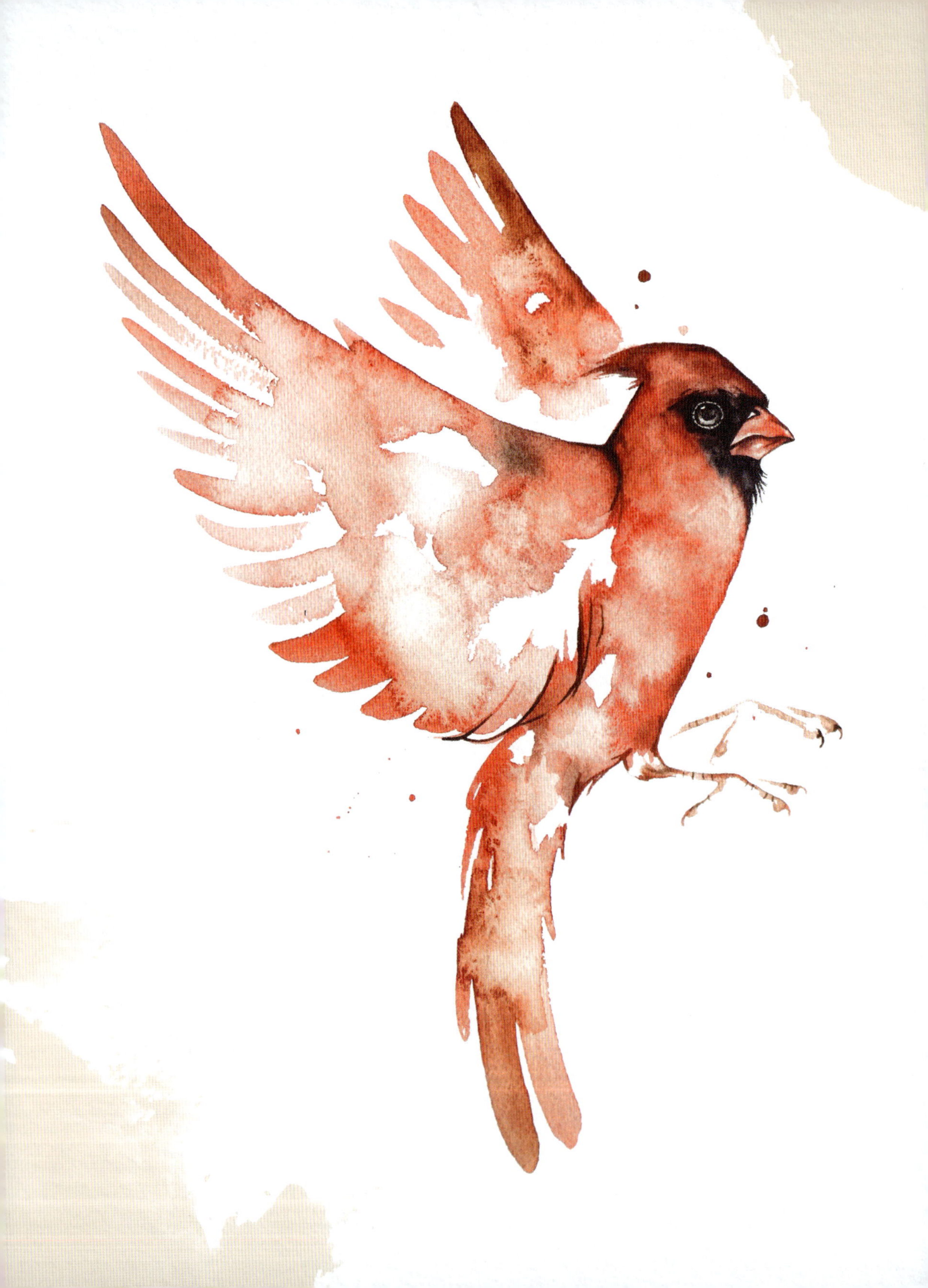

Feathered Flyers

Birds are my favorite animals to paint and are what got me back into painting with watercolors. You can find birds for inspiration by just looking out your window or visiting a nearby park. When I first started painting birds, I would often look through field guides to identify the birds I saw in my neighborhood, and then I would paint them.

In this section, you will start off by painting small, detailed song-birds and then move on to creating portraits of larger birds. You will still be creating details like you learned in the first chapter, but you will also utilize some loose watercolor techniques by creating wings and feathers with quick, expressive brushstrokes. These mark-making techniques will also convey a sense of movement and lightness to your feathered friends. For the larger portraits at the end of the chapter, you will be able to let go a little and allow the watercolor to do its thing by creating larger, abstract washes to contrast against the details.

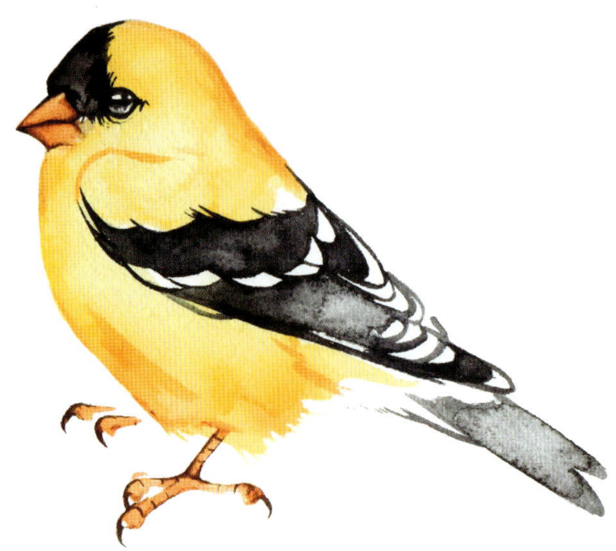

American Goldfinch

I love seeing these beautiful yellow birds at the feeders picking out thistle seeds. The males are bright yellow except during the winter when they match the females' subtle yellow-brown color. In this project, you will start off with a layer of yellow and then add dark details on top of the yellow using a wet-on-dry technique in order to keep the yellow clean and bold. You will also use a fine-tipped brush to carefully paint this finch's delicate feet.

Step 1

Create a drawing of the goldfinch by using the drawing template on page 155. For this painting in particular, it is important to have your pencil lines really light so they don't show through the yellow paint. If your lines are too dark, gently erase them a little with an eraser.

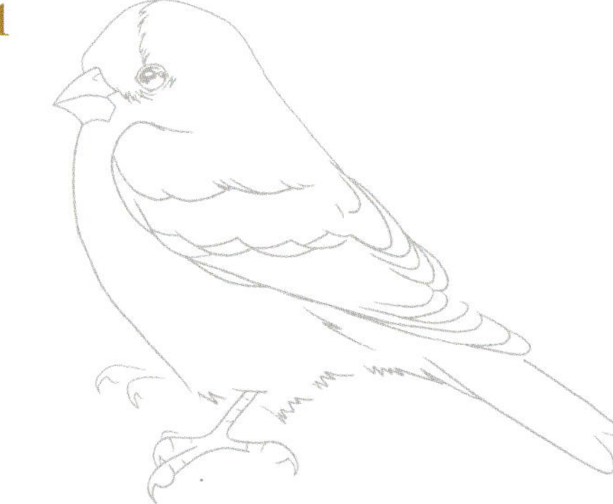

1

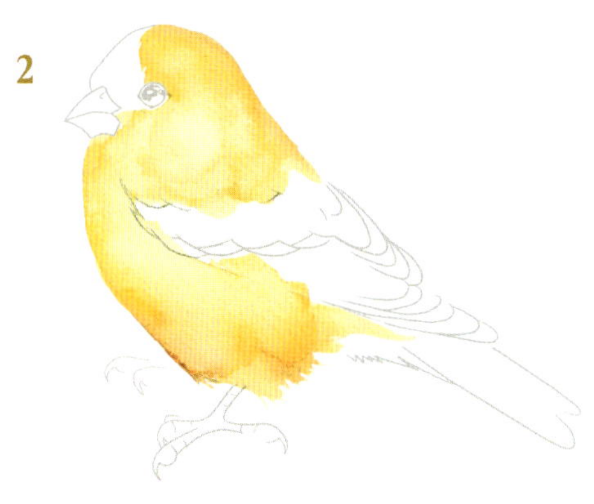

Step 2

Add Cadmium Yellow Medium Hue paint to the body of the goldfinch using a medium-sized round brush. While the wash is still wet, dab in a small amount of Yellow Ochre to the wash at the back of the head and near the legs. Next, use your small round brush to pull out little feather marks near its feet and tail feathers.

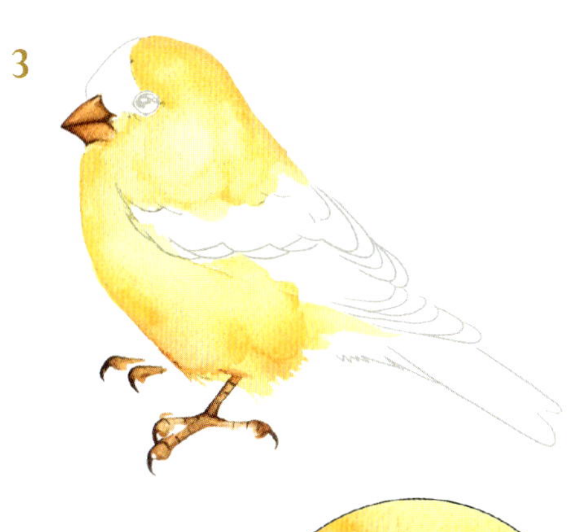

Step 3

For the beak and feet of the goldfinch, mix together Burnt Sienna and Cadmium Yellow Medium Hue to get a warm orange, using a 50:50 ratio. Next, add some extra water to the orange you just mixed to dilute it. Apply this lighter orange color to the beak and feet of the goldfinch using a small round brush.

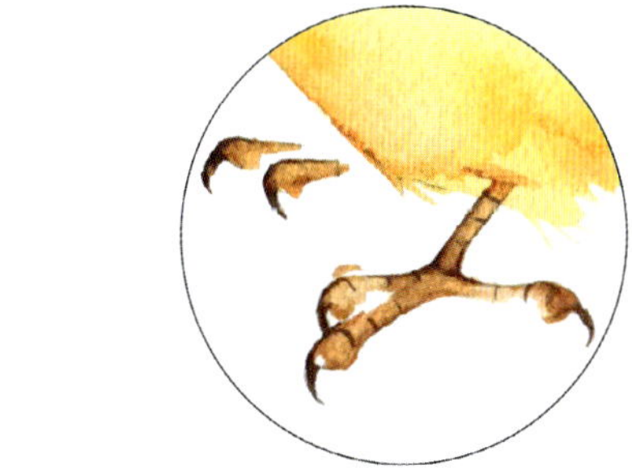

After the layer of orange paint dries, add claws and stripe details to the goldfinch's feet and define the beak with Raw Umber paint and a small round brush.

Step 4

In this step, you will use a wet-on-dry technique to paint the eye and the black patch on its head. Paint the eye using Payne's Gray. You will want the gray paint to be lighter inside the eye and darker for the outside details and for the pupil. Make sure to leave some white dots inside the eye for the highlights. This will make the bird appear more lifelike. For the black patch at the front of its head, use Payne's Gray as well, keeping the paint saturated.

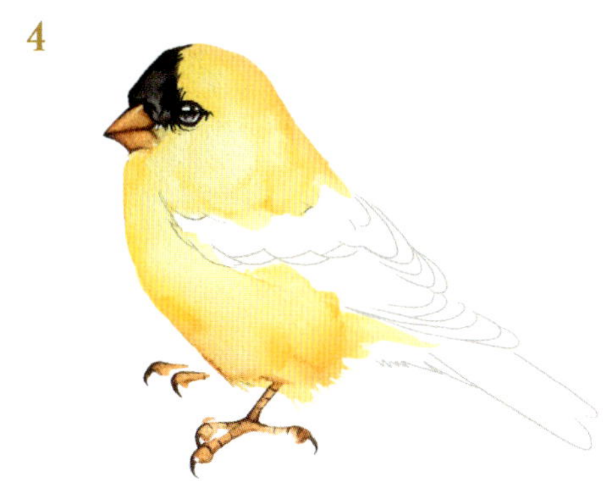

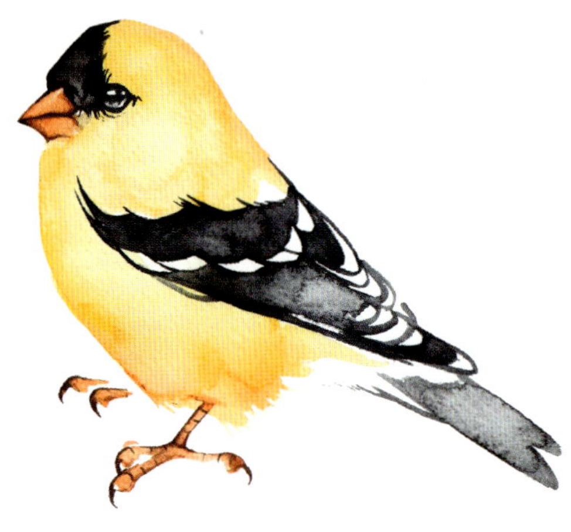

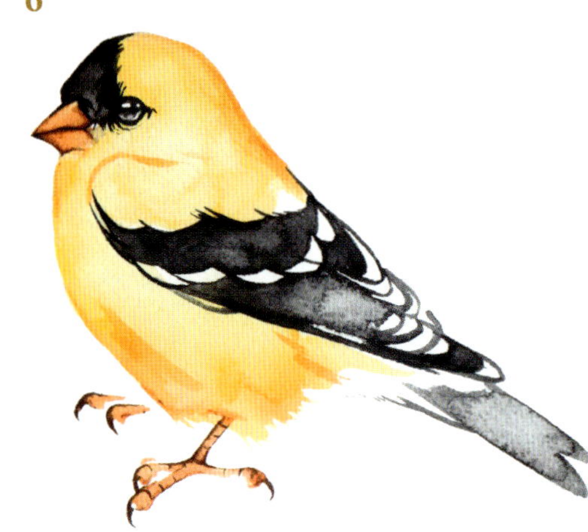

Step 5

Now you will be painting the wings and tail of the goldfinch using Payne's Gray paint. For the fine details, use your small round brush, and for filling in the larger spaces of black, use your medium-sized round brush. To create the tail feathers, load up your medium round brush with Payne's Gray paint and starting at the end of the tail feathers, drag your brush toward the body. Apply this wet paint to dry paper.

Step 6

Your goldfinch is almost complete! Now you just need to add some details to the body so it doesn't appear so flat. Add hints of Yellow Ochre with your small round brush throughout the yellow portion of its body and make sure to outline the top of its wing.

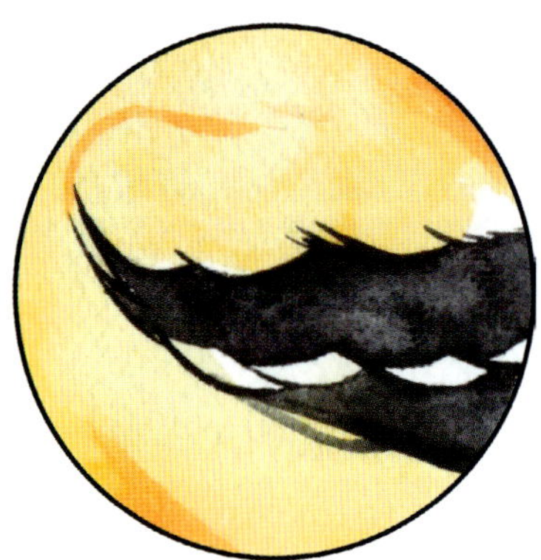

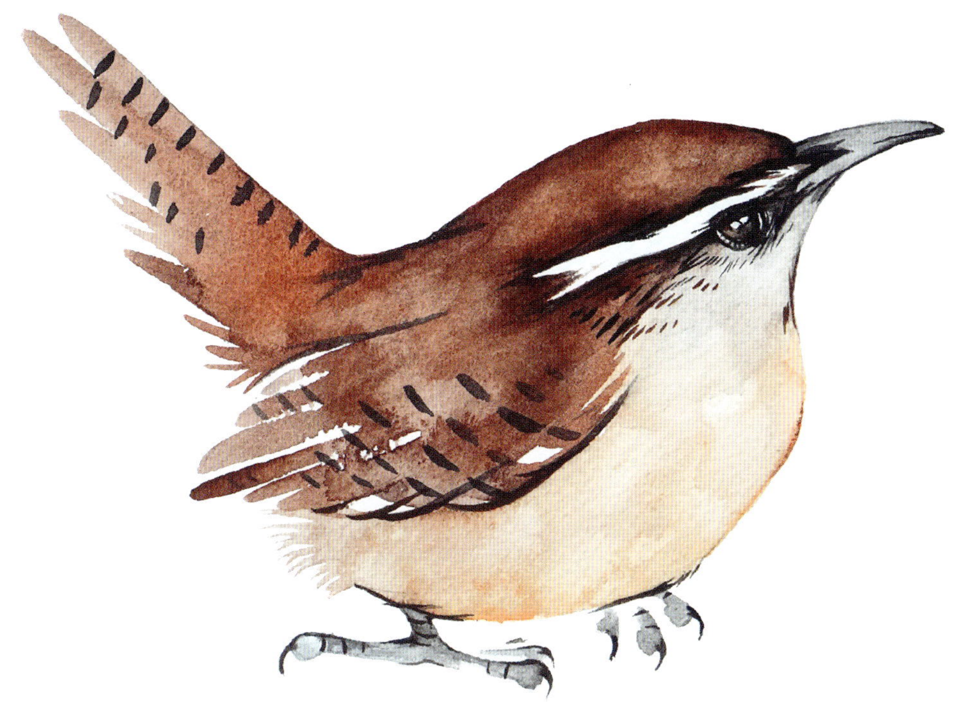

Carolina Wren

Wrens are tiny birds that sing beautiful songs but can also scold with an alarm-like chatter. They have short wings and a tail that usually sits straight up. They are often referred to as being a little feisty. In this project, you will be combining fine details on the face of the wren with impressionistic feather marks on its wings and tail. You will be using a few neutral tones to create this tiny bird, such as Burnt Sienna, Yellow Ochre and Payne's Gray.

Lesson
Wet-on-dry technique to create small details and feather patterns

Colors
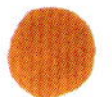 Burnt Sienna

Payne's Gray

Yellow Ochre

Brushes
Medium Round Brush

Small Round Brush

Step 1

Create a sketch of the wren by tracing the drawing template on page 155.

Step 2

Start by applying Burnt Sienna with a medium round brush to the top of the wren's head and upper back, making sure to leave some white for the stripe on its head. Using the same brush, create feather marks for the wren's wing. To create the feathers, start at the tip of each feather and drag your brush to the Burnt Sienna wash on its upper back.

Step 3

Create the tail feathers with the same technique you did for the wings, using Burnt Sienna and a medium-sized round brush. Then for the few small feathers below its tail feathers and near its wing, use the same paint but with a small round brush. Add a little extra Burnt Sienna to blend the tail feathers with the rest of the body.

After the Burnt Sienna is fully dry, use your small round brush and Payne's Gray paint to add small stripes to the wing and tail feathers. Also add some Payne's Gray details along the back and around the white stripe.

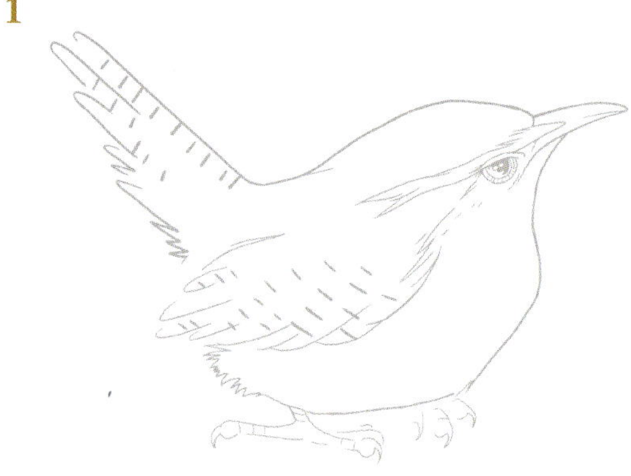

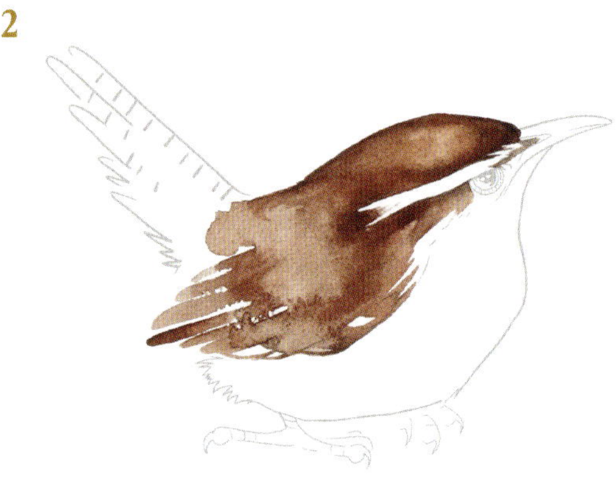

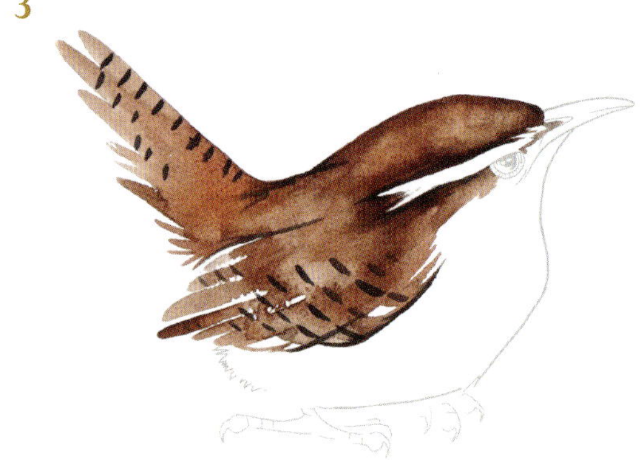

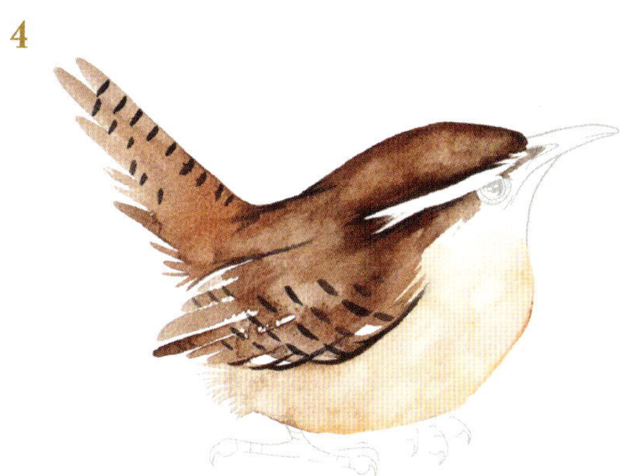

Step 4

For the underside of the wren, you will add a light wash using Yellow Ochre, starting at its breast. While the Yellow Ochre wash is still wet, drag out tiny feather marks using a small round brush.

Step 5

Now you will be adding details to the face of the wren. For the beak, add a light wash of Payne's Gray to the entire beak and after it dries, add details using a saturated amount of Payne's Gray. Start filling in the eye with Burnt Sienna, leaving some white for the highlight in the eye, and then paint around the outside of the eye using a saturated amount of Payne's Gray paint. Lastly, add some small marks with gray paint around the head to represent its feather pattern.

Step 6

For the feet, add a light layer of Payne's Gray using your medium round brush. After the paint dries, switch to using your small round brush and a saturated amount of Payne's Gray to add the claws and small lines on each foot.

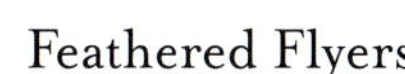

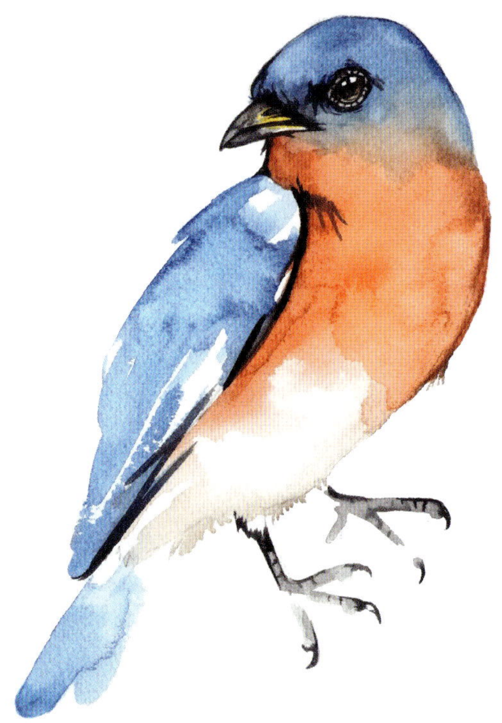

Eastern Bluebird

Bluebirds are quite rare to see, but when I do, it is super exciting. The males have bright blue heads and wings paired with a rust-colored throat, while the females are a little more subdued. Many people set out nest boxes in the hopes of attracting these birds to their backyards. In this lesson, you will be painting a subject using complementary colors, or colors that are opposite to each other on the color wheel. Though these are the bluebird's natural colors, using complementary colors can add a lot of contrast to your piece. You just have to be careful to not muddy up the colors when they are placed next to each other.

Lesson

Painting a subject with complementary colors

Colors

 Burnt Sienna

 Raw Umber

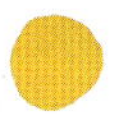 Cobalt Blue

Cadmium Yellow Medium Hue

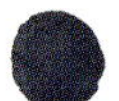 Payne's Gray

Brushes

Medium Round Brush

Small Round Brush

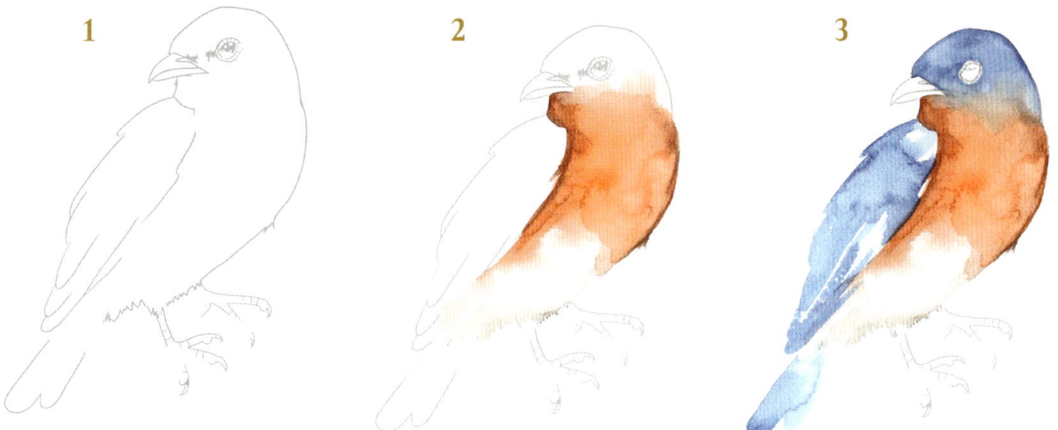

Step 1

Create a drawing of the eastern bluebird using the template on page 155.

Step 2

To start this painting off, add Burnt Sienna to the breast of the bluebird with your medium round brush. Have the orange paint end above the legs of the eastern bluebird. Toward the tail of the bluebird, add a light wash of Raw Umber, and while the wash is still wet, drag out small hair marks using your small round brush. Make sure that this wash is completely dry before moving on to the next step.

Step 3

Now you will be adding color to the top of the eastern bluebird's head and painting out its wing and tail feathers with a bright blue. Fill in the bird's head with Cobalt Blue using a medium round brush and be careful to not add too much pigment where the blue and orange meet. For the wing, start by filling in the top portion of the wing with Cobalt Blue. After filling in half of the wing with blue, create wing feathers by swiping your medium round brush upward into the wash, starting at the tip of the wing feather and then using a similar technique for the tail.

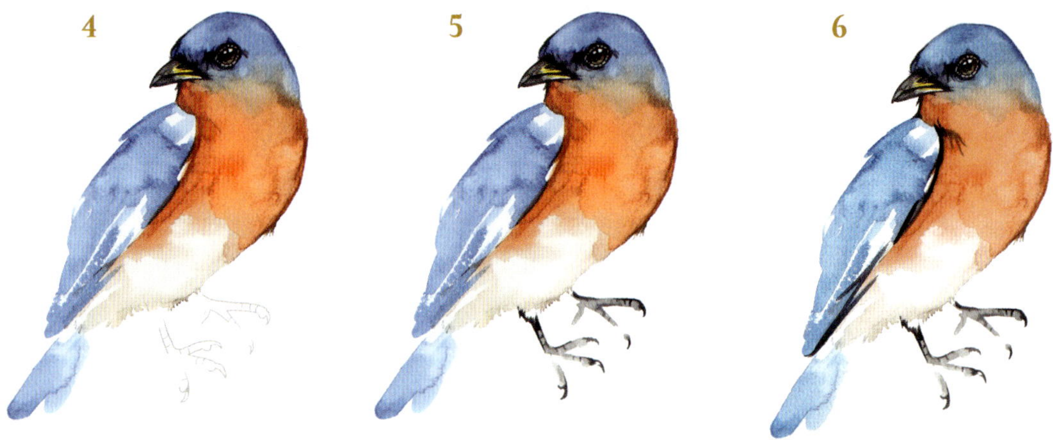

Step 4

Now you will paint the beak and eye. For the beak, start off by applying Cadmium Yellow Medium Hue paint to the back half of the beak. After the yellow is fully dry, paint the rest of the beak using Payne's Gray paint.

For the eye of the bluebird, paint the inner eye with a light layer of Raw Umber. While that paint dries, paint the ring around the bluebird's eye with a diluted amount of Payne's Gray paint. Once this first layer is dry, paint the details inside and outside of the eye using a saturated amount of Payne's Gray paint.

Step 5

Next, you will be painting the feet of the bluebird. Start off using a diluted amount of Payne's Gray paint. To get the paint lighter, just make sure to add additional water to the pigment. Using your medium round brush, paint out an impression of the feet. After this layer dries, paint out small details and claws on the feet using a saturated amount of Payne's Gray.

Step 6

In order to increase the contrast and to add more definition to the wings of the bluebird, add a saturated amount of Payne's Gray paint around the wing. Feel free to add in a background such as a fence post to create an environment, or you can go more abstract and add some paint splatters.

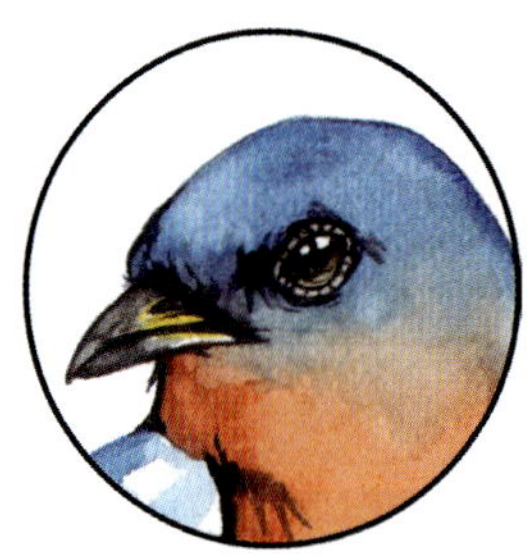

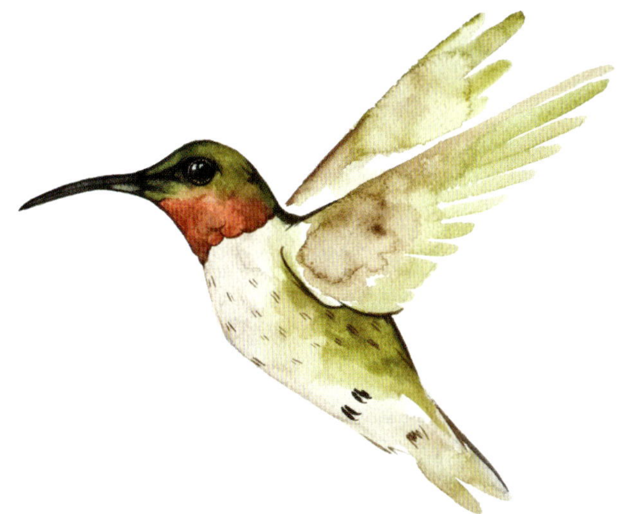

Ruby-Throated Hummingbird

These little guys beat their wings so fast that it sometimes looks like they don't even have any! And they have feet so small they cannot walk; they just perch when it's time to rest. These hummingbirds have long beaks for gathering nectar from flowers and the males have bright red throats that give them their name. In this project, you will be painting the flying wings using just a few brushstrokes. By keeping the wings gestural, you will give the impression that they are moving quickly and are slightly blurry.

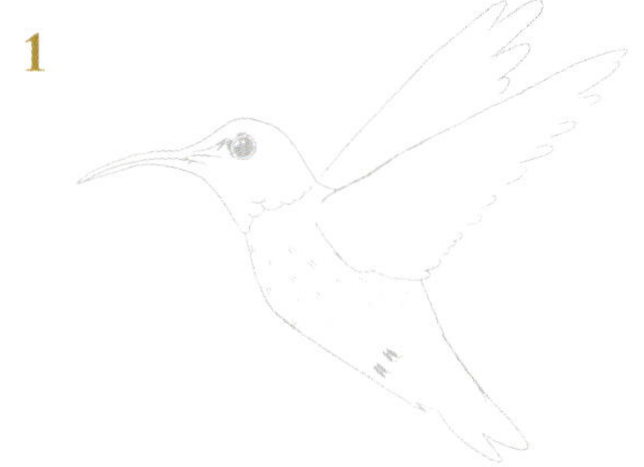

1

Step 1
Create a sketch of the hummingbird by using the template provided on page 157. Make sure to keep the sketch light, especially for the wings and tail feathers.

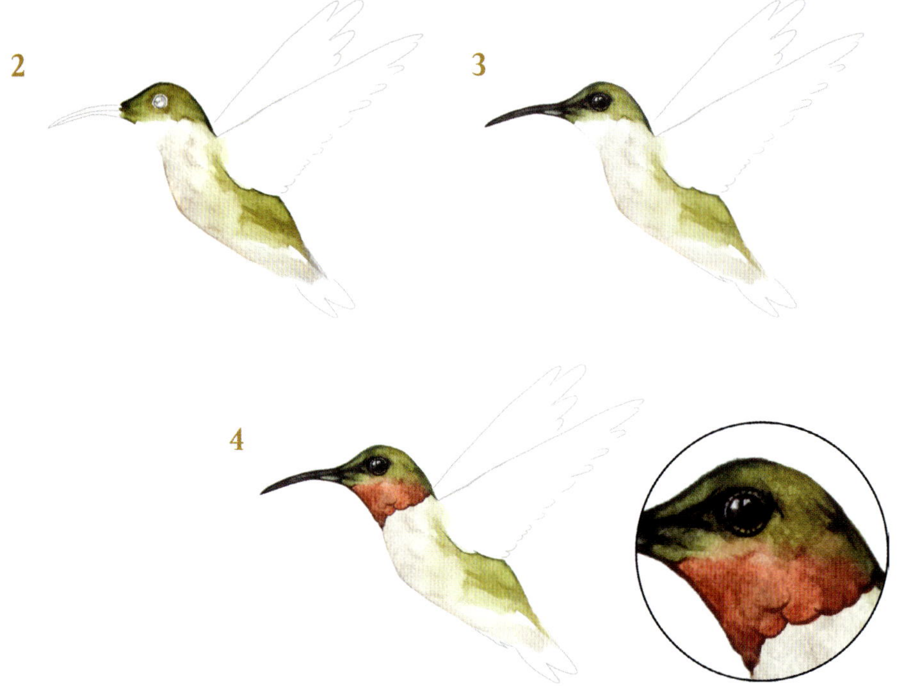

Step 2

Fill in the front of the hummingbird's chest with a light wash of Raw Umber using a medium round brush. While this wash is still wet, add Olive Green to the back of the hummingbird, below its wings, and lightly blend it with the Raw Umber. Next, paint the top of the hummingbird's head with Olive Green. You may need to switch to a small round brush for some of the tighter areas.

Step 3

After the Olive Green paint from the last step is dry, start painting the beak using Payne's Gray paint and your small round brush. Using the same brush and paint, paint the eye of the hummingbird, making sure to leave white highlights. Next, add some shadows in front of the eye using Payne's Gray as well.

Step 4

Create a 50:50 water-to-paint ratio with Cadmium Red Medium Hue paint, and cover its entire neck. After your first layer dries, use a wet-on-dry technique to create small details using your small round brush and a saturated amount of Cadmium Red Medium Hue mixed with a small touch of Raw Umber to deepen its color. The paint ratio should be about 75:25 Cadmium Red Medium Hue to Raw Umber.

5

6

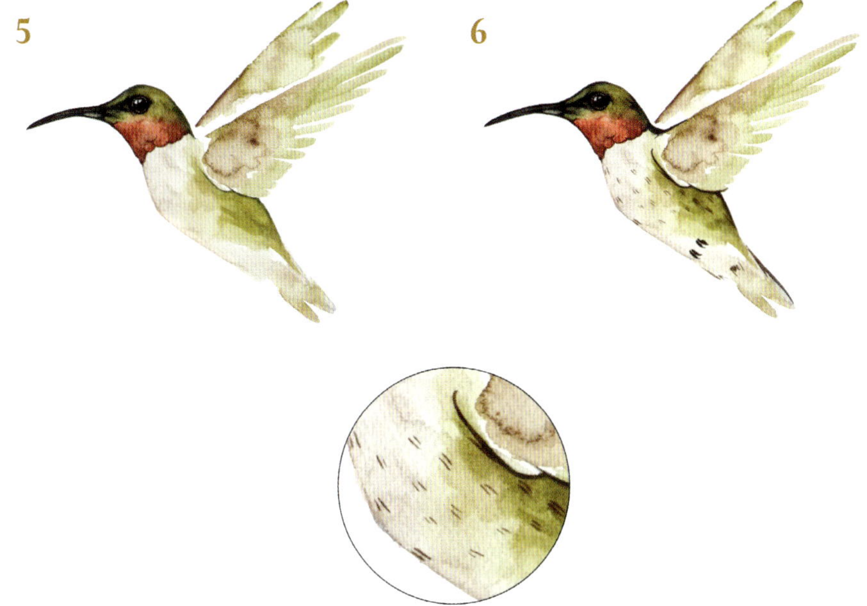

Step 5

Before you paint the flying wings of the
hummingbird, make sure that your pencil
lines are fairly light. If they are not light
enough, lightly erase them until they
almost disappear. For this step, start off
with the closer wing, adding a diluted
amount of Raw Umber to the area of the
wing that comes out of the body. Then,
using your medium round brush and
Olive Green paint, start at the tip of each
wing feather and drag the paint into the
Raw Umber wash.

For the back wing, use the same technique,
making sure to leave a little white between
the two wings so they don't become one.
For the tail feathers, use Raw Umber with
a medium-sized round brush and just two
upward brushstrokes on dry paper.

Step 6

For this next step, make sure that
everything is dry as you will be using
a wet-on-dry technique to create small
details. You will need your small round
brush and a saturated amount of Payne's
Gray to paint out the small feet of the
hummingbird. Then add some to its
shoulder, below its wing and to the back
of its tail. Next, using Raw Umber with a
small round brush, paint out small lines
on its breast.

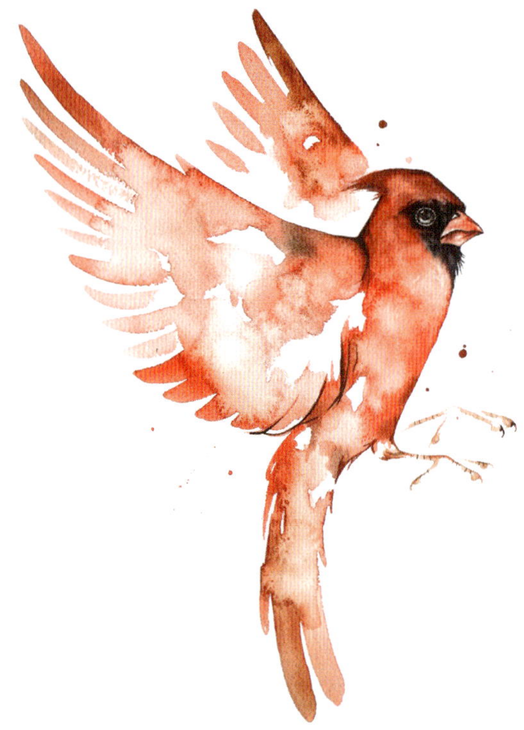

Northern Cardinal

The northern cardinal is a favorite bird to many, and it is easy to see why: its bold, red color and distinct song capture one's attention whenever it flies by. They are often also believed to be a symbol of a loved one who has passed.

The goal of this painting is to create a bird that appears to be in motion by using quick brushstrokes to create the wing feathers and by using watercolor blooms to create a soft, lightweight effect. For this painting, you will only be using two different brush sizes, one to fill in the color quickly and to create the feathers, while the other will be used for the tiny details on its eye, beak and feet.

Lesson
Using watercolor blooms to create motion

Colors
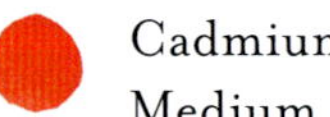 Cadmium Red Medium Hue

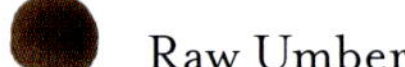 Raw Umber

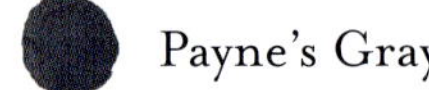 Payne's Gray

Brushes
Medium Round Brush

Small Round Brush

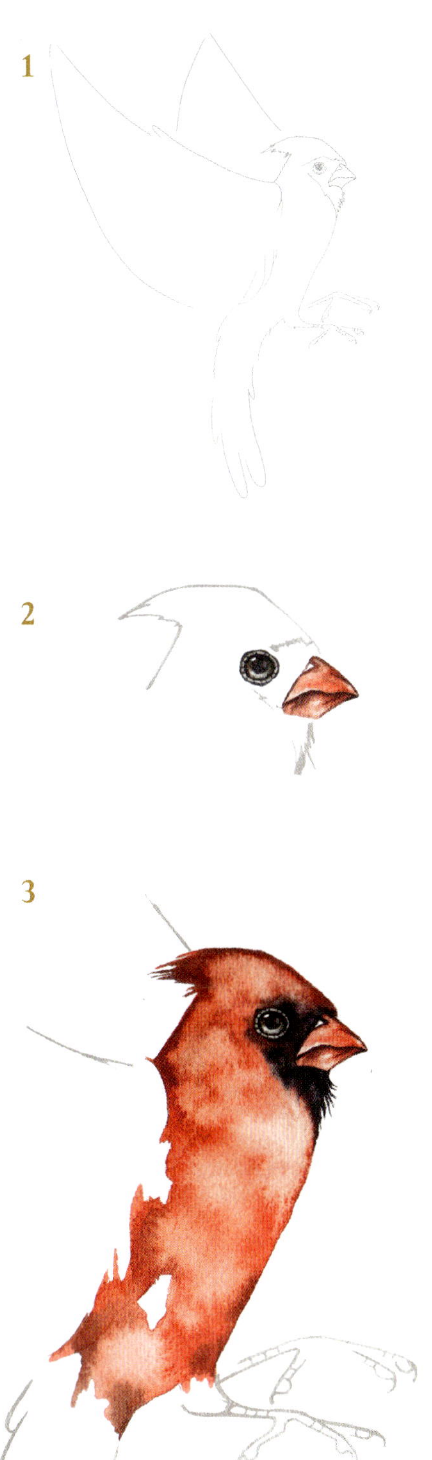

Step 1

Trace the drawing template found on page 157. Make sure you keep the pencil lines light so they don't show through your watercolor paint.

Step 2

Paint the cardinal's beak using Cadmium Red Medium Hue paint and a small round brush. Once the beak is dry, you can add a thin line of Raw Umber to separate the lower and upper beak. Next, fill in the inner eye with Raw Umber, keeping the value darker at the top of the eye and lighter toward the bottom. Paint the details outside of the eye as well as the pupil with Payne's Gray, making sure to leave a highlight. This gives the eye a lifelike shine.

Step 3

First load a medium-sized round brush with Cadmium Red Medium Hue paint and add it to the body. For the cardinal's crest, switch back to a small round brush to drag out the tiny feathers. Next, add some Payne's Gray to the area around the beak and the eye. Before your wash fully dries, you will create blooms in your wash by dipping clean water into the wash while it is lightly damp. Start by adding one dab of water and watch the magic happen. If you like this effect, add a few more blooms of water throughout your wash.

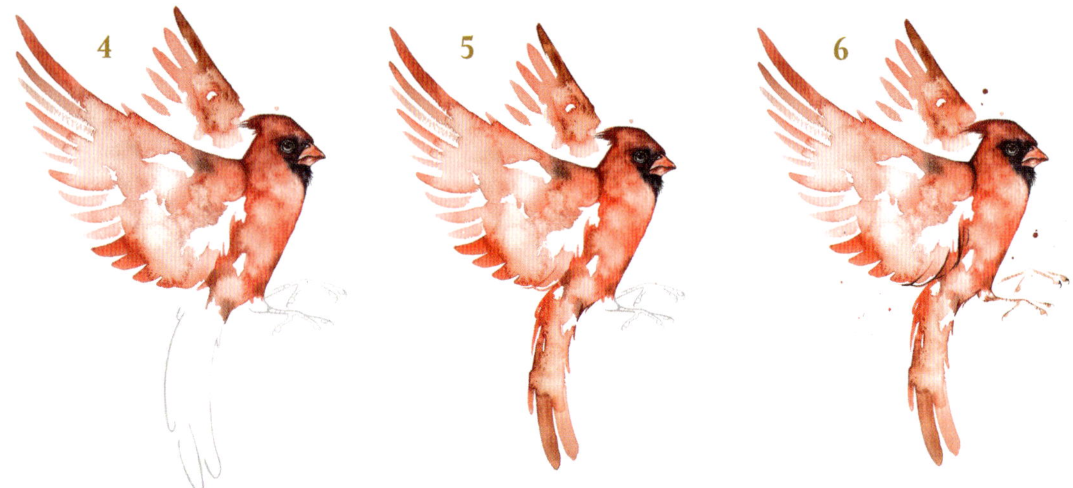

Step 4

Add a wash of Cadmium Red Medium Hue paint to the area closest to the body with a medium round brush, leaving some white of the paper showing. Next, create wing feathers with Cadmium Red Medium Hue paint. Starting at the edge of the curved pencil line and drag it into the wash. After painting the first wing, repeat this process for the back wing. While the wash is still damp, you can create more blooms.

Step 5

Mix together about a 25:75 ratio of Raw Umber to Cadmium Red Medium Hue paint. Adding just a slight amount of Raw Umber pigment to the Cadmium Red Medium Hue paint will help create some variation and depth to the color. Next, load up your medium round brush with this mixture and paint out the tail feathers. Then add blooms to the wash while the paint is damp.

Step 6

Paint out the thin feet using a wet-on-dry technique, using a small brush and diluted amount of Cadmium Red Medium Hue paint. You want the feet to appear light and impressionistic. Add Payne's Gray for the talons and small dash marks on the legs.

Using your Payne's Gray again, add some small details on the feathers right next to the cardinal's body; this helps separate the feathers from the rest of the body. To give additional movement to the painting, create some light splatters around the cardinal.

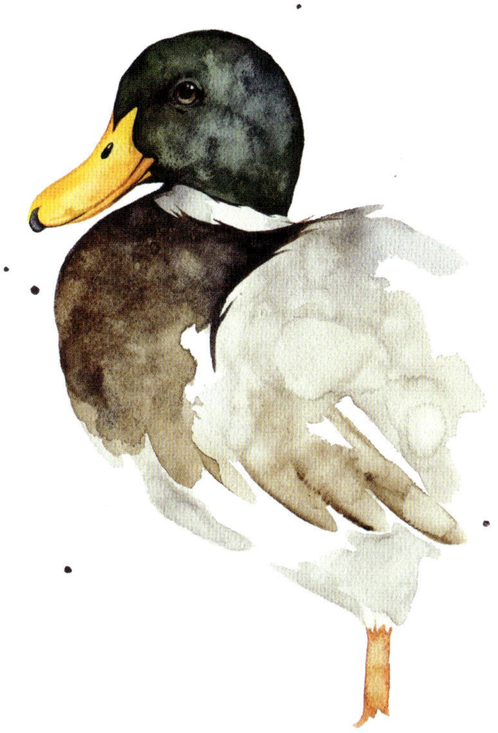

Mallard Drake

Mallards are one of the most recognizable duck breeds and are the ancestor to many domesticated ducks. Male mallards, known as drakes, have a striking iridescent-green head that will be the focal point of this painting. For this project, you will be creating a portrait that is cropped as opposed to being centered on the paper. The head of the drake will be detailed and lifelike and the painting will slowly abstract and become looser on the body, where you will use expressive brushstrokes to create the wing feathers.

Lesson
Creating a cropped portrait

Colors
Cadmium Yellow Medium Hue

Burnt Sienna

Payne's Gray

Raw Umber

Cascade Green

Brushes
Medium Round Brush

Small Round Brush

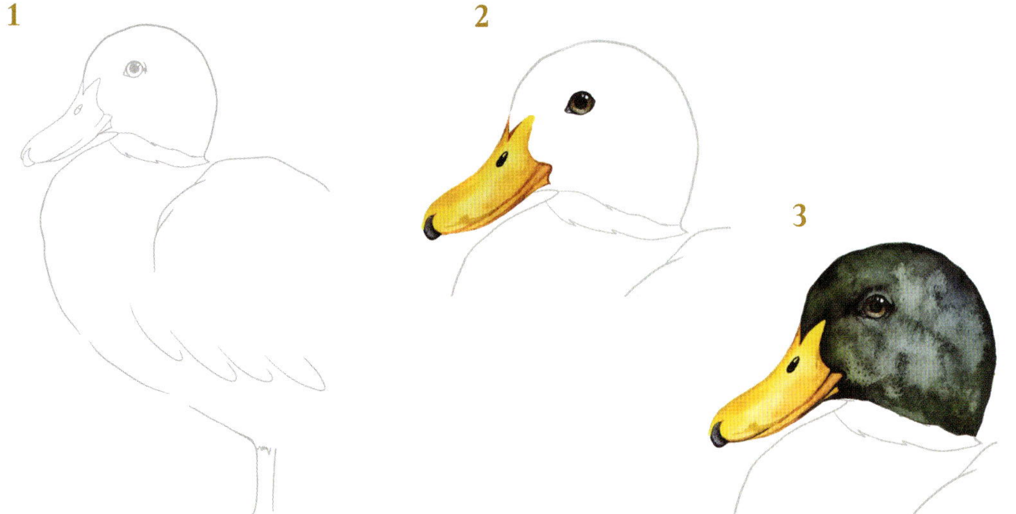

Step 1

Create a sketch of the duck on watercolor paper by tracing the template provided on page 157. Draw the portrait so that it hugs the bottom-right side edge of your paper because you will be painting a cropped image. If you feel like a challenge, try lightly sketching the duck using the template only as a visual aid. This is good practice and can allow you to paint a larger duck if you would like.

Step 2

Start by painting the bill of the duck with Cadmium Yellow Medium Hue. Fill in the whole bill other than the tip. While the yellow paint you just added is still wet, add Burnt Sienna for the details on the bill. Last, after the first layer is fully dry, paint in a nostril and the tip of the bill with Payne's Gray using a small round brush.

Next, paint the eye of the duck. Start by filling in the eye with Raw Umber paint. After the Raw Umber paint is dry, outline the eye with a saturated amount of Payne's Gray and paint the pupil with Payne's Gray as well.

Step 3

In this step, fill in the duck's head with Cascade Green using a medium round brush, and then add a small amount of Payne's Gray around the front of the duck's eye and around its bill to increase the value. While your wash on the duck's head is still damp, dab small drops of clean water into the wash to create a texture.

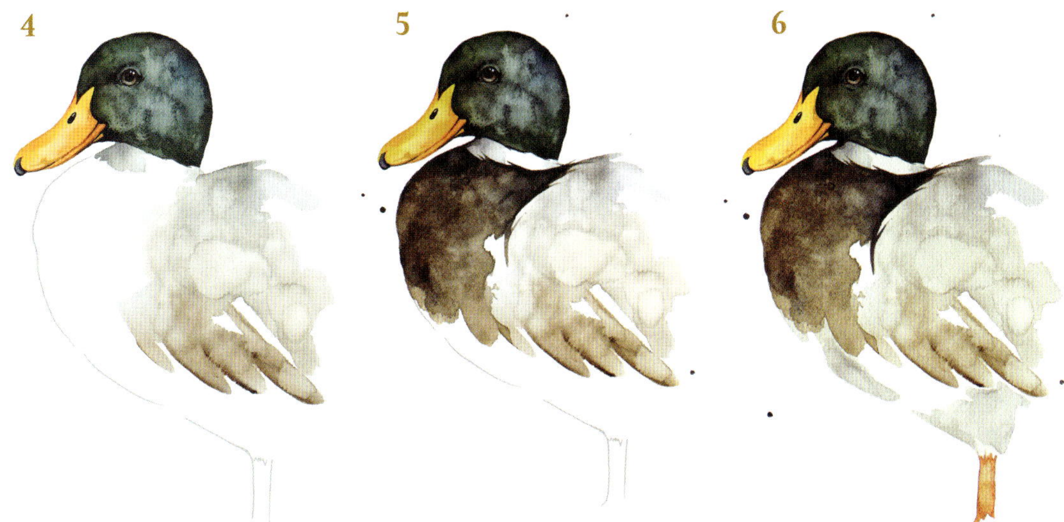

Step 4

Now you will start loosening up the body of the duck. Add a diluted wash of Payne's Gray around the ring of the duck's neck to its back. Next, add a mixture of diluted Raw Umber next to the gray you just added while the gray paint is still wet. Lastly, load up your medium round bush with Raw Umber paint and create feather marks to represent the wing feathers. Before the wash fully dries, dab some clean water onto the wash to create blooms.

Step 5

Add a wash using a mixture of Payne's Gray and Raw Umber to the breast of the duck using your medium round brush, and then add more green paint to the top portion of the wash. Using a small round brush, paint out a harsh edge around the ring of the duck's neck and by its wing using Payne's Gray. If you would like, create some paint splatters around the duck's body using your medium round brush and Raw Umber paint.

Step 6

Since this piece is meant to have a cropped look, you won't be completing the tail and foot of the duck. Finish the body of the duck by creating a light wash with Payne's Gray and also add some of this paint above its foot.

For the duck's leg, mix Cadmium Yellow Medium Hue and Burnt Sienna together to create an orange color, and then fill in the leg with your medium round brush.

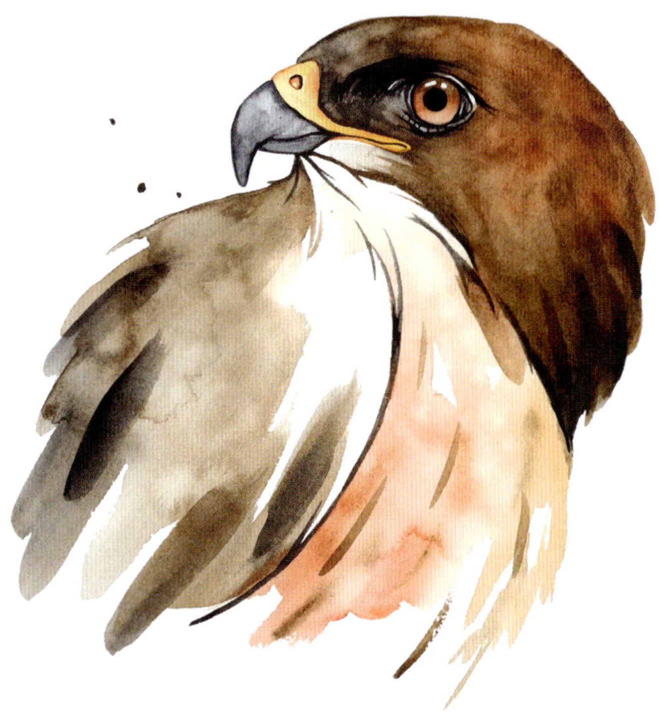

Red-Tailed Hawk

I see these hawks all the time. They are usually seen on top of telephone poles throughout the country, their eyes watching the grass for their next meal. This hawk has a sharp, curved beak and large eyes. In this project, you will create a realistic rendering of the beak using a blending technique and adding fine details. The piercing eye will also be pretty detailed, but the rest of the portrait will be created using a loose wash combined with dry brush marks for texture. You will be leaving some white of the paper showing through your washes that will allow the imagination to fill in the gaps.

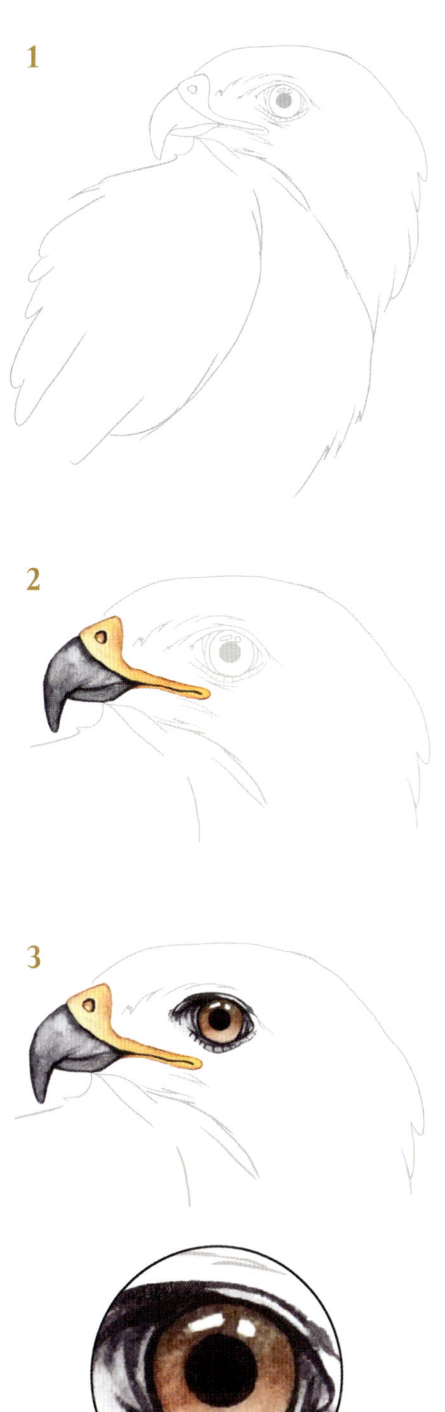

Step 1

Draw out the hawk using the template provided on page 159. Create more details around the face of the hawk, especially around the beak and the eye. Loosely and lightly draw out the shape of its breast and feathers.

Step 2

Start off by painting the beak of the hawk. Paint the yellow portion first to avoid contaminating it with the gray color. Fill in the top portion of the beak starting with Cadmium Yellow Medium Hue and then blending in Burnt Sienna around the outer edges while things are still wet.

After this layer is dry, paint the nostril with Burnt Sienna and the front part of the beak with Payne's Gray. For the front of the beak, make sure the value shifts from dark to light to give it a shiny appearance.

Step 3

In order to give the eye a piercing look, create a gradient in the iris going from a saturated Burnt Sienna at the top of the eye to a diluted Burnt Sienna toward the bottom of the eye, making sure to leave highlights in the eye. While the center of the eye is drying, paint the area around the eye, starting with a diluted amount of Payne's Gray. Next, use a saturated amount of Payne's Gray with a small round brush to create the details. Lastly, add the pupil to the eye of the hawk using a saturated amount of Payne's Gray.

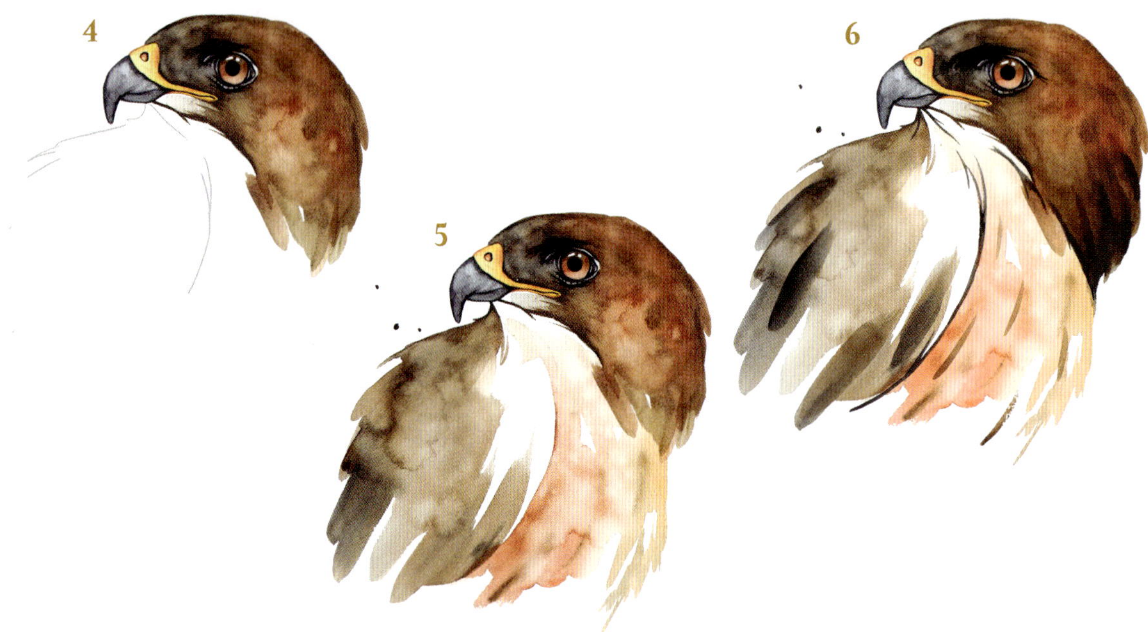

Step 4

Now you will be loosening up a little and creating larger washes. Using a medium round brush, start filling in the head with Raw Umber. While the wash is still wet, add Payne's Gray to the wash around the eye of the hawk. Next, dab a small amount of Burnt Sienna into the wash for some variation and warmth. Toward the back of the hawk's head, create a few feathers by creating bold brushstrokes with your medium-sized round brush and Raw Umber paint.

Step 5

Start by adding a light layer of Yellow Ochre to the top portion of the chest and a light wash of Burnt Sienna at the bottom, and then blend the two colors together.

Next, paint the wing of the hawk starting with a loose wash of Raw Umber. Towards the bottom of the wash, create some feather marks using Payne's Gray.

Step 6

After your last step is dry, paint small marks on the breast using Raw Umber paint with a medium round brush. Then, still using Raw Umber, paint some feather details along with the neck and the wing.

Add extra Payne's Gray around the eye of the hawk to deepen the color. Last, add some more feather marks to the wing and to the back of the head using both Payne's Gray and Raw Umber.

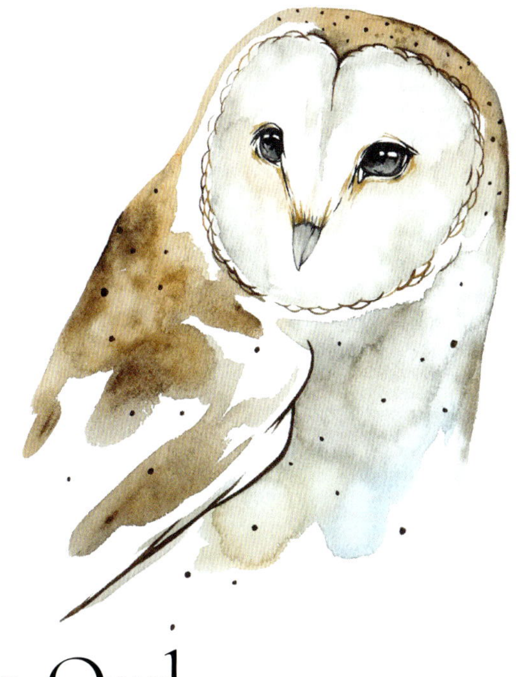

Barn Owl

Barn owls have heart-shaped faces with dark, round eyes. They have small, stiff feathers along the side of their facial discs, which focus sound and direct it to their ears. This project will demonstrate how you can create these unique feathers with a scalloped pattern. The eyes of this owl will be bold and dark with a small beak centered between them. You will also be creating beautiful wet-on-wet washes, mixing earth tones with a hint of cool blue.

Lesson
Creating a scalloped pattern

Colors

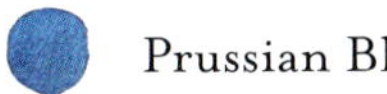 Prussian Blue

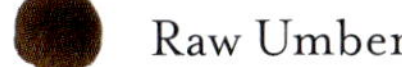 Raw Umber

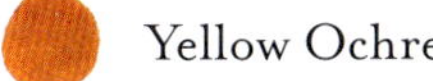 Yellow Ochre

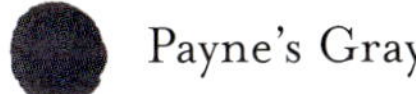 Payne's Gray

Brushes
Medium Round Brush

Small Round Brush

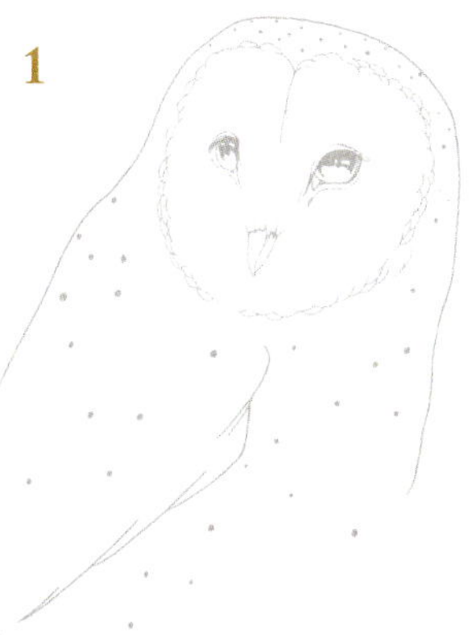

1

Step 1
Create a sketch of a barn owl portrait by using the template provided on page 159.

Step 2

Using your medium round brush, create a wash using Prussian Blue and Raw Umber. While the wash is still wet, add in a small amount of Yellow Ochre near the wing. Once the wash is lightly damp, splash some clean water onto the wash to create texture.

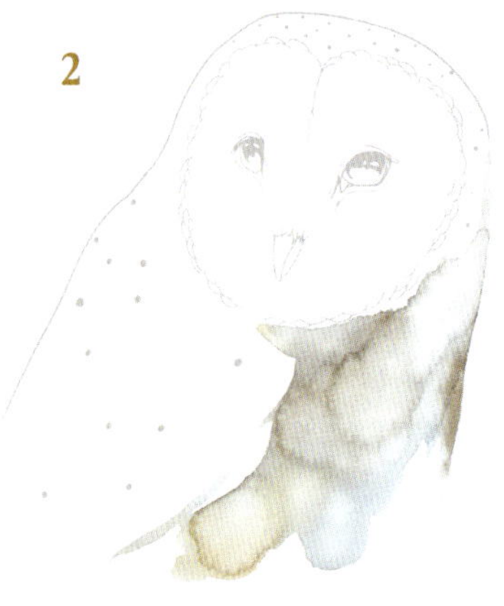

Step 3

For the wing, add a wash using Raw Umber and Yellow Ochre paint. Also create a couple feather marks using your medium round brush and Raw Umber paint. On the top of its head, use the same two colors.

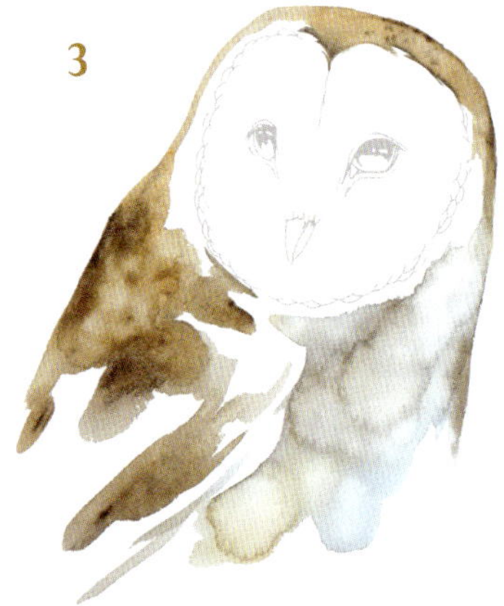

Step 4

Next, dilute your Raw Umber paint with quite a bit of water until the color appears very light. Add this light wash of Raw Umber to the face of the barn owl using your medium round brush, making sure to leave some of the white of the paper showing at the center of the owl's face. While the wash is still wet, add Yellow Ochre around the eyes. After the wash is dry, add small feather details around the barn owl's head using a saturated amount of Raw Umber and a small round brush.

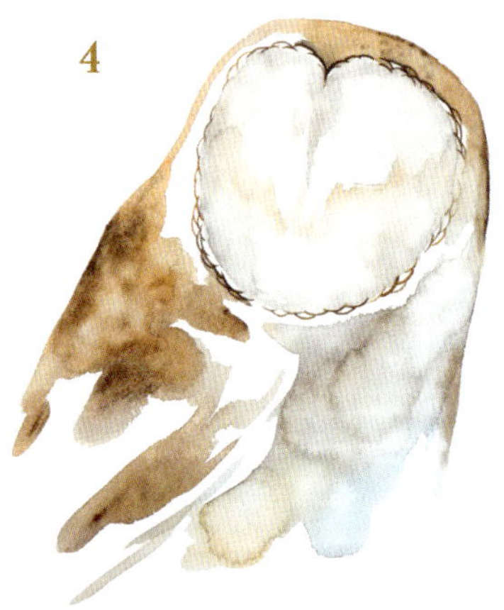

Small feather details around
the barn owl's head

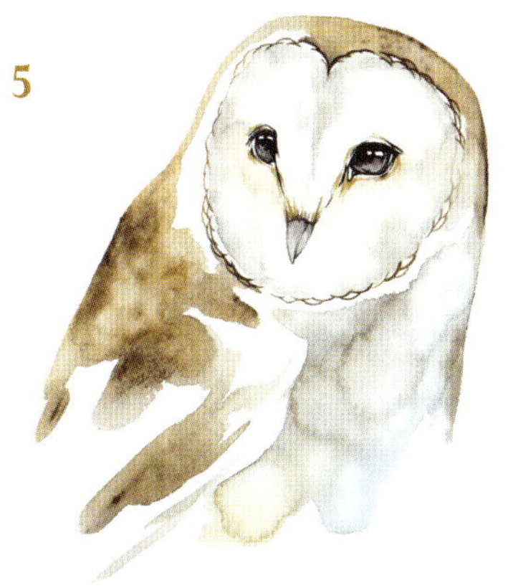

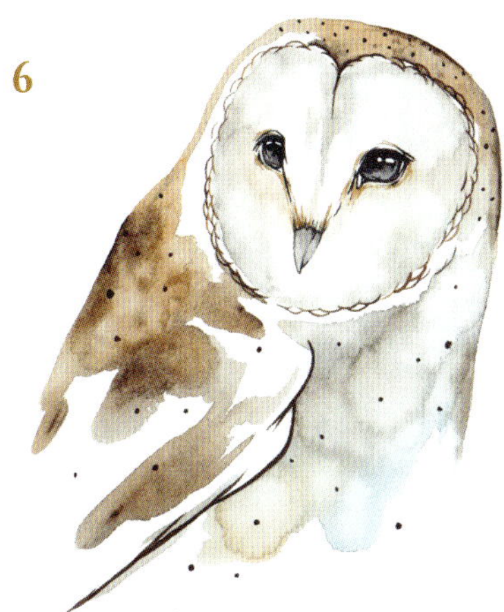

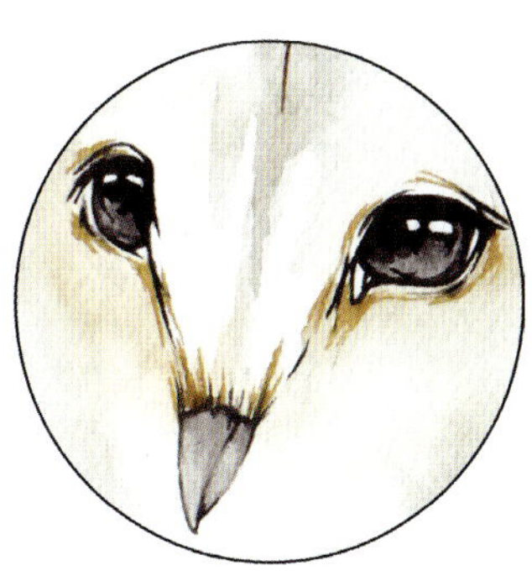

Step 5

Start with a light wash of Payne's Gray paint in the center of the eye with a medium round brush. While the wash is still wet, add in the saturated gray paint to the top portion of the eye and the inner corners.

After that wash is dry, paint details around the eyes using a saturated amount of Payne's Gray paint and a small round brush. Then add a pupil to the center of the eye, making sure to leave some white for the highlights.

Next, using the same brush, paint the beak using a diluted wash of Payne's Gray paint. Finally, add details around the beak and eyes using Raw Umber and Yellow Ochre.

Step 6

Using your small round brush and a saturated amount of Payne's Gray, add small dots all over your barn owl. Depending on the size of your brush, you can either just dab the paint on or you will have to paint tight circles. Lastly, add some thin lines to define the wing of the barn owl also using a saturated amount of Raw Umber paint.

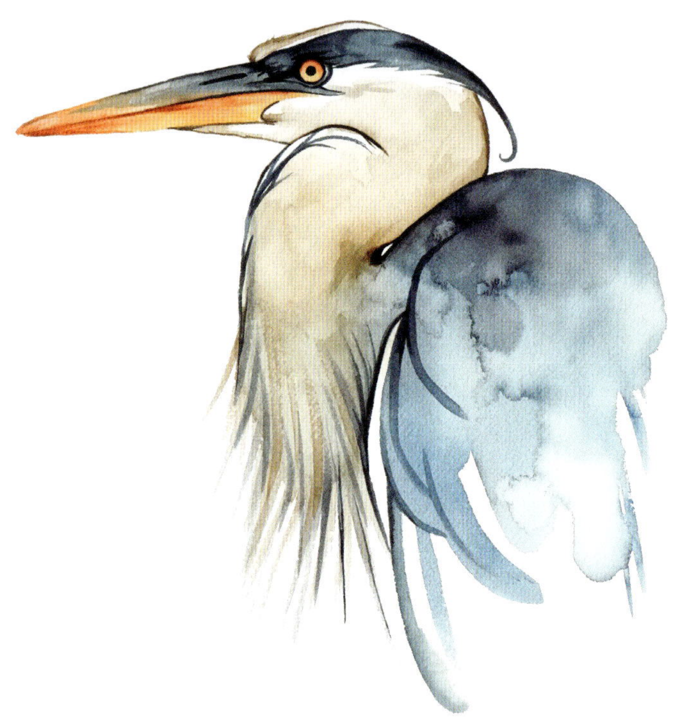

Great Blue Heron

Great blue herons are some of my favorite birds. Once, I was going on a walk around my neighborhood and stumbled upon a heron rookery in the river. This experience got me into bird watching and painting birds. Great blue herons are large birds standing 3 to 4 feet (92 to 122 cm) tall with a wingspan of up to 6 feet (1.8 m).

Most of your time on this project will be spent painting the head of the heron, where the fine details are. You will then loosen up and paint faster for the chest and wing. The wing of the heron will be created using a simple, textured wash with just a few brushstrokes to represent the feathers. Next, you will paint the long, fringe-like feathers on its chest. In order to paint these unique feathers, you will create long, sweeping brushstrokes.

Lesson

Using a dry brush technique to create thin, fringe-like feathers

Colors

Cadmium Yellow Medium Hue

Burnt Sienna

Prussian Blue

Payne's Gray

Raw Umber

Brushes

Medium Round Brush

Small Round Brush

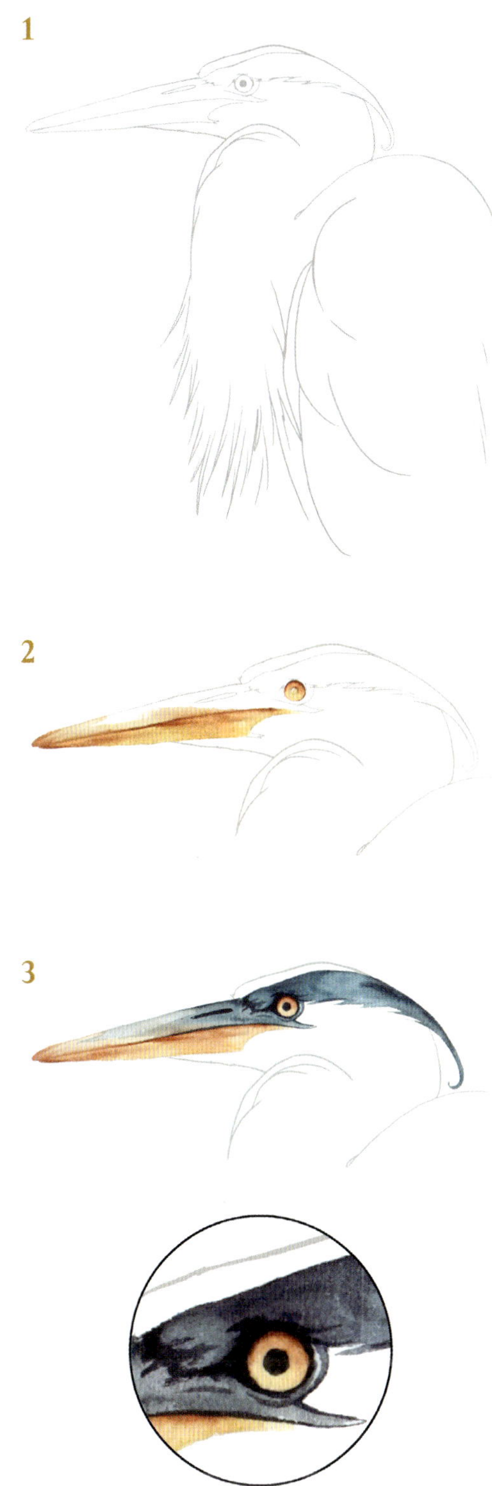

Step 1

Create a sketch of a great blue heron by using the drawing template provided on page 159. You can either draw this piece in the center of your paper or you can give it a cropped look by aligning it to the bottom right.

Step 2

Apply Cadmium Yellow Medium Hue paint to the lower beak using a wet-on-dry technique and a medium round brush, and then add this color to the eye. While the yellow paint is still wet, add Burnt Sienna to both the beak and the top portion of the eye. Next, add a line of Burnt Sienna to separate the top and bottom beak of the heron.

Step 3

After the last step is fully dry, add Prussian Blue to the top portion of the beak, concentrating more pigment near the eye. Also add Prussian Blue to the crest on top of the heron's head using a medium-sized round brush. You can switch to a small round brush for the tighter details if you need to. After the blue paint dries, use Payne's Gray to paint details on the beak and the eye with a small round brush.

Step 4

For this next section of the painting, you
will use a medium round brush with a
diluted amount of Raw Umber to fill in
the neck of the heron. Then add Prussian
Blue to the back of the heron using a
medium-sized round brush. You will
want to use a little bit more water to paint
this wash. Create a solid wash at the top
of its back, and at the bottom, add some
brushstrokes to represent its feathers on
its wing.

Next, while the wash is still damp, dab
in some clean water into the wash to
create blooms. You can use a hair dryer
to quickly dry these washes. Last, after the
wash on the neck is dry, use a small round
brush and a saturated amount of Raw
Umber paint and outline the neck and
head to define its shape.

Step 5

In this step, you will start adding the fine
strands that come off the heron's chest.
In order to do this, first apply a watery
light wash of Raw Umber to the lower
chest stopping at where the strands will
start. Then, using your medium-sized
round brush, start at the tip of the strand
and drag it into the wash. Add variety by
creating some strands by using a diluted
amount of Raw Umber and some using
Prussian Blue.

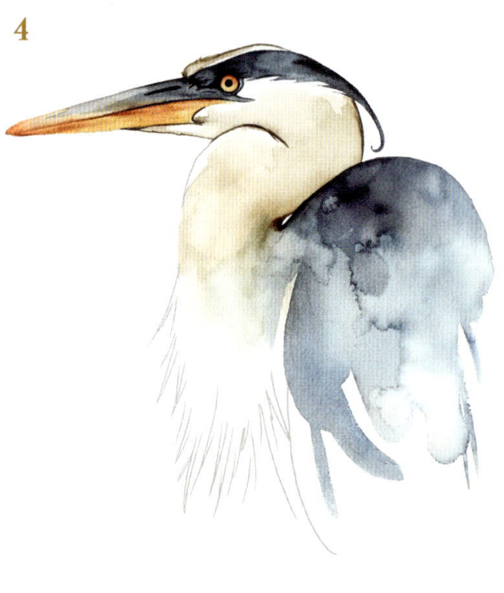

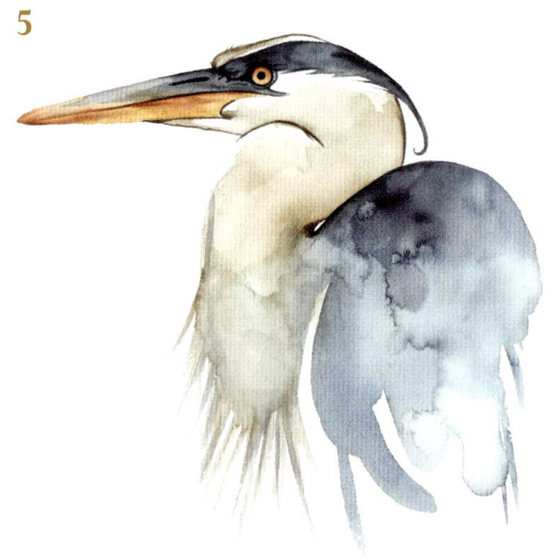

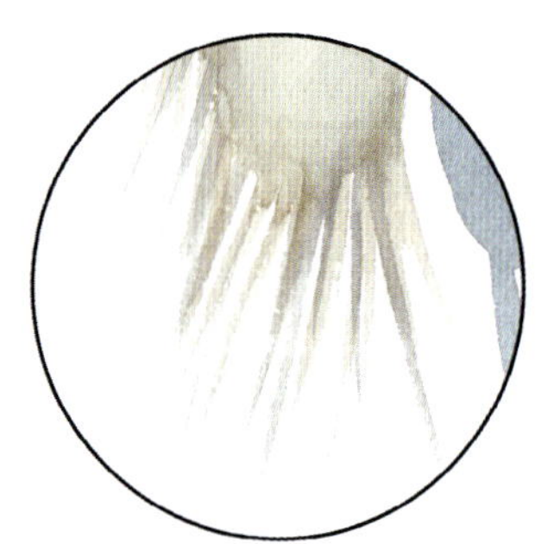

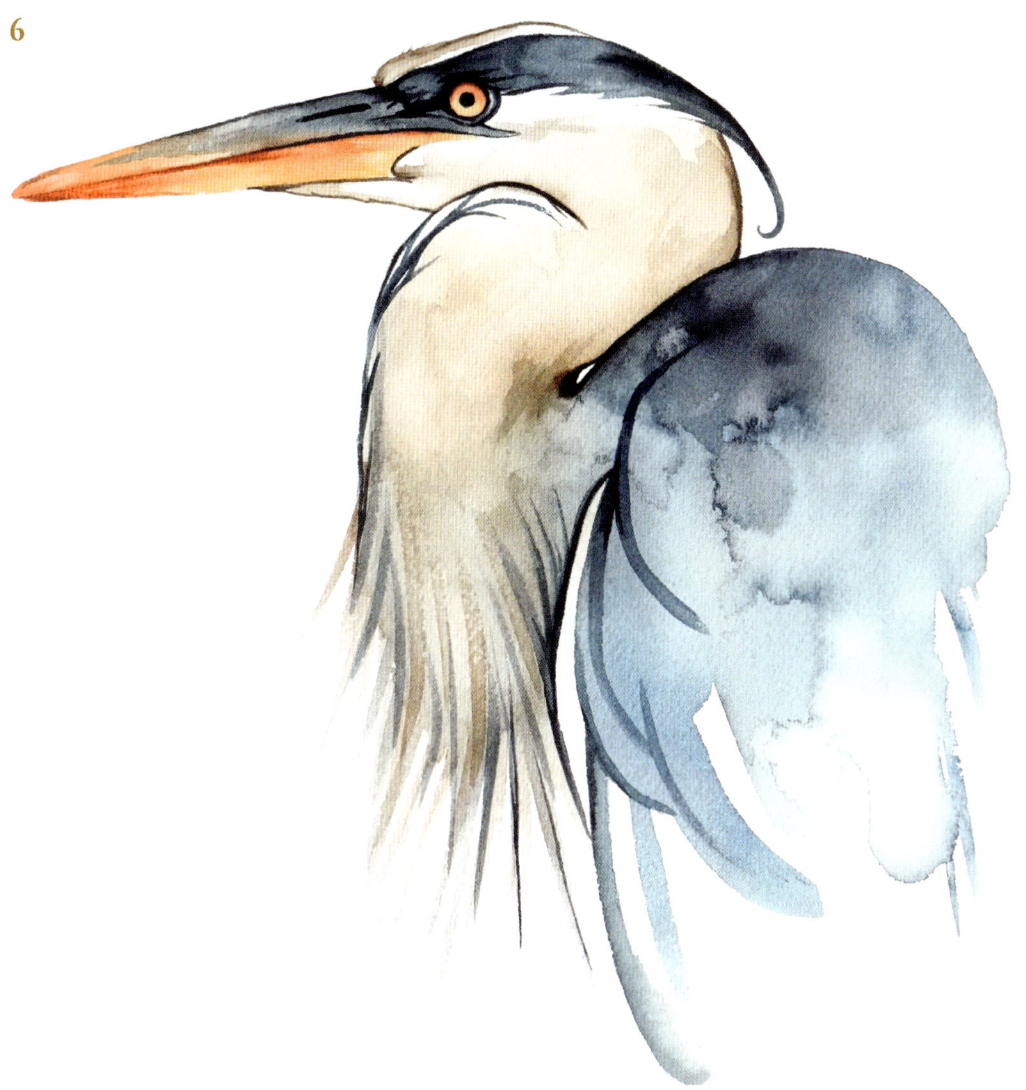

Step 6

In this final step, you will be adding the finishing details. Use a saturated amount of Prussian Blue and a small round brush to define the neck as well as the wing of the heron. Then, using a wet-on-dry technique, add more thin strands to the heron's chest, using both Raw Umber and Prussian Blue paint with your medium round brush.

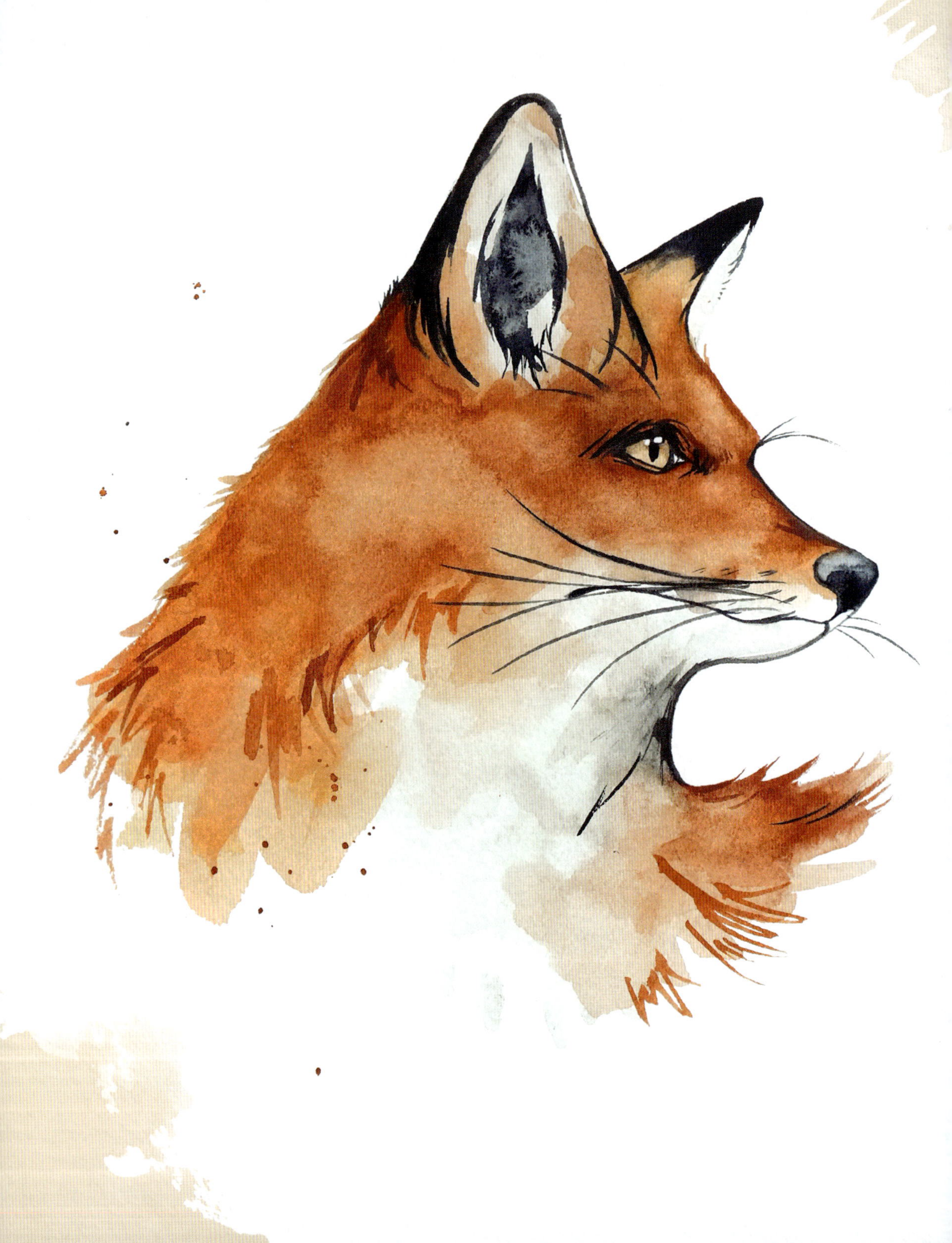

Furry Friends

When painting an animal, it is important to showcase its distinct characteristics. You can do this by emphasizing specific features of that animal. What makes it special? Does it have large ears? Bright, shiny eyes? An interesting pattern on its fur or a fluffy tail? In order to not overwork your painting, I want you to focus on adding details to the animal's most prominent features.

Painting animals can be a little intimidating at first, but once you break down the process into a few simple steps, it is a lot of fun! In order to create the impression of fur without painting every single hair, we will be focusing on creating beautifully textured, layered washes. These washes will not only save you time and frustration but add a sense of depth and visual interest to each piece.

Turn the page and get started on loosening up even more to create quick, expressive portraits of widely beloved animals such as a red fox, white-tailed deer and sea otter!

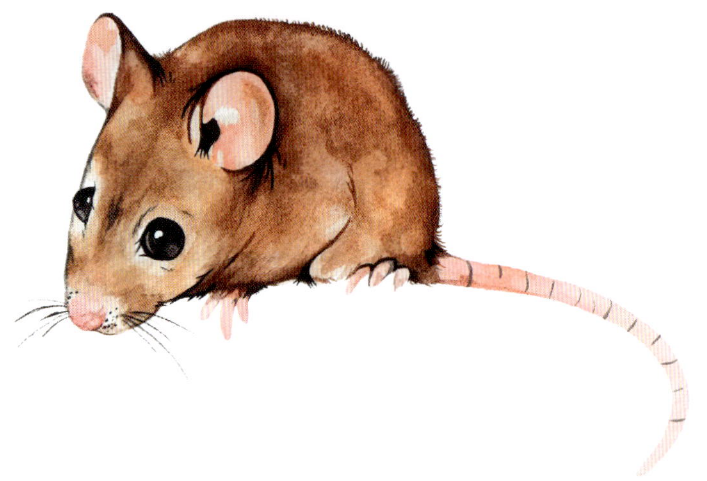

Deer Mouse

This small rodent has a furry body, big eyes and a long, skinny tail. They can be found in many different environments, from forests to urban areas. You might find this little guy adorable or quite the pest.

For this mouse painting, you will start off with a textured wet-on-wet wash. This textured wash will help give the appearance of fur without having to paint every single hair and save you time on your painting. You will then add its most prominent features, such as its large, dark, shiny eyes, its round, pink ears and its long, thin tail.

Step 1

Create a sketch of the mouse on watercolor paper by using the template on page 161. I would recommend using a hard pencil for this process but remember to sketch lightly so your pencil lines can be easily covered by your watercolor paint.

1

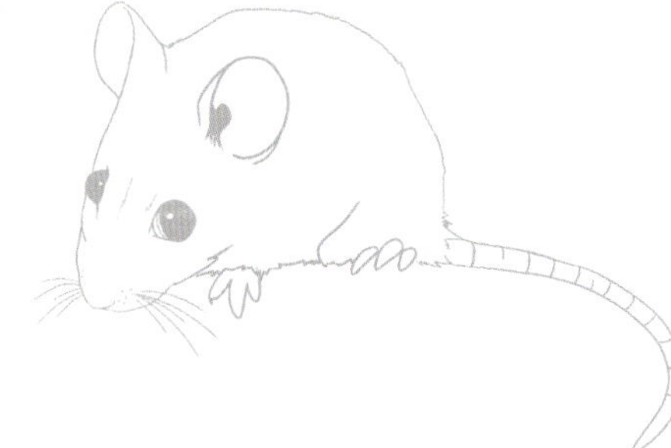

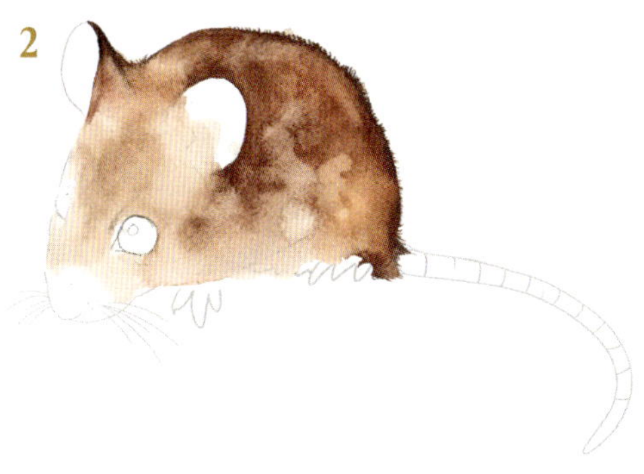

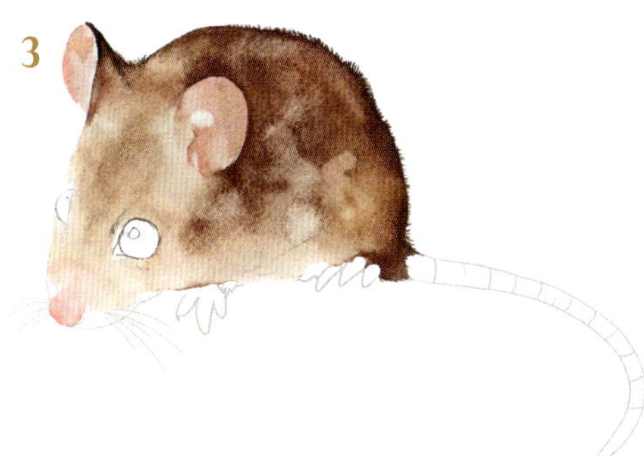

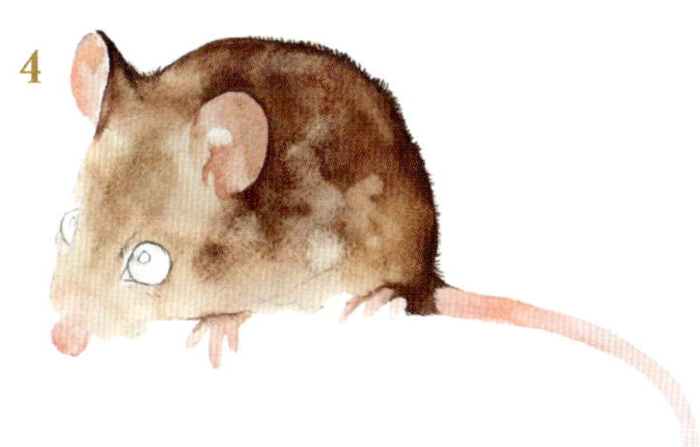

Step 2

Fill in most of the body other than the tip of the mouse's snout with a wash of Raw Umber paint using a medium-sized round brush. While the wash is still wet, add small amounts of Burnt Sienna paint to its body. Then dab some diluted Yellow Ochre onto its face and body. Then, while the wash is still wet, use a small round brush to drag out small hairs on the edge of its body. Lastly, while the wash is lightly damp, dab some clean water into the wash to create a mottled, textured effect to its fur.

Step 3

Either allow the previous step to fully dry or use a hair dryer to speed up the drying process before moving to the next step. Add Rose Doré to the nose and ears of the mouse using a medium round brush. For the ears, add extra pigment of Rose Doré to the inner ear to create shadows.

Step 4

Next, you will add Rose Doré paint to the front and back legs of the mouse. For this step, you may need to switch to a small round brush to paint these small feet. Then paint the mouse's tail using the same color. For the tail, you can either carefully fill it in with a small round brush or use a medium-sized round brush to paint out the entire tail in one single brushstroke for a looser look. Since the mouse's tail isn't fluffy, try to keep the wash either flat or a smooth gradient.

Step 5

In this step, you will be adding some definition to the mouse's body. Using a saturated amount of Raw Umber paint and a small round brush, outline the shape of the mouse's ears, snout and legs. On the head of the mouse, add a light layer of Burnt Sienna with a medium round brush between the eyes and to its back in order to increase the value.

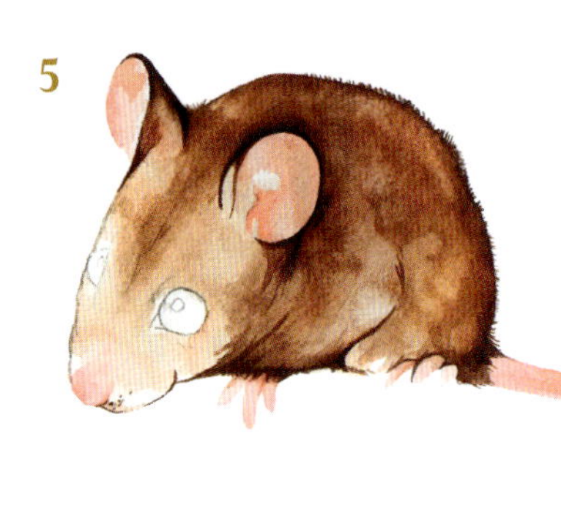

Step 6

Paint the eyes of the mouse using Payne's Gray paint and a small round brush. Using the same brush and color, add details to the ear and tail as well. The last step is to paint small dots on the mouse's snout and then paint thin lines for the whiskers. If you find it challenging to create small, thin lines, you can also use a fine-tipped pen for this process; just make sure that the pen you are using is a waterproof pen.

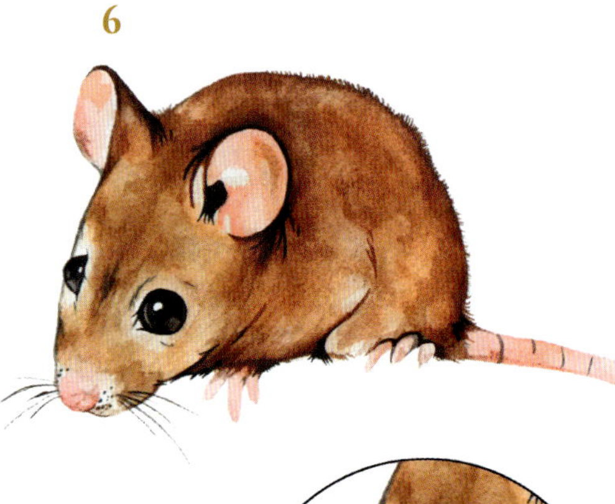

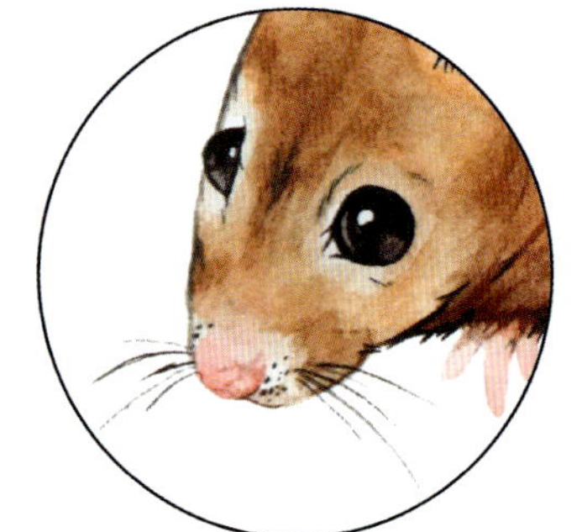

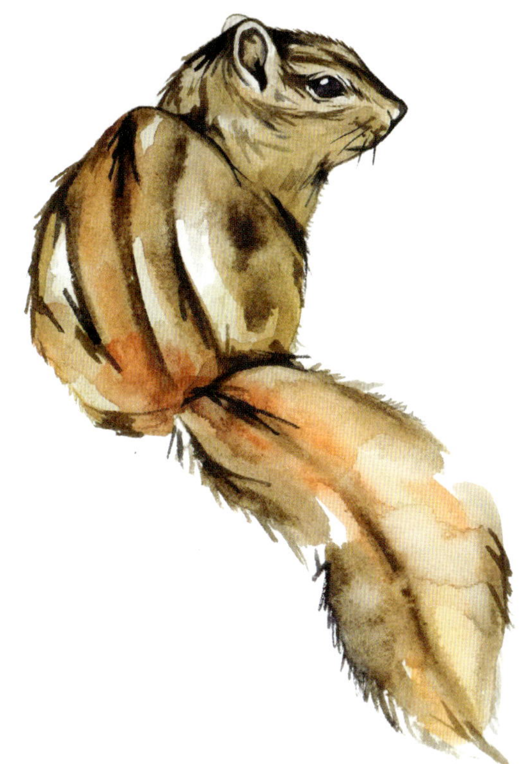

Striped Chipmunk

Chipmunks are small, ground-dwelling rodents that are part of the squirrel family. They have fluffy tails and a striped pattern on their backs and tails. They have cheek pouches that they use to store and carry nuts and seeds.

For this painting, you will try painting a little faster on some of the more gestural elements, such as on the chipmunk's tail. By moving quicker, you will create more expressive brush marks and avoid overworking your piece. In this lesson, you will be creating a striped pattern once again, but this time using a wet-on-wet technique to create a soft appearance.

Using a wet-on-wet technique to create soft, striped fur

Colors

Raw Umber

Yellow Ochre

Burnt Sienna

Payne's Gray

Brushes

Medium Round Brush

Small Round Brush

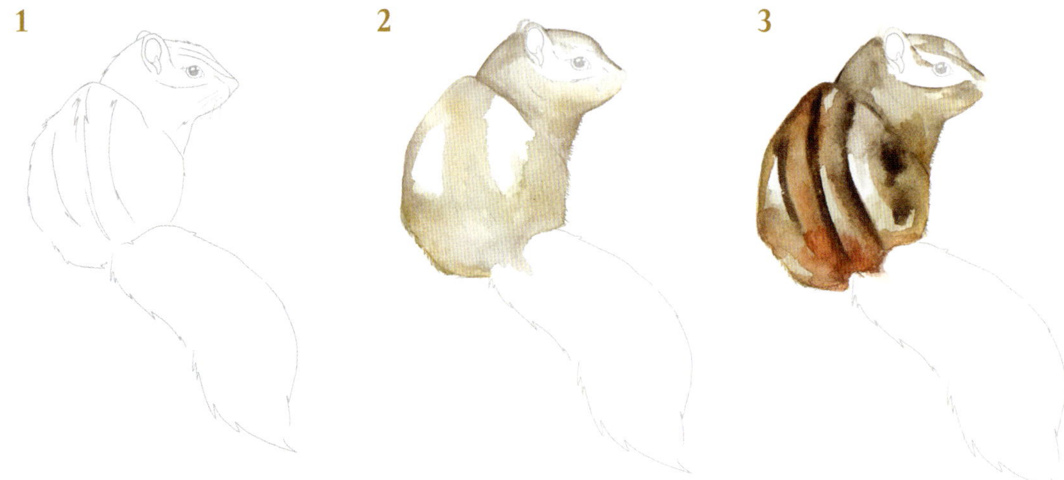

Step 1

Trace the image from page 161. Create the outline of the chipmunk and draw out the striped pattern on the chipmunk's back. For the tail pattern, loosely draw the stripe; it doesn't need to be exact.

Step 2

Apply a layer of diluted Raw Umber to the chipmunk's head and back using a medium round brush. While the wash is still wet, dab in some Yellow Ochre paint. Make sure to leave some white of the paper showing on the back of the chipmunk.

Step 3

After the last step is dry, start by adding another light layer of Raw Umber wash to the head and back using a medium round brush. Then, using a wet-on-wet technique, dab some Burnt Sienna into the wash on the lower back of the chipmunk.

For this next step, wait until your wash is just damp. You can tell if the paper is damp if it is still wet but not shiny. Then add stripes to the chipmunk using a saturated amount of Raw Umber and a small, fine-tipped round brush. Adding a saturated amount of paint to damp paper will make sure that the lines still appear but are not quite as bold as if you added them to dry paper.

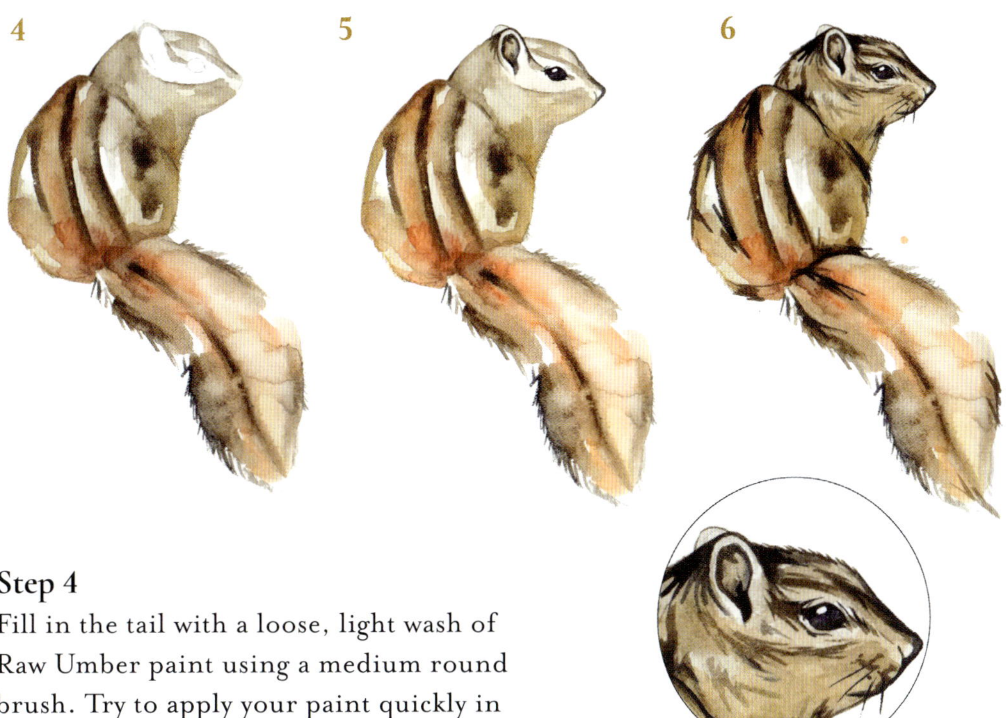

Step 4

Fill in the tail with a loose, light wash of Raw Umber paint using a medium round brush. Try to apply your paint quickly in the general shape of the tail. It is okay if the shape isn't fully filled in and some white is showing. Next, while the wash is still wet, using a small round brush, paint small hairs on the edge of the wash with a 50:50 mixture of Raw Umber and Payne's Gray.

Then, using wet-on-wet techniques, dab small touches of Burnt Sienna paint into the wash and paint a saturated line of Raw Umber down the center of the tail.

Step 5

Paint the eye using Payne's Gray paint and a small round brush, making sure to leave a small dot for the highlight. Next, add some Raw Umber to the front of the face and the nose to define the shapes, and then paint the ear using the same paint color.

Step 6

Add some fur marks throughout the chipmunk using both Raw Umber and Payne's Gray paint with a small round brush using a wet-on-dry technique. For these fur marks, create hard, jagged lines. These harsh lines will create a graphic effect that will contrast against the softness of the wash. As a final touch, paint in the stripes on the chipmunk's face and add some whiskers.

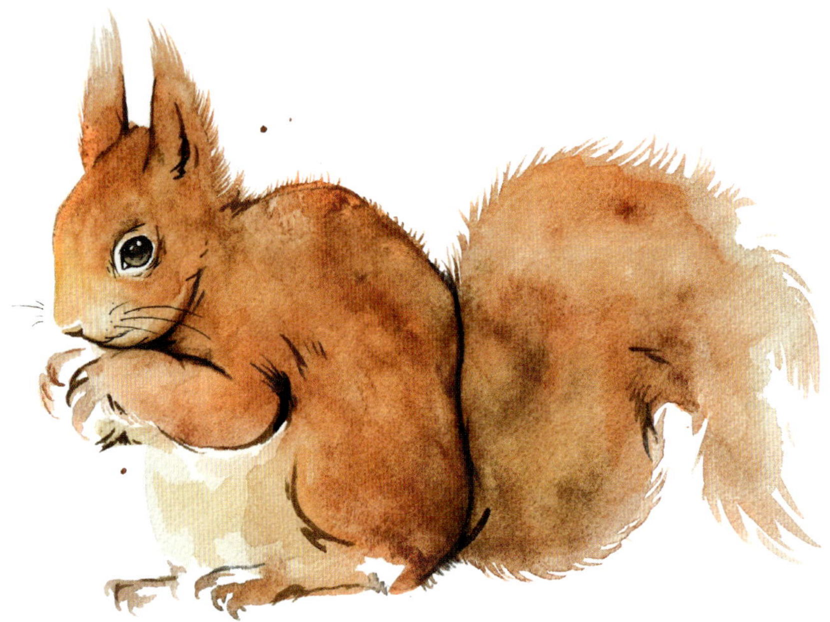

Red Squirrel

Red squirrels have tails that are about the same size as their bodies. These large tails help them stay balanced as they run and jump among the tree branches. These large, bushy tails will be the focal point of this painting, and you will start off by creating a wash and then gently pulling out small hairs to create the tail. You will begin this painting by creating large washes made up of a variety of warm hues, and then after the washes are dry, you will add thin, illustrative details to add definition to the squirrel's body and facial features.

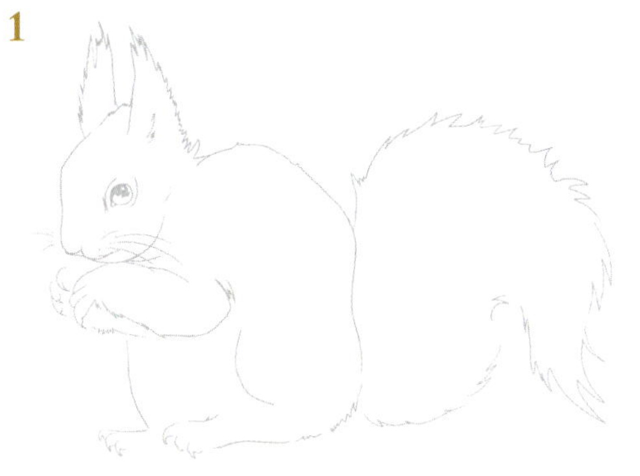

Step 1

Create a sketch of the squirrel by tracing the drawing template on page 161. Keep the tail portion of the sketch very light, as you will mostly be freehand painting it.

Step 2

Use a medium round brush to add Burnt Sienna to the majority of the body but add Yellow Ochre to the front of its face and to its belly. Make sure to leave some white for the eye, around the jaw and under the front leg. While the wash is still wet, use your small round brush to pull out fur marks on the squirrel's ear and on the back of its neck. While your wash is still slightly damp, dab in clean water to create blooms.

Using the same brush and Burnt Sienna, paint out the squirrel's claws, making sure to use less water for this process.

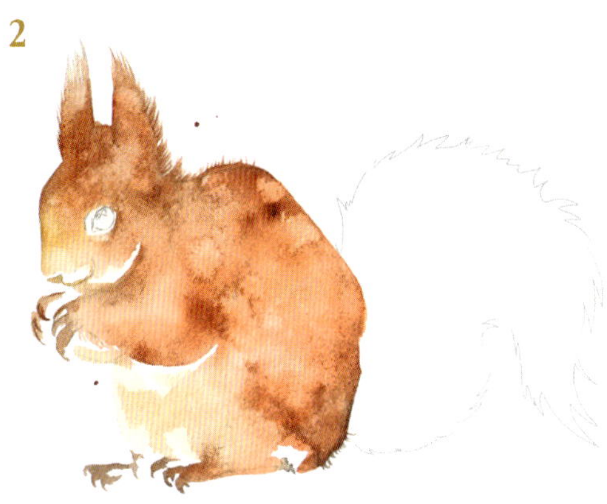

Step 3

In this step, start off by using your medium round brush and Burnt Sienna paint to loosely paint a general shape of the tail. While the wash is still wet, dab in Raw Umber in the area where the tail comes out of the squirrel's body. Then drag out hairs out of the wash using a small round brush. Last, add some drops of clean water to the wash while it is still damp to create blooms. Allow the wash to dry.

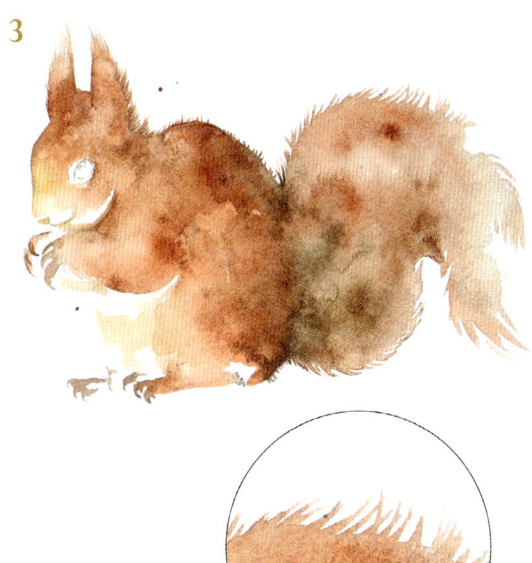

Step 4

In this step, you will be defining the squirrel's shape by using a wet-on-dry technique after the last step is dry. Using your small round brush and a saturated amount of Raw Umber, paint out thin lines around the head and legs and to separate the body and tail. Then add small hair mark details to the fur using the same brush and paint.

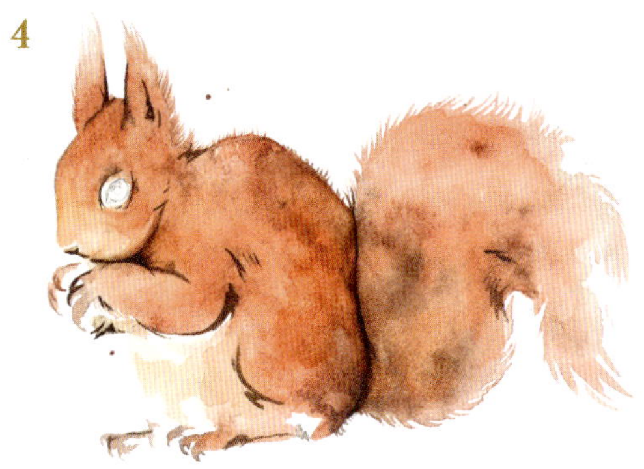

Step 5

Start by adding a light layer of Raw Umber paint to the eye using a small round brush, making sure to leave a white dot in the eye for the highlight and a white ring around its eye. After your layer of Raw Umber paint is fully dry, paint around the eye shape using Payne's Gray paint with a small round brush and fill in the pupil. Using the same brush, paint out the squirrel's mouth and some small dots on its cheeks.

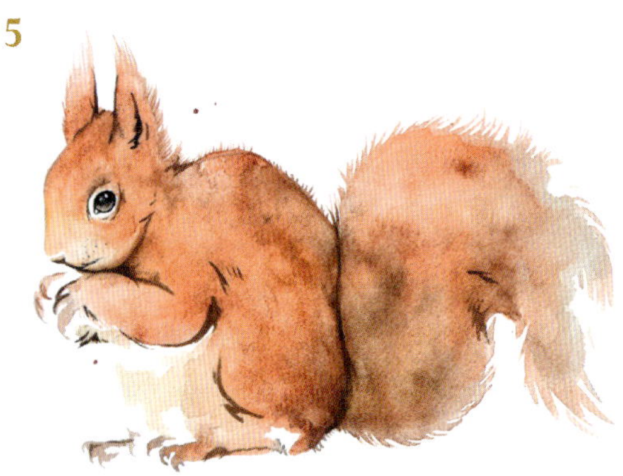

Step 6

In this step, start by mixing together Yellow Ochre and Burnt Sienna. After mixing an equal amount of the two colors, add some extra water so the color is diluted. Using your medium round brush, add this mixture to the squirrel's head, back and tail to even out and deepen the color. After the wash dries, add whiskers to the squirrel using a small brush and a saturated amount of Payne's Gray.

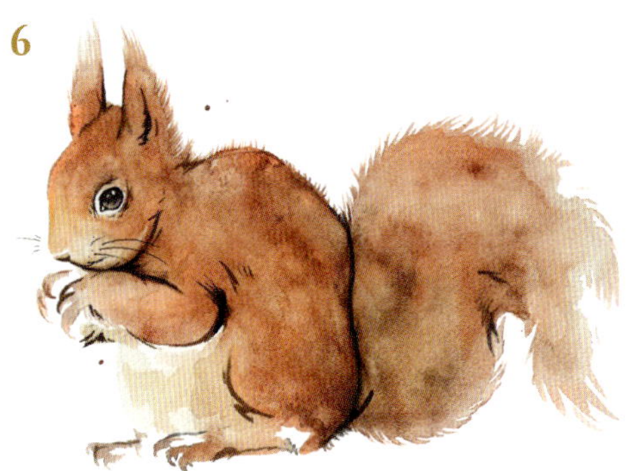

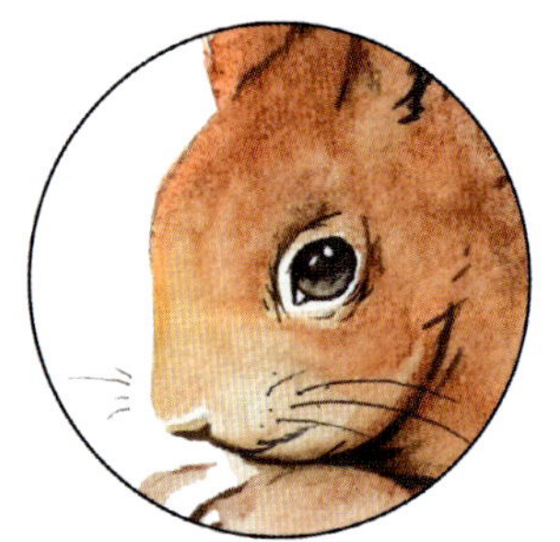

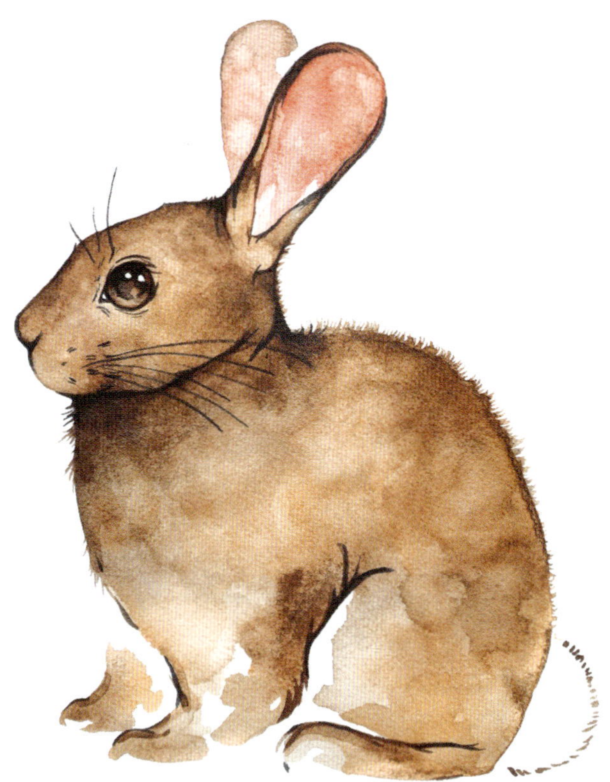

Cottontail Rabbit

Named after their little cotton ball–like tails, these rabbits stay hidden during the day and come out to eat in the evening. The mottled coloring of their coats helps them blend into their surroundings by using camouflage. They avoid predators by running in a zig-zagging pattern if pursued.

In this lesson, you will create a little rabbit using large, textured washes with small hair details on the outer edges of its body. The legs and feet will be painted quickly to give the impression that this bunny is ready to jump. Most of your time will be spent adding details to the face, where you will create a realistic eye that is on the lookout.

Lesson

Painting a mottled fur texture on an animal without painting out every little hair detail

Colors

 Raw Umber

Yellow Ochre

 Rose Doré

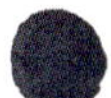 Payne's Gray

Brushes

Medium Round Brush

Small Round Brush

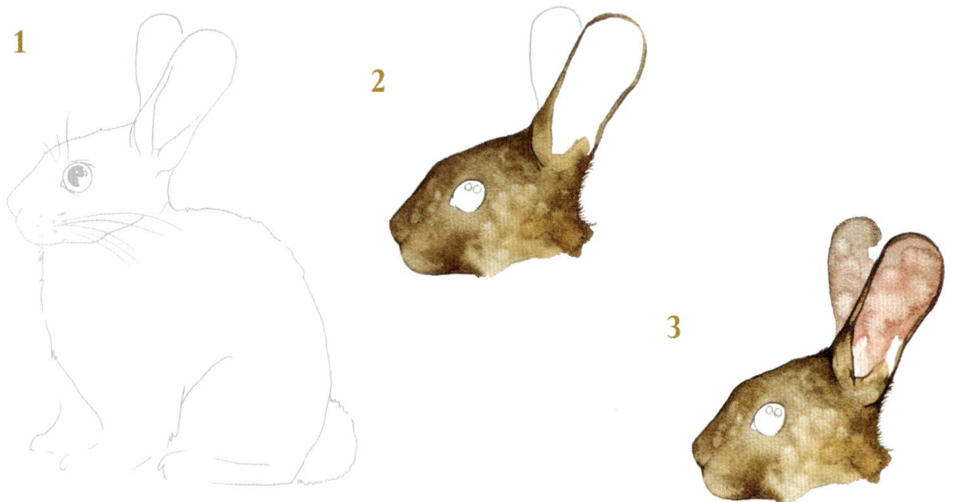

Step 1

Create your rabbit sketch by tracing the drawing on page 163. If you would like a challenge, try sketching the rabbit's shape on your own. This is a good option if you want to paint it bigger.

Step 2

Start with using Raw Umber and then dab in small amounts of Yellow Ochre to the area around the mouth and the back of the head. While the wash is still wet, add some extra texture to your wash by dabbing in small amounts of water to create blooms. This will help give the rabbit that mottled fur pattern. After filling in most of the face, avoiding the eye, use your small round brush to paint the outline of the closest ear and to paint out small hairs on the back of the rabbit's neck.

Step 3

Fill in the front ear with Rose Doré paint. For the farther ear, create a wash with both Raw Umber and Rose Doré paint. Start by adding Raw Umber at the top of the ear and then adding the Rose Doré at the bottom of the ear, and then blend the two colors together. Making the farther ear lighter and less detailed gives the painting depth and helps distinguish the closer, more detailed ear.

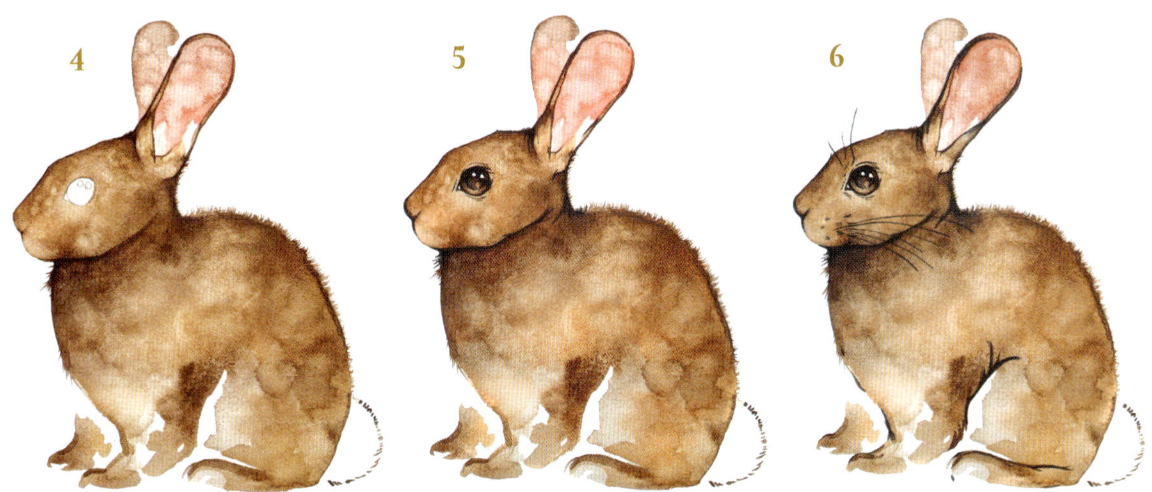

Step 4

Using a medium round brush, start filling in the rabbit's body with a mixture of Raw Umber and Yellow Ochre. Use a larger amount of paint and water to quickly fill in the shape. Loosely paint out the legs and feet, using a few brushstrokes to show the curve of its toes to give an impressionistic look. After filling in the body with paint, add extra Raw Umber to the lower back of the rabbit and below the jaw. Then, while the wash is still damp, you can add small dabs of water to it to create more blooms.

With a small brush, pull out of the wash to create fine hair marks. With a small brush and Raw Umber paint, add hair marks around the outside of the rabbit's small, white tail. Some gaps between the brushstrokes make the tail look fluffier.

Step 5

Fill in the eye with Raw Umber paint, making sure to leave some white for the highlights. After the Raw Umber paint fully dries, use your small round brush and Payne's Gray paint to fill in the pupil and to add details around the eye. Using this same brush and paint color, add some paint to define the nose as well.

Step 6

Start by adding a light layer of Raw Umber to the head to increase the value. After that dries, start painting out the whiskers using a small round brush and a saturated amount of Payne's Gray paint; add the whiskers to the cheek and above the rabbit's eye. To the body of the rabbit, add a small amount of Raw Umber below the jaw to increase the contrast, and then add a thin line to the rabbit's front leg to separate it from the rest of the wash.

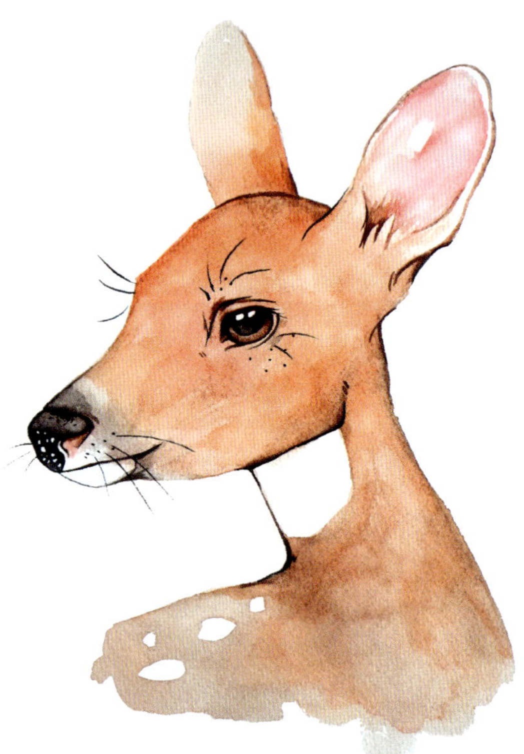

White-Tailed Deer Fawn

White-tailed deer fawns are usually born in late May or early June. They are often born as a set of twins and have a rust-colored coat covered in white spots; the spots will stay on their coat until they are three to four months old.

In this project, you will be painting a portrait of a cute, little fawn looking over its shoulder. The fawn will be made up of large washes on its head, neck and back. While painting the wash you will leave its distinctive white spots by painting around the shape of them. On the head of the fawn, you will create a detailed nose and bright, expressive eyes.

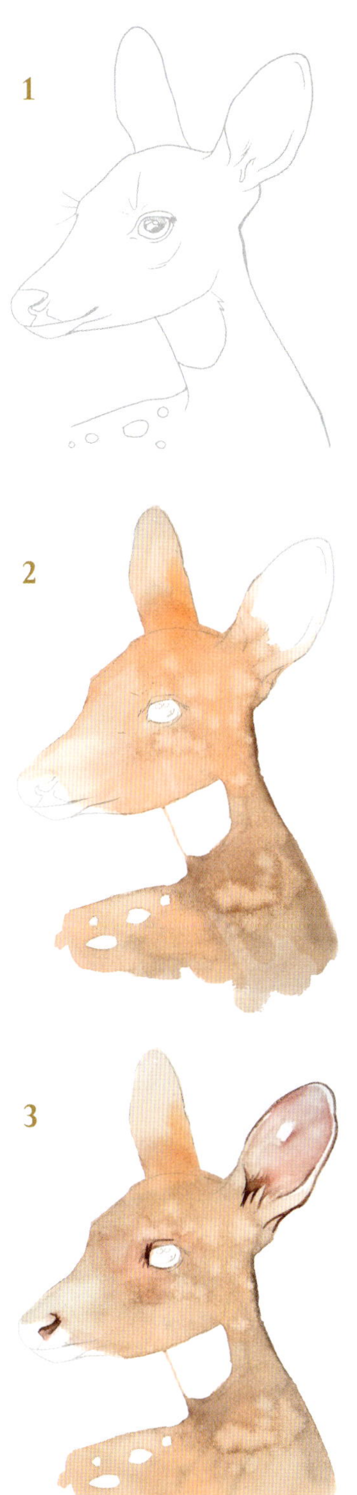

Step 1

Create your fawn drawing by using the outline provided on page 163.

Step 2

Mix together Yellow Ochre and Burnt Sienna, using an equal amount of each color. Then, using a medium-sized round brush, start filling in the deer's head and neck. Make sure to leave the area on the neck white and also leave some white spots on the deer's back. Also, only paint the farther ear, as the closer ear is facing a different direction and will be painted in a later step.

Step 3

Once the last step has dried, add Rose Doré to the ear, to the corner of the eye and to the nostril. You can leave some white of the paper showing in the ear of the deer, to represent a highlight. Let the pink dry and then use a small round brush and Raw Umber to add shadows in the ear, eye and nostril. Have the value of the shadows go from dark to medium by blending the paint into a gradient using a wet brush.

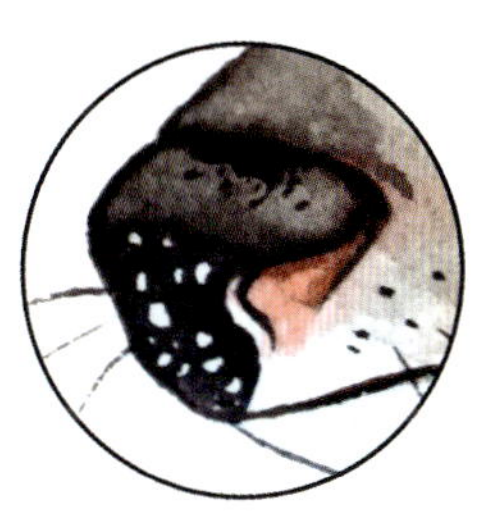

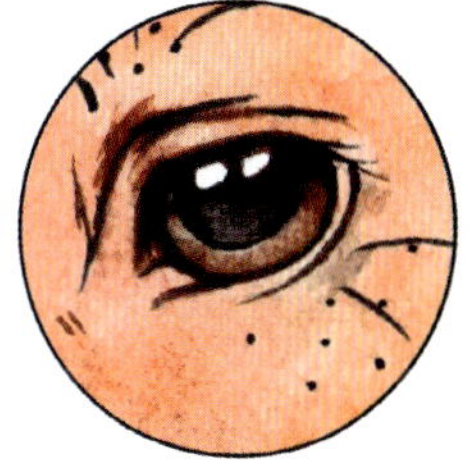

Step 4

Paint the eye by applying Raw Umber first. After the layer of Raw Umber is dry, paint the pupil using a saturated amount of Payne's Gray, making sure to leave two dots for the highlights. For the nose and mouth of the deer, use your Payne's Gray as well. On the nose, make sure to leave little white spots and carefully paint out a line for the mouth. Lastly, add a diluted wash of gray to the area outside of the fawn's muzzle.

Step 5

Add thin, dark lines of Raw Umber around the ear and along the jaw of the deer using a small round brush. After adding the Raw Umber details, mix together a 50:50 ratio of Raw Umber to Yellow Ochre, making sure to add extra water to dilute it. Apply the light wash with a medium round brush, adding the paint to the head, neck and back of the deer. This wash will help deepen the color.

Step 6

After the previous layer dries, add whiskers around both the eye and snout of the deer. Use a small round brush and a saturated amount of Payne's Gray, or you can use a black pen. Lastly, add some Payne's Gray to the front of the neck to define that area.

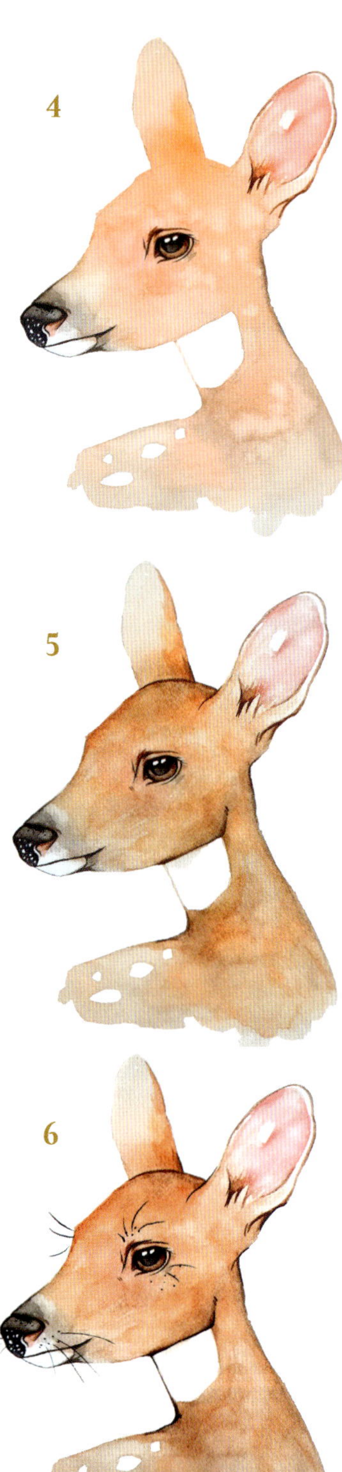

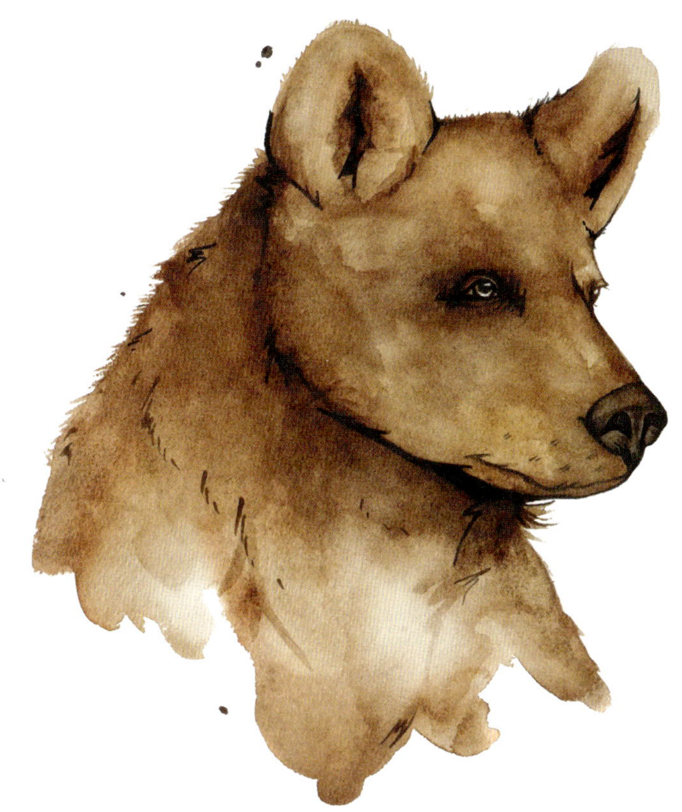

Brown Bear Cub

Brown bear cubs are born during hibernation. Most litters
have two to three cubs, and they form strong bonds with
their mothers as they are fully dependent on them. Their
cries can even sound like they are saying "Ma!"

This painting will be pretty simple because you will first
create one large wash that covers the entire portrait of
the bear. You will then add in the facial features using a
wet-on-dry technique and build up value to add dimension
to this mainly monochromatic subject. Despite being all
one color, you will be using a warm- and cool-toned
brown paint to add depth.

Creating shadows with a
limited color palette

Colors

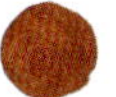 Burnt Umber

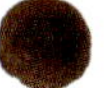 Raw Umber

 Payne's Gray

Brushes

Medium Round Brush

Small Round Brush

Step 1

Create a drawing of a bear cub by using the drawing template provided on page 165.

Step 2

In this step, you will be creating a wash using Burnt Umber with your medium round brush. For this wash, make sure the color is more saturated along the back, under the chin, on the bridge of the nose and in the center of the ears. While the wash is still wet, create little hair marks using your small round brush. Allow this wash to either air-dry or use a hair dryer to speed up the process.

Step 3

Now you will paint the bear's nose. To paint the nose, first fill it in with an even layer of Raw Umber using your medium round brush. Allow this layer to dry and after it dries, paint the nostrils and the mouth with a saturated amount of Payne's Gray paint and a small round brush.

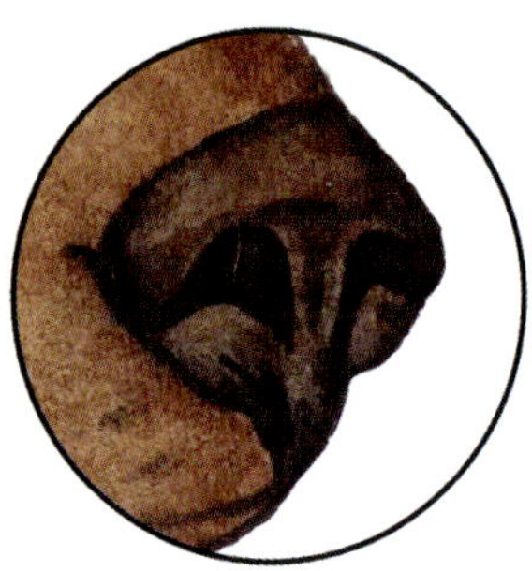

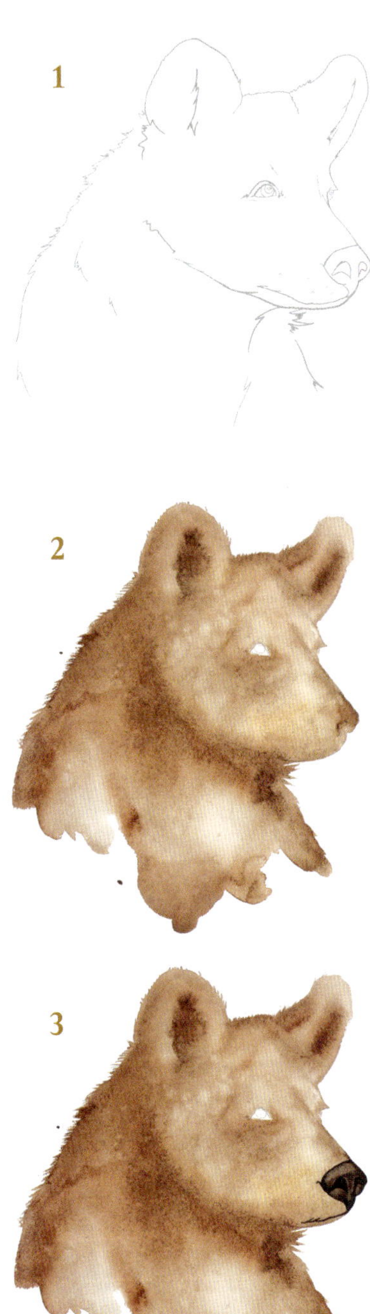

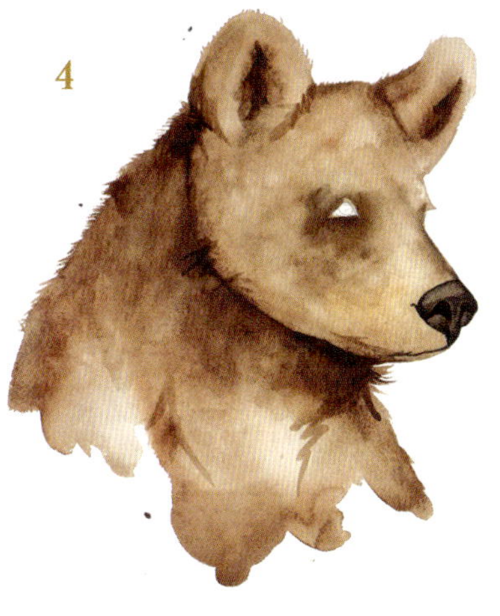

Step 4

In this step, you will be adding further definition and value to the fur of the bear. Add a light layer of Raw Umber below the head of the bear in order to separate it from the rest of its body. Then add some Raw Umber around the ears and eyes.

Step 5

Now you will paint the eyes of the bear using Raw Umber and Payne's Gray paint. Start with a light layer of Raw Umber for the iris and for the creases surrounding the eyes. After this layer of paint fully dries, add pupils using Payne's Gray paint and a small round brush.

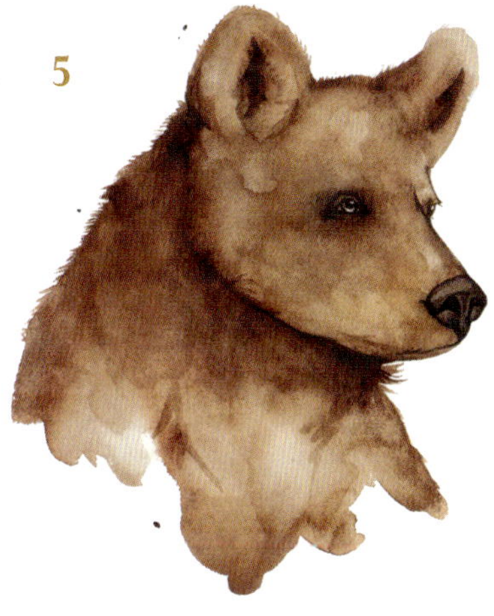

Step 6

Next, add a light layer or Burnt Umber to the head of the bear to increase the value. After adding this layer of paint, add small fur details throughout the bear using a saturated amount of Raw Umber and a small round brush.

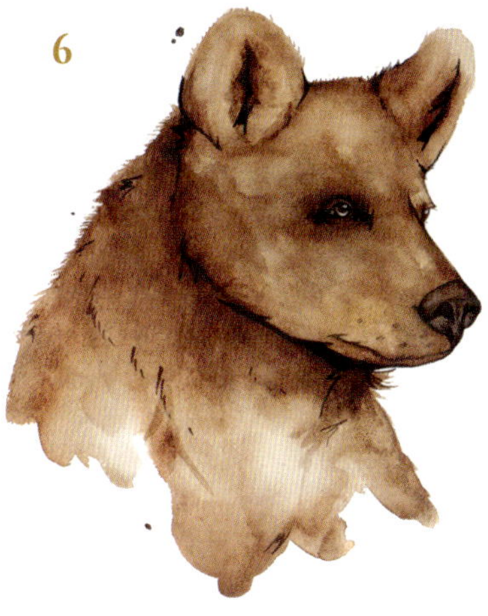

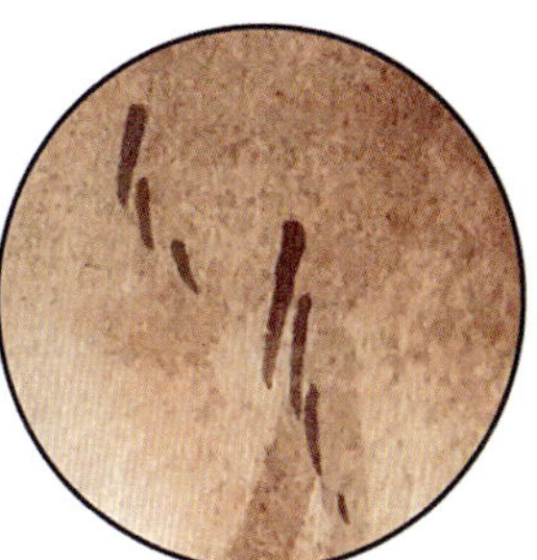

Fur Details

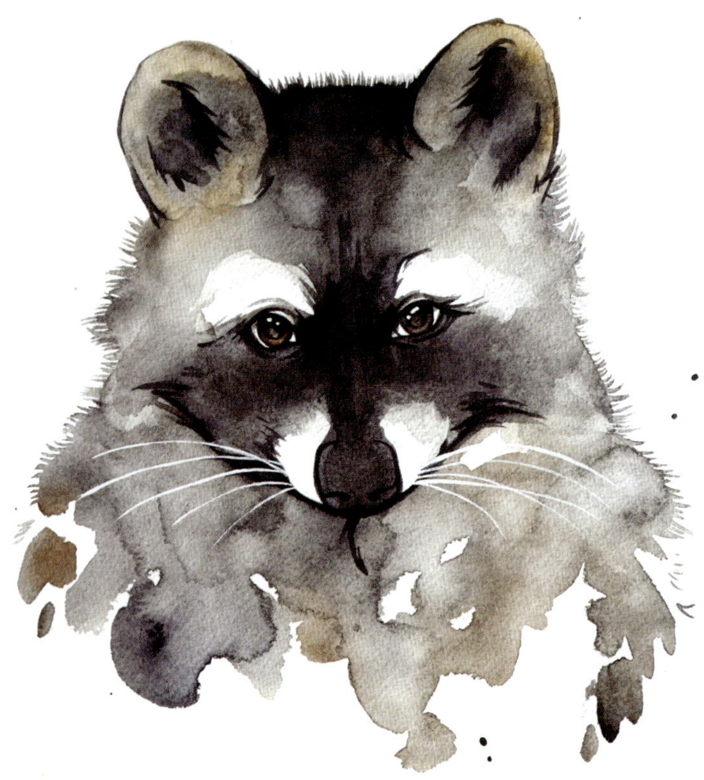

Masked Raccoon

This easily recognizable animal has a dark mask on its face and a bushy tail with rings on it. Raccoons are very adaptable and thrive in a variety of habitats. Raccoons are nocturnal, coming out at night to find food.

For this project you will be focusing on creating multiple layered washes before painting on the raccoon's distinctive mask. The edges of this painting will be abstracted and surrounded by splashes of paint for an expressive water-color portrait. The saturated paint around the eyes, nose and ears will contrast against the fur wash.

Lesson

Creating a portrait that ends with a loose, abstracted wash

Colors

Raw Umber

Payne's Gray

Yellow Ochre

Brushes

Medium Round Brush

Small Round Brush

Extra Supplies

White ink or gel pen

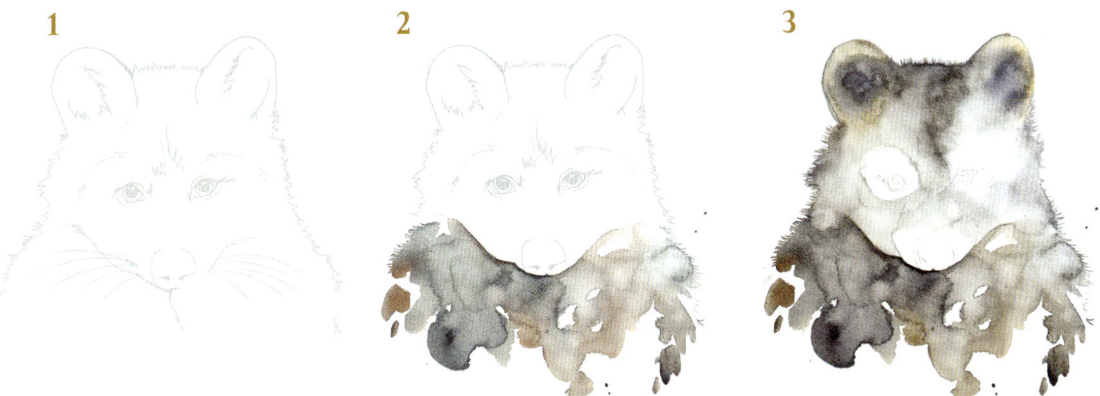

Step 1

Create a portrait of a raccoon by tracing the template on page 165. Keep your lines light so the paint will cover them.

Step 2

In this step, you will be creating a loose wash using Raw Umber and Payne's Gray paint. For this wash, use a medium round brush and make sure to load up your brush with plenty of paint and water. Start by adding Raw Umber underneath the nose and chin of the raccoon. Then add a watery mixture of Payne's Gray. It is okay if the value of your wash is uneven and goes from light to dark.

While the wash is still wet, paint out small hair lines using a small round brush. To complete the loose watercolor look, splatter some gray paint around the racoon's portrait using your medium round brush.

Step 3

In this step, you will continue adding a wash to the head of the raccoon. You will create a 75:25 ratio mixture of Payne's Gray to Raw Umber. Start by adding a diluted wash of the Payne's Gray and Raw Umber mixture to the lower portion of the head, making sure to leave the white of the paper around the eyes and nose. Next, add a light wash of Yellow Ochre to the ears.

Add a darker mixture of Payne's Gray and Raw Umber to the top portion of the head. While the ears are still damp but not too wet, add some Payne's Gray to the center of the ears using a wet-on-wet technique.

Lastly, pull out small hair marks while the wash is still damp. If you need to reactivate the paint, add some extra water to the edge of the wash. While the wash is damp, you can also dab some clean water into the wash to add texture. Allow to air-dry or use a hair dryer to speed up the process.

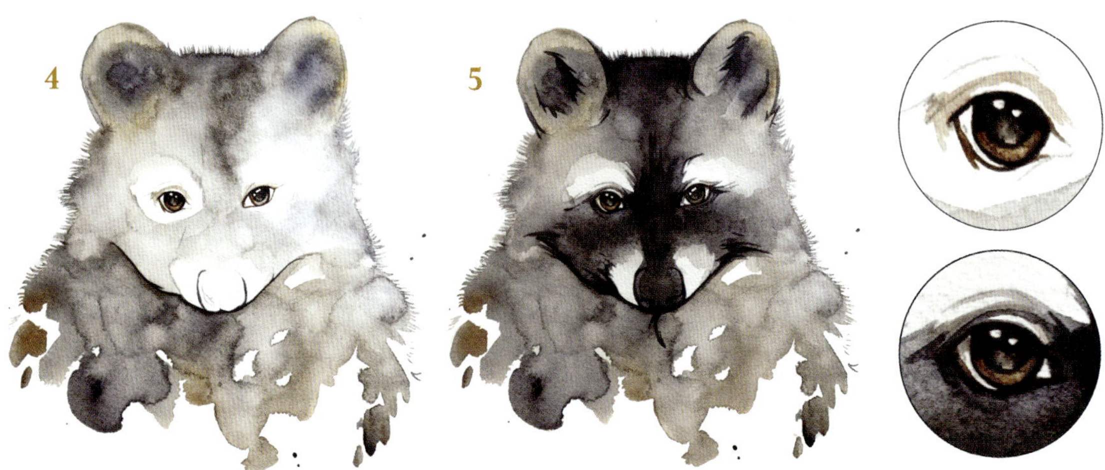

Step 4

After your washes in previous steps are fully dry, paint the eyes of the raccoon. Add Raw Umber to the irises of the eyes, making sure to leave two white dots in each eye for the highlights. Create the rest of the details around the eyes using Raw Umber as well. After the Raw Umber in the eyes dries, add pupils with Payne's Gray. Next, you will paint an outline of the nose using Raw Umber.

Step 5

In this step, add a saturated Payne's Gray wash to create the dark mask on the raccoon's face and nose. Add a slightly lighter layer of Payne's Gray to the top of its head between its two ears. After your washes are fully dry, paint out the nostrils on the nose and add small details around the eyes and ears of the raccoon using a saturated amount of Payne's Gray and a small round brush.

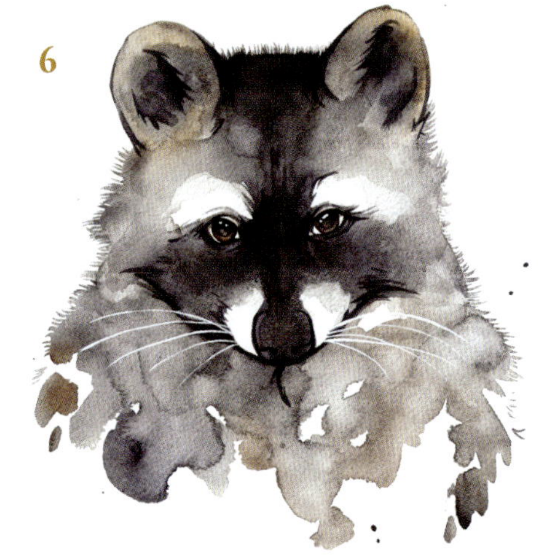

Step 6

In this final step, you will be adding white whiskers to the raccoon. To create whiskers, use a white gel pen, white opaque ink or paint. If you choose to use ink or paint, make sure to use a small, fine-tipped brush.

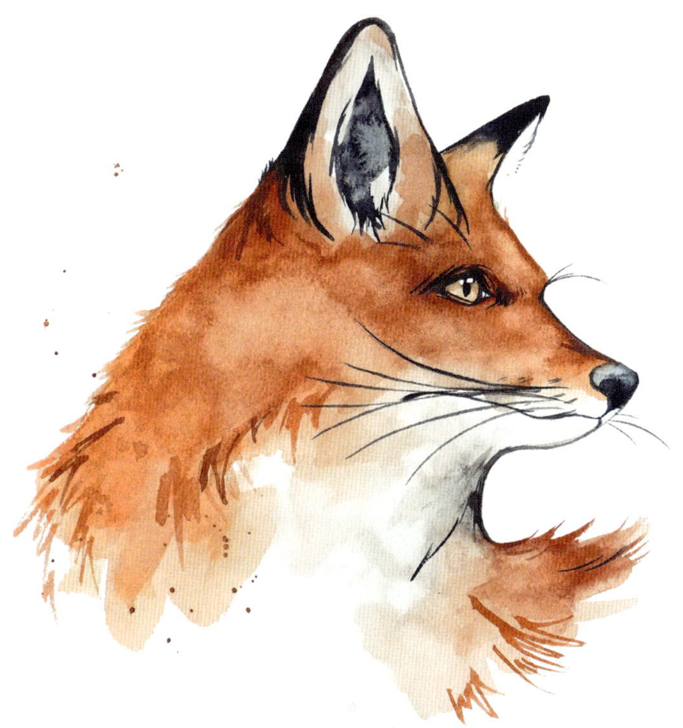

Red Fox

Despite their name, these foxes' coats can come in a variety of colors, from rusty red to silver and black. For this project, you will be creating a fox with the iconic rust-colored fur. Red foxes can be found on multiple continents, so there is a chance you have seen one yourself!

Red foxes have large, triangular ears with black tips and a pointed snout. This portrait will have bold, saturated details on its face and transition into an abstract wash. The loose wash will be layered with paint splatters and jagged lines that represent the fox's fur.

Lesson

Using jagged lines to create fur texture

Colors

Burnt Sienna

Yellow Ochre

Raw Umber

Payne's Gray

Brushes

Medium Round Brush
Small Round Brush

Step 1

Trace the drawing template of the fox on page 167.

Step 2

Create a wash using a 50:50 mixture of Burnt Sienna and Yellow Ochre with a medium round brush. Add these colors to the top portion of the fox's head and the back of its neck. Concentrate Burnt Sienna around the eye of the fox to create a shadow. Before your wash fully dries, use a small round brush to drag out small hairs on the back of the fox's neck; rewet your paint if needed.

Step 3

In this step, add a diluted wash of Raw Umber to the ears, mouth and neck area. While the light wash of Raw Umber around the neck is still wet, dab in a little Payne's Gray to darken the area. On the neck and shoulder area, add your Burnt Sienna and Yellow Ochre mixture from the last step, and then create hair marks using your medium round brush.

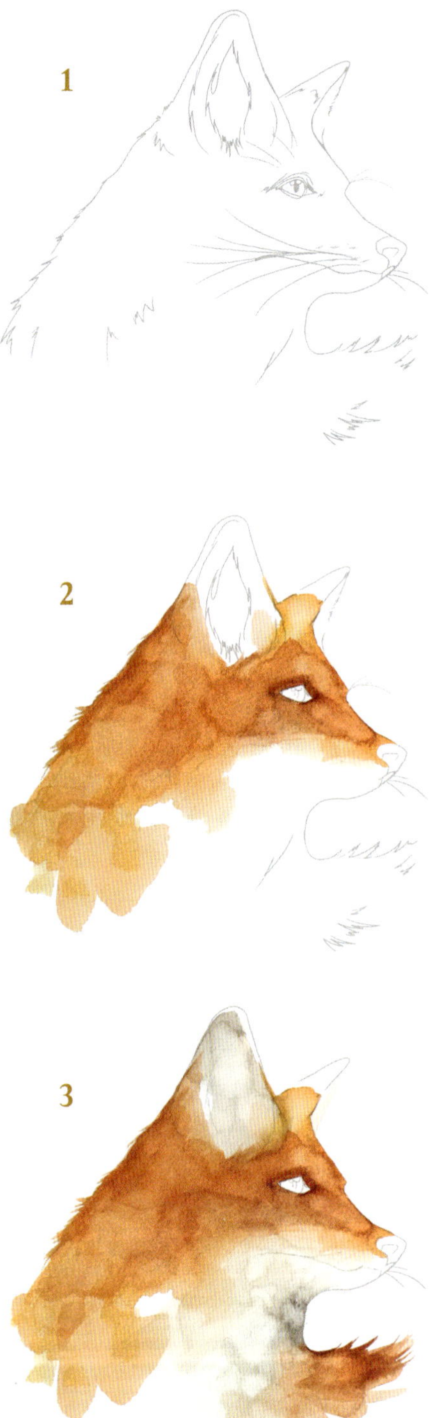

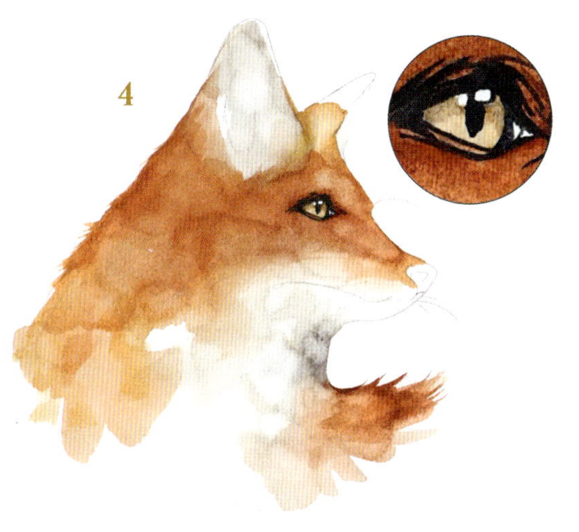

Step 4

Start by adding Yellow Ochre to the lower portion of the eye and Raw Umber to the top portion of the eye. Blend the two colors together to create a gradient. While filling in the eye with these colors, make sure to leave two white dots for the highlight of the eye. After this paint dries, outline the eye using Payne's Gray, and then paint a pupil using a small round brush.

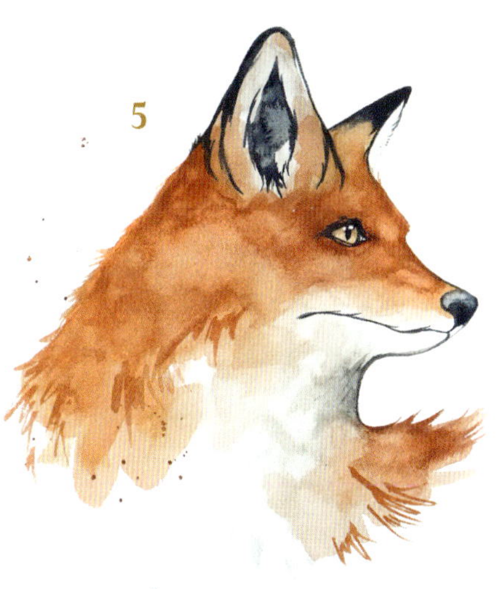

Step 5

In this step, you will add Payne's Gray paint to the tips of your fox's ears, keeping the paint pretty saturated to keep the color dark. Add this same color to the inside of the ear using more water with your paint so that the color appears lighter.

Next, paint the nose and mouth of the fox with Payne's Gray. For the nose, make sure the value is lighter on the top of the nose and darker for the nostrils. Lastly, create fur marks on the fox using your medium round brush and Burnt Sienna paint.

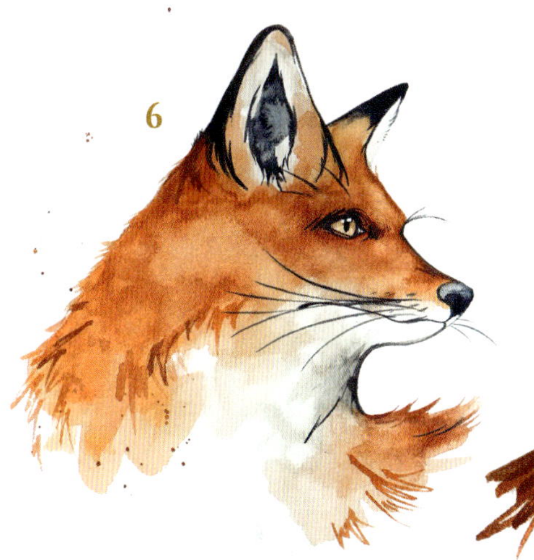

Step 6

In this final step, add whiskers to the fox using your small round brush and a saturated amount of Payne's Gray paint. Add more details around the eye and neck using the same brush and paint. Next, add a few more fur lines to the fox's body using a saturated amount of Burnt Sienna.

Fur mark-making created using fast, jagged brushstrokes

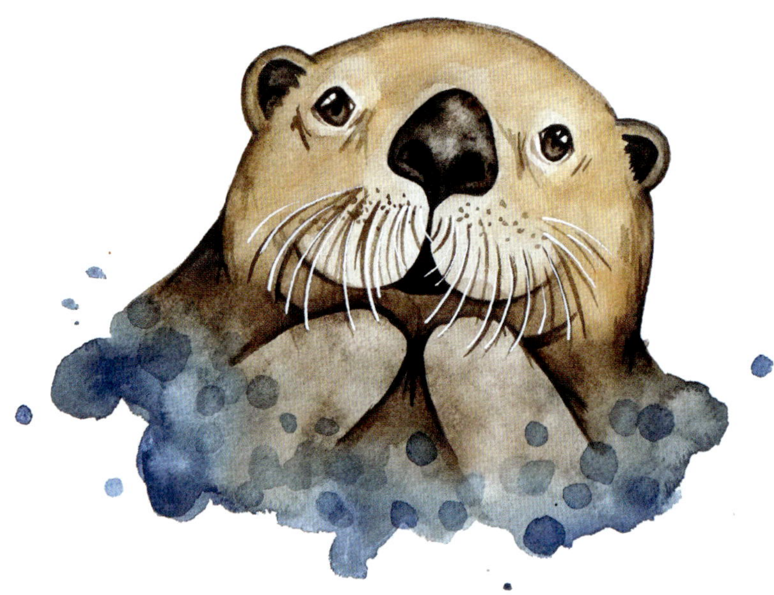

Sea Otter

This marine mammal spends most of its life in the water and can be found along the Pacific Coast. They have very buoyant bodies that allow them to float on the surface of the water, and a group of resting otters is called a raft.

This otter is very playful-looking as it peeks out of the surface of the water with its paws up to its opened mouth. You will add to this playful feeling by layering blue bubbles that frame the otter portrait. For this project, you will also practice painting whiskers using either white ink or paint.

Lesson
Painting layered water effect

Colors

Raw Umber

Prussian Blue

Payne's Gray

Yellow Ochre

Brushes
Medium Round Brush
Small Round Brush

Extra Supplies
White ink or gel pen

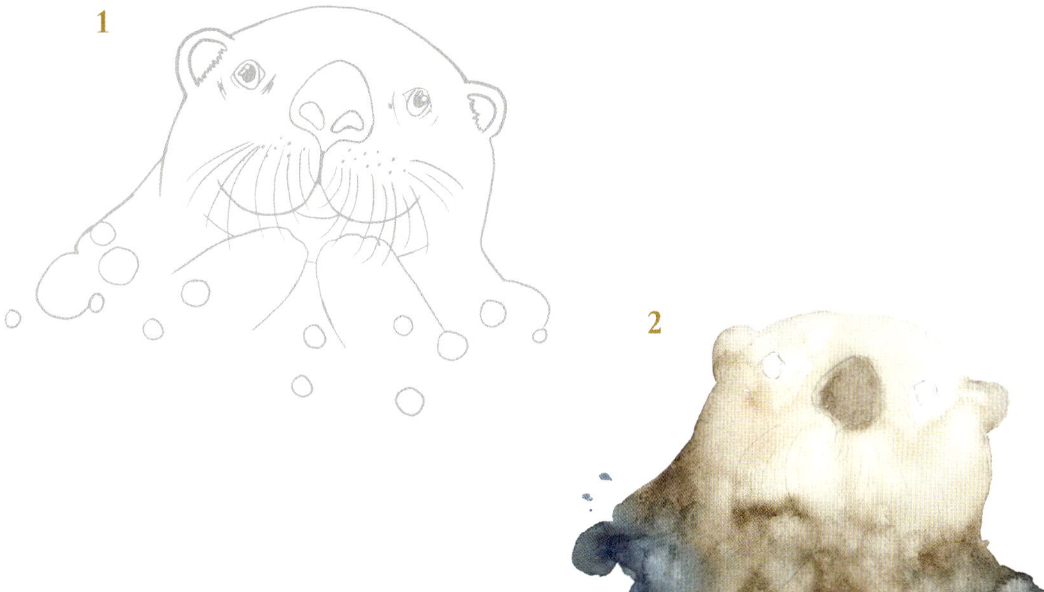

Step 1

Trace the outline found on page 169. Keep the drawing light so it doesn't show through your paint. You can draw the water bubbles exactly like they are in the drawing, or you can add additional ones if you like.

Step 2

For this painting you will start off with a wash that transitions from Raw Umber to Prussian Blue. Start off your wash by adding a light layer of Raw Umber to the head of the otter, and make about an 80:20 water-to-paint ratio. While that wash is still wet, add a more saturated amount of Raw Umber to the nose of the otter and to the middle of the wash, about a 50:50 water-to-paint ratio. Last, add Prussian Blue to the bottom third of the wash. Use a hair dryer to dry the wash or allow it to air-dry before moving on to the next step.

Optional

Add a few splashes of water into the wash to create some texture, and you can also splatter some paint around the outside of the portrait.

3

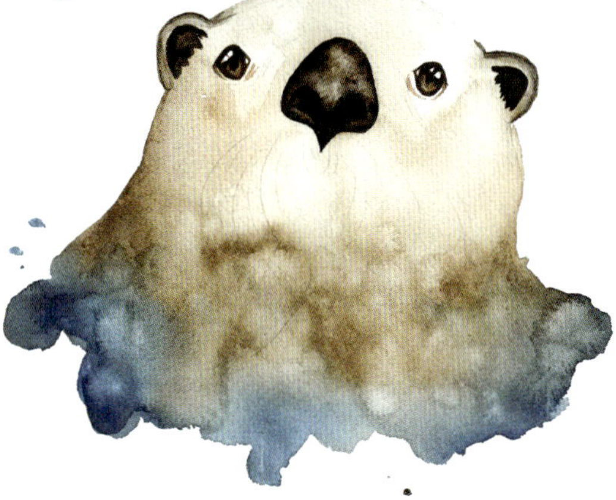

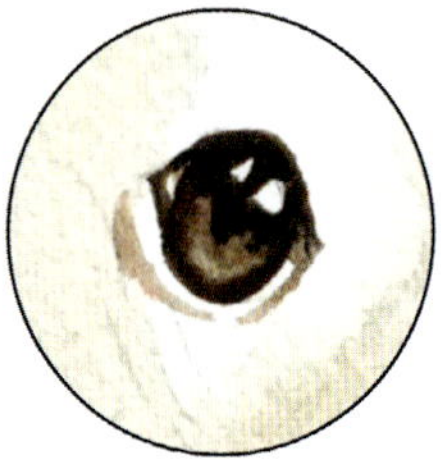

4

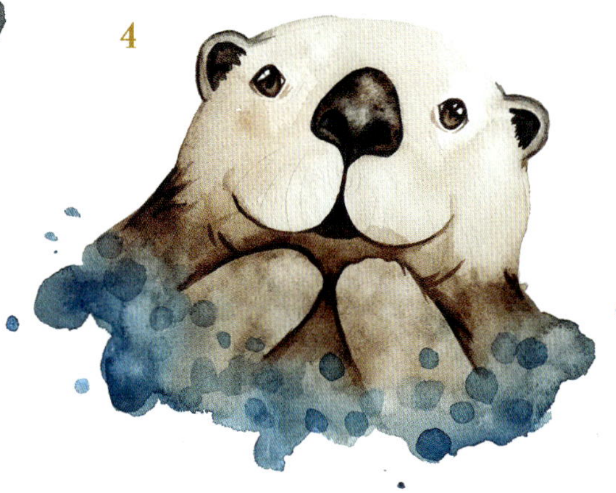

Step 3

Use Raw Umber with your medium round brush to fill in the iris of the eyes, the nose, and ears. While filling in the eyes, make sure to leave a couple white dots for the highlights. After adding Raw Umber, switch to using a saturated amount of Payne's Gray and a small round brush to add the nostrils to the nose and the pupils to the eyes.

Step 4

Start by creating an outline for the mouth and front paws of the sea otter with Raw Umber paint and a medium round brush. Don't use too much water so you can control the paint easier. Next, add a light wash of Raw Umber around the neck and the paws of the otter. Then add small hair marks to the otter using the same paint and brush. Lastly, add small bubbles of Prussian Blue for the bubbles in the water. The bubbles can vary in size and saturation.

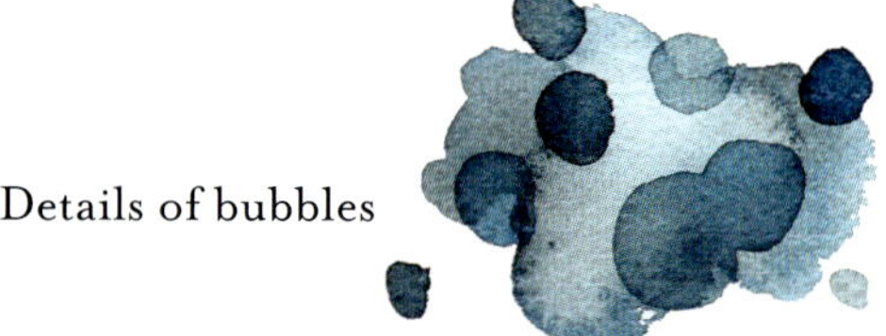

Details of bubbles

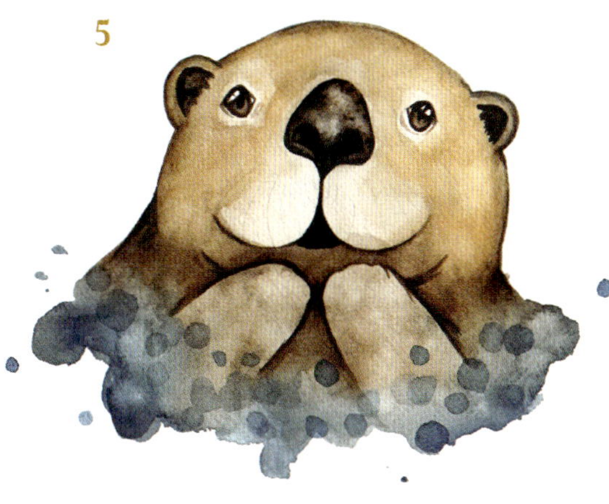

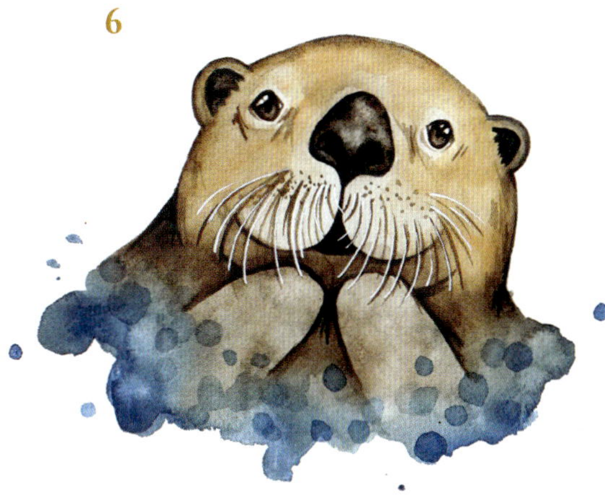

Step 5

In order to warm this piece up, add a light layer of Yellow Ochre paint using your medium round brush to the top of the head, avoiding around the eyes and mouth. Make sure the paint is diluted so it doesn't appear too dark when you add it. Allow this layer to air-dry or use a hair dryer to speed up the process.

Step 6

Add dots to the cheeks of the otter using Raw Umber paint and a small round brush. Using the same brush and paint, add small lines around the otter's eyes and along the side of its face.

Next, paint the first layer of the otter's whiskers with Raw Umber and a small round brush. After the paint for the whiskers dries, add more whiskers, this time using either a white gel pen or white ink.

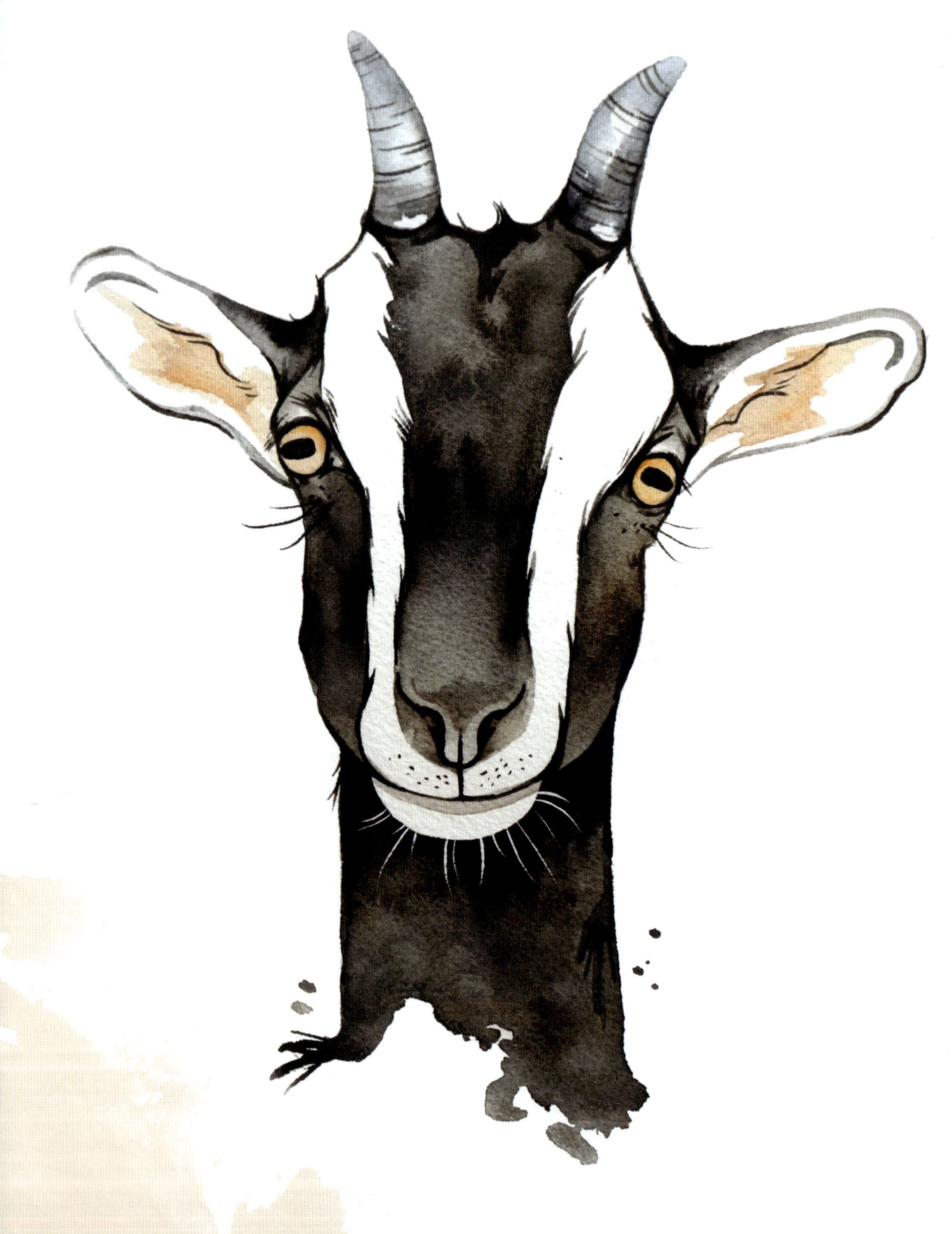

Farm Animals

Now that you have been practicing painting expressive animal portraits with watercolors, let's go visit the farm! There is a variety of different types of animals that can be found on a farm, such as chickens, goats, cows and horses. All of these animals have been domesticated to live alongside humans; maybe one of them lives at your home!

In this final round of paintings, you will be combining all of the techniques you learned in the previous chapters with a few new ones, such as painting a very light-colored animal like a sheep or painting the spotted texture on a cow's nose. When you paint your animals, think of how you can express their personalities, such as creating the alert expression of an energetic Border Collie or a sweet, timid piglet covered in mud.

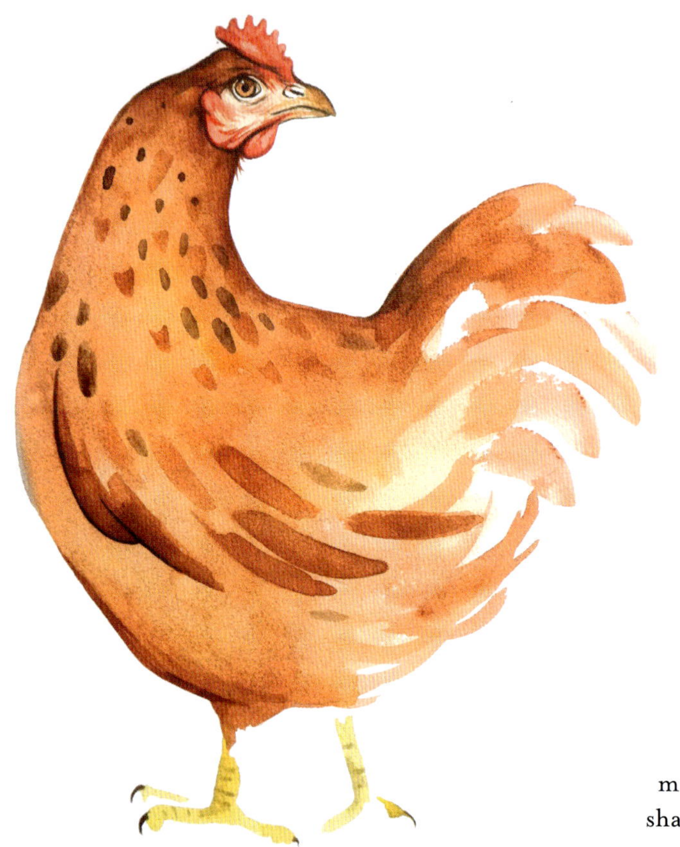

Red Hen

Similar to other domesticated animals, hens are usually bred for different purposes: most for eggs, some for their meat, others for companionship. Humans usually keep their chickens in coops to keep them safe. At night they like to go somewhere high to roost because this is when they are most vulnerable. We take care of laying hens like this one and in return we are rewarded with their eggs.

In this project, you will paint a hen with an impressive tail made up of a variety of curved brushstrokes. You will also use the tip of your paint brush at different angles and pressure amounts to create a pattern on its neck.

Lesson
Creating different mark-making patterns and shapes with your paint brush

Colors
Yellow Ochre

Burnt Sienna

Cadmium Red Medium Hue

Payne's Gray

Cadmium Yellow Medium Hue

Raw Umber

Brushes
Medium Round Brush
Small Round Brush

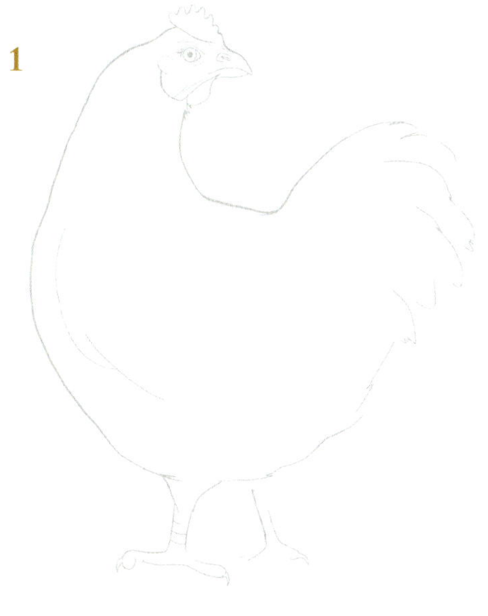

Step 1

Create a sketch of the hen by using the template provided on page 167. Add details to the face, but loosely draw out the tail feathers and feet.

Step 2

Fill in the body of the hen with a wash of a 50:50 mixture of Yellow Ochre to Burnt Sienna using a medium-sized round brush. While the wash is still wet, dab in extra Burnt Sienna around the head and neck in order to increase the value. You may have to switch to a small round brush to paint the tighter areas.

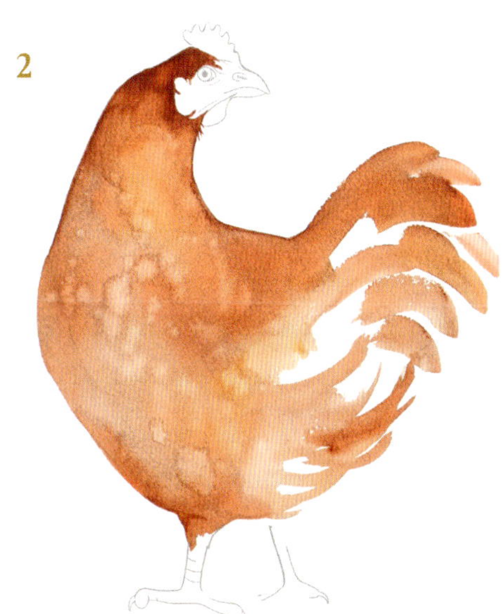

Next, create loose tail feathers using your medium-sized round brush and the same paint mixture. Most of the feathers should be applied directly to dry paper, with some of them meeting the wet wash. To create the feathers, move your brush using a curved hand motion and use the edge of the brush with more pressure to create larger, curved brushstrokes. Allow some of the white of the paper to show through. Allow the wash to air-dry or gently use a hair dryer to speed up the process.

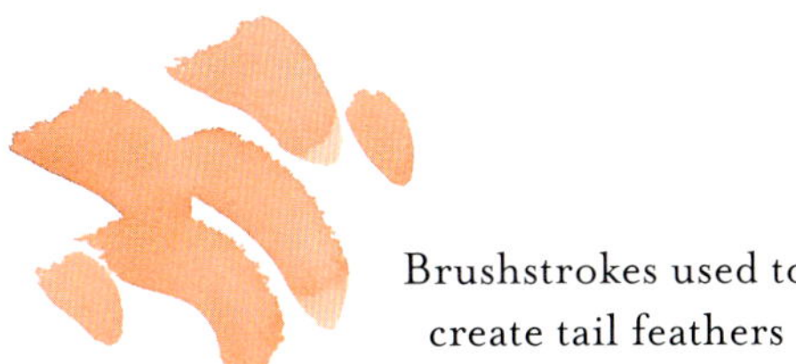

Brushstrokes used to create tail feathers

Step 3

After the last layer is completely dry, apply a light, diluted wash of Yellow Ochre with a medium-sized round brush to the face of the hen, starting at its beak and ending below its eye. Fill in the comb and wattle (the red parts on the chicken's face) with a diluted wash of Cadmium Red Medium Hue paint. After that first layer dries, add a saturated amount of Cadmium Red Medium Hue paint with a small round brush to paint the details.

Step 4

In this step, you will be adding more details to the face of the hen. Start by adding Yellow Ochre and Burnt Sienna to the tip of the beak and to the hen's eye using a small round brush. Next, add small details to the beak and the inner and outer eye with your small round brush using Payne's Gray paint. Add shadows using Payne's Gray below the comb and wattle of the chicken.

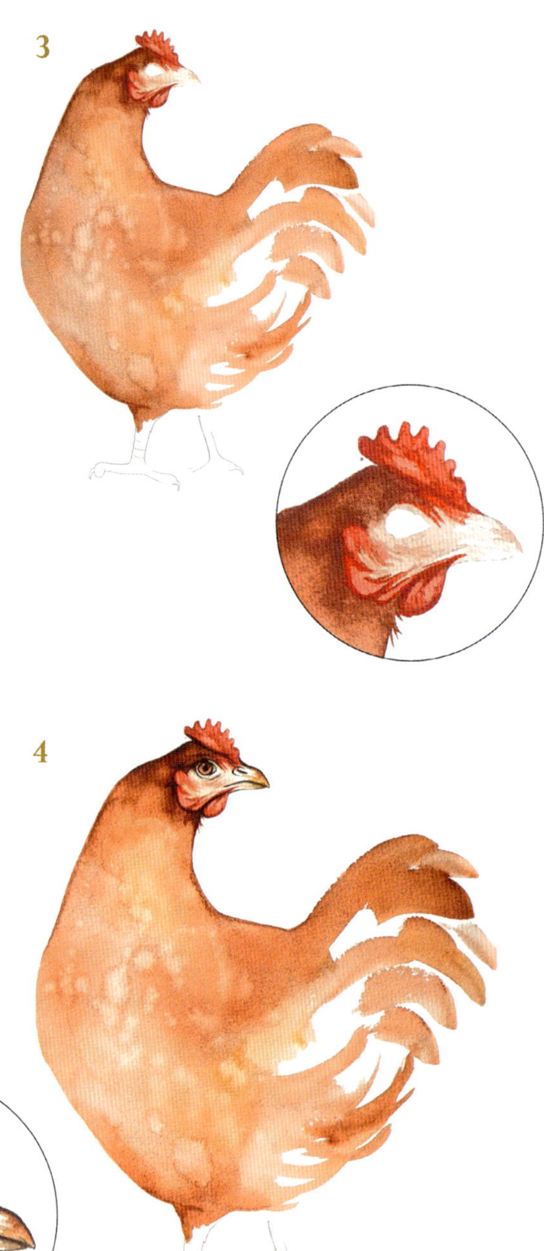

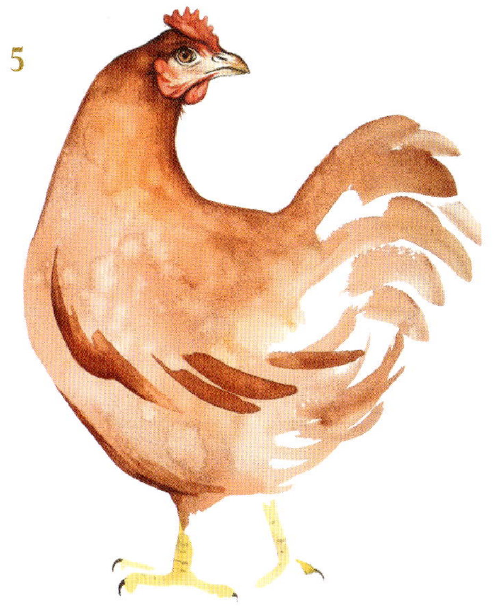

Step 5

Loosely paint the hen's feet with Cadmium Yellow Medium Hue paint and a medium-sized round brush. Add talons using a small round brush and Payne's Gray paint. While the feet are still damp, add thin lines to them with Raw Umber paint. Near the hen's leg, add some Burnt Sienna paint to create a shadow.

Next, paint feathers on the hen with a medium-sized round brush and a saturated amount of Burnt Sienna paint, about a 30:70 water to paint ratio. To create thinner lines for the features, apply less pressure than you did for the tail feathers.

Step 6

In this final step, add a light wash of Yellow Ochre to the body of the hen, avoiding its tail feathers, to warm things up. After that wash dries, create the pattern on its neck and back using your medium round brush and Raw Umber and Burnt Sienna paint. Apply different amounts of pressure and position your brush at different angles to get different shapes. For more circular shapes, gently touch your paper without too much pressure; for the more ovular shapes, angle your brush.

Lastly, add thin lines of saturated amounts of Payne's Gray with a small round brush to define the wing shape.

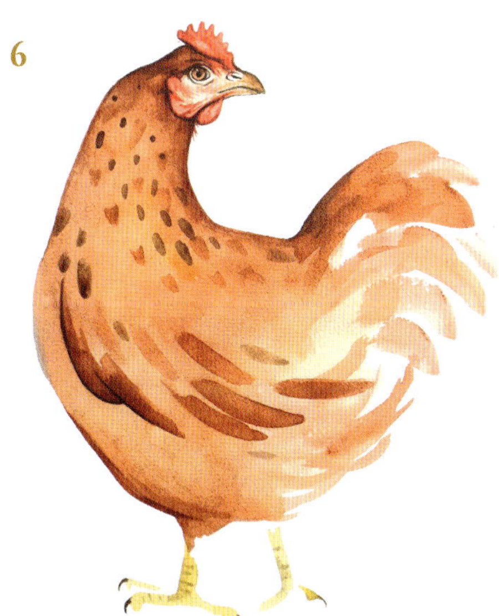

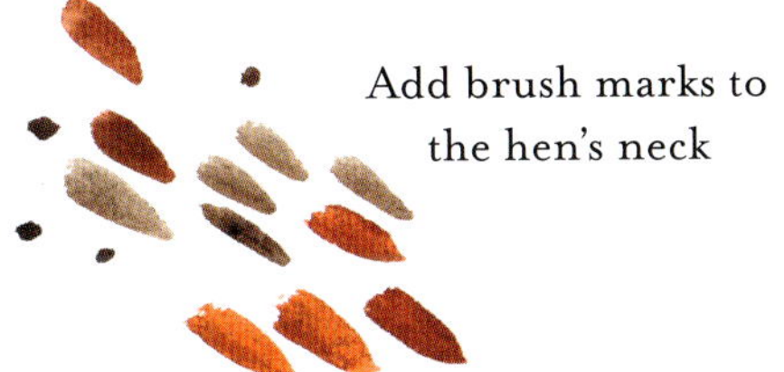

Add brush marks to the hen's neck

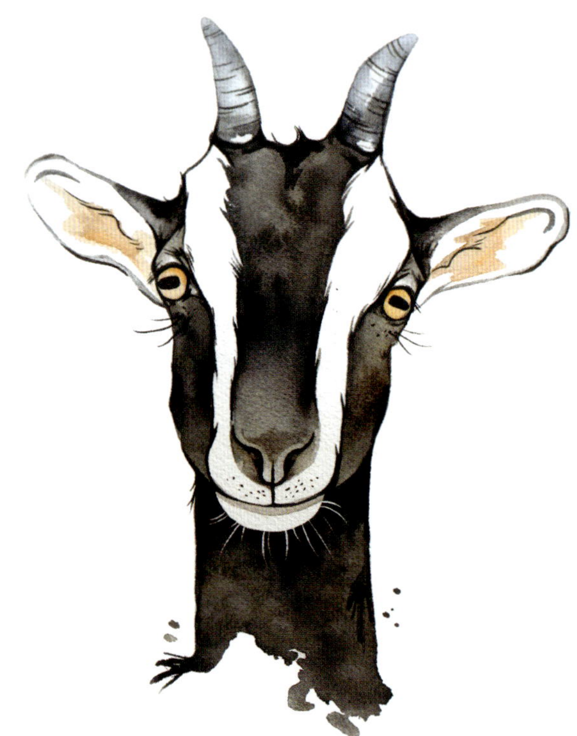

Baby Goat

Domestic goats are descendants of mountain goats, which makes them great climbers—they are known to even climb to the tops of trees! Both male and female goats have horns. The horns on their heads help them regulate their body temperature and protect them.

This goat will be painted using just a few colors, as it is a black and white animal, but instead of painting the black fur with black paint, you will mix together a blue-toned gray with brown and blue paint to add some depth to the color. The main focus of this piece is the goat's horns, but the goat you will be painting has fairly small horns since it is a young goat.

 Payne's Gray

Raw Umber

 Prussian Blue

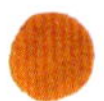 Yellow Ochre

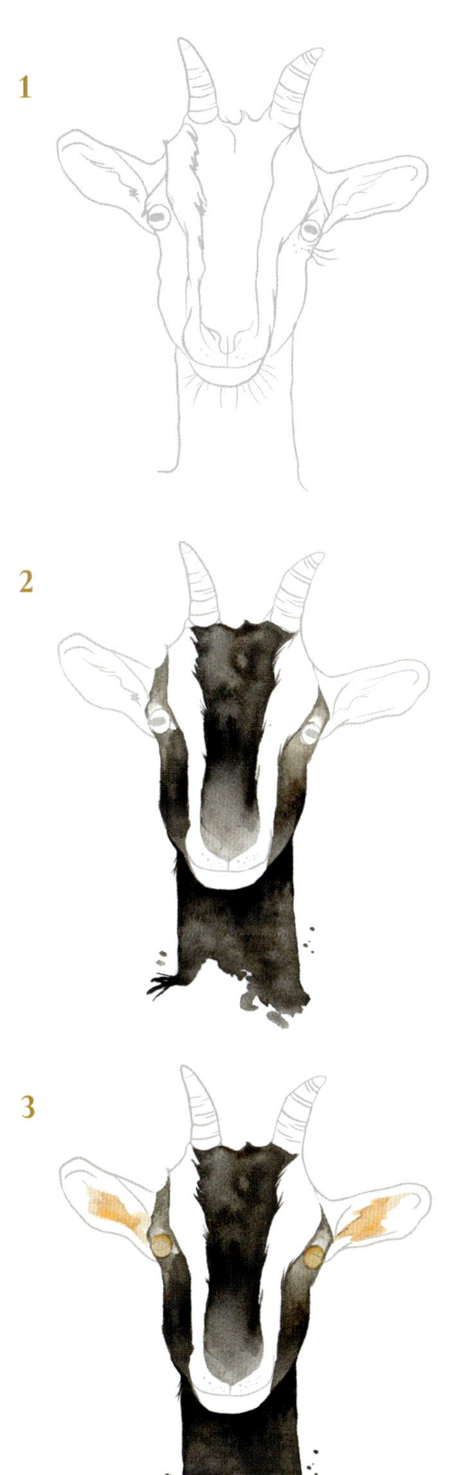

Step 1

Draw the portrait of your goat by using the template provided on page 169.

Step 2

Fill in the black areas of the goat using Payne's Gray paint. Use a medium-sized round brush to fill in the majority of the shapes. For the small hair details, move to your small round brush. While the wash is still damp, dab in small amounts of Raw Umber and Prussian Blue paint to add some variation to the gray. You can also add some small paint splatters at the end of the goat's neck where the portrait ends if you would like.

Step 3

Add Yellow Ochre paint to the ears of the goat using a wet-on-dry technique. Next, add Yellow Ochre to the goat's eyes, making sure the gray paint surrounding them is dry so the colors don't bleed together. Allow this layer to dry before moving onto the next step.

Payne's Gray wash with dabs of Prussian Blue and Raw Umber

Step 4

For this layer, you will only be using
Payne's Gray to paint in some of the
facial features. Use a saturated amount
of Payne's Gray paint with a small round
brush to paint around the eye and to fill
in the pupil. Paint around the mouth
and nostrils using a saturated amount of
Payne's Gray as well. Below the mouth,
add a light wash of gray. Lastly, paint
in the goat's ears by painting over your
pencil lines and filling in the area that
connects to the head.

Step 5

Mix together equal parts Payne's Gray
and Prussian Blue paint. Then dilute the
paint with water before adding it to the
goat's horns with a medium round brush.
Leave some white showing in the center
of the horns. After the first wash is dry,
paint out small horizontal lines using a
small round brush to give a realistic
horn texture.

Step 6

In this last step, add fine lines to the ears
and the whiskers below the goat's eye
using Payne's Gray paint. Around the
mouth, add small dots using Payne's Gray
as well, but for the whiskers around the
mouth, use either a white gel pen or white
ink to paint them.

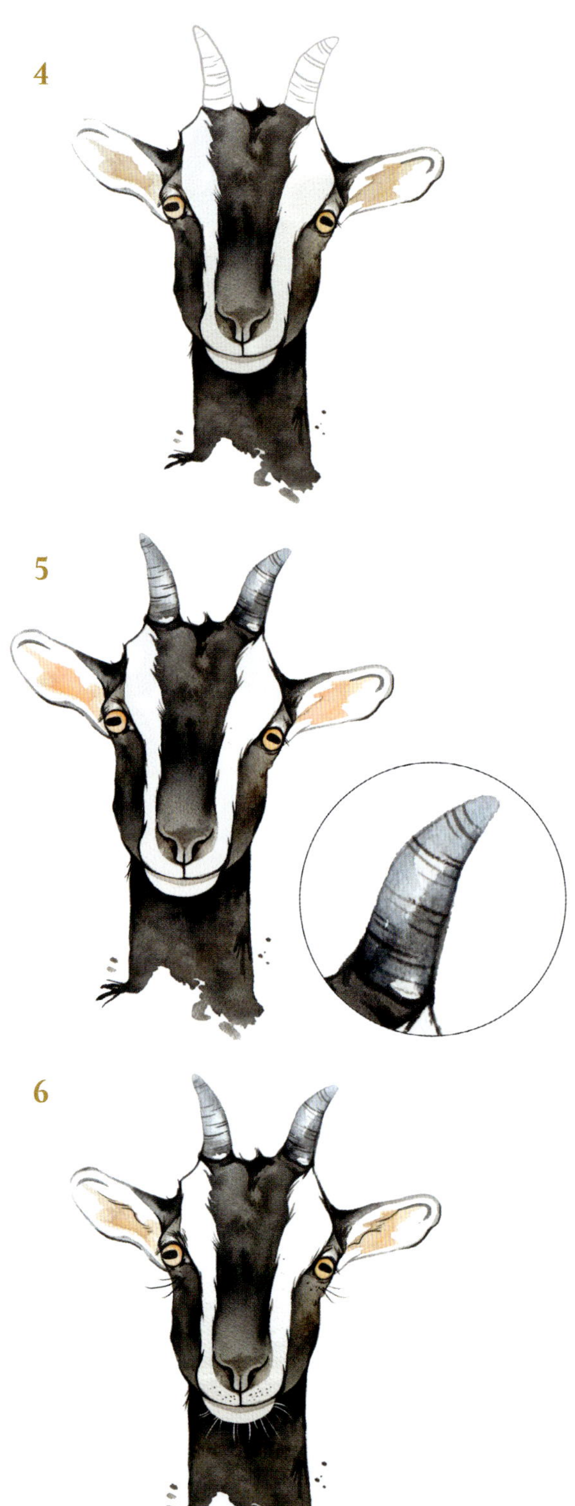

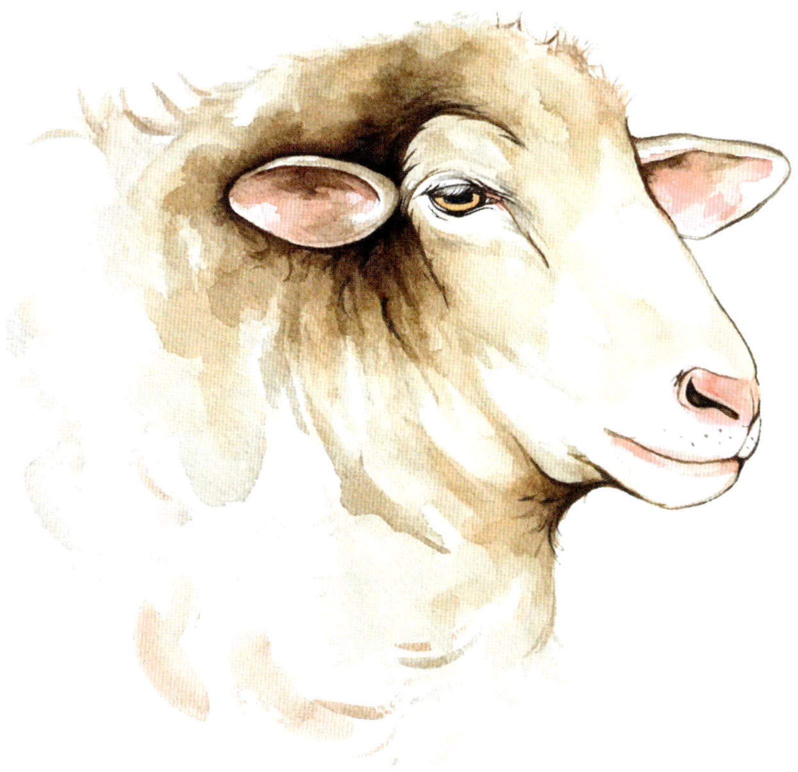

Fluffy Sheep

Sheep are gentle animals that gather in large flocks for protection from predators. One of their most prominent features is their fluffy wool. Sheep wool comes in different types and is used to create a variety of things such as scarves, blankets and even rugs!

In this tutorial, you will practice painting their light-colored wool using diluted paint and creating curled brushstrokes to represent the texture of their wool. The initial wash will be the largest step of this painting, and then you will increase the value around the sheep's head and add its adorable facial features.

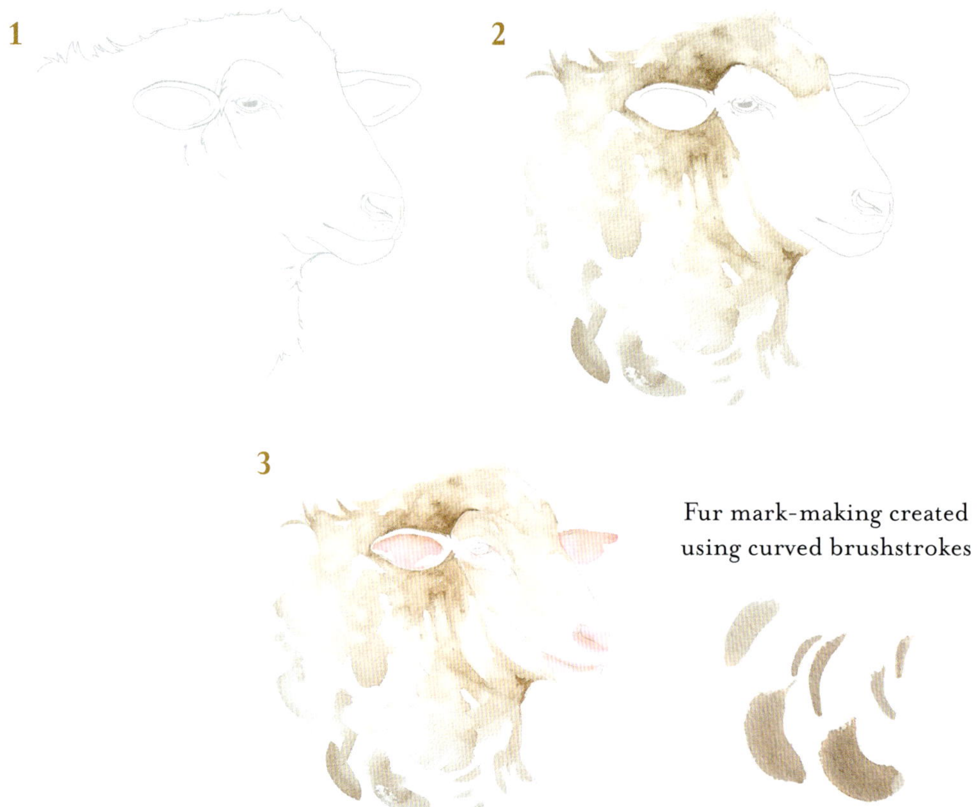

Fur mark-making created
using curved brushstrokes

Step 1

Create a sketch of a sheep by tracing the template on page 171.

Step 2

For the wash, start by applying a diluted amount of Yellow Ochre paint around the face of the sheep, allowing some of the white of the paper to still show.

For the brush marks on the outer edge of the wash, mix in a small amount of Raw Umber with your diluted Yellow Ochre to darken the color a little. Then create curved marks around the portrait with a medium-sized round brush. While the wash is still wet, dab in some Raw Umber around the ear and below the neck, and then drag out small fur marks on its back.

Step 3

In this step, you will be adding some Rose Doré paint to the ears, nose and mouth of the sheep after the wash from the last step is dry. Next, add a light wash of Yellow Ochre to the face of the sheep, making sure to leave some white of the paper showing on the bridge of its nose, around its eye and under its cheek bone.

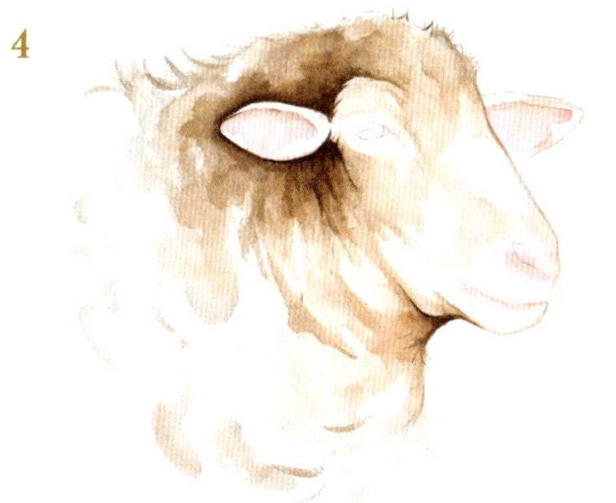

Step 4

Add a layer of Raw Umber around the ear and along its neck to create shadows. By adding dark values to your painting, it allows the light areas to appear even brighter. Next, use a dry brush technique and both a small round brush and a medium round brush to create more curved hair marks in the sheep's wool around its head.

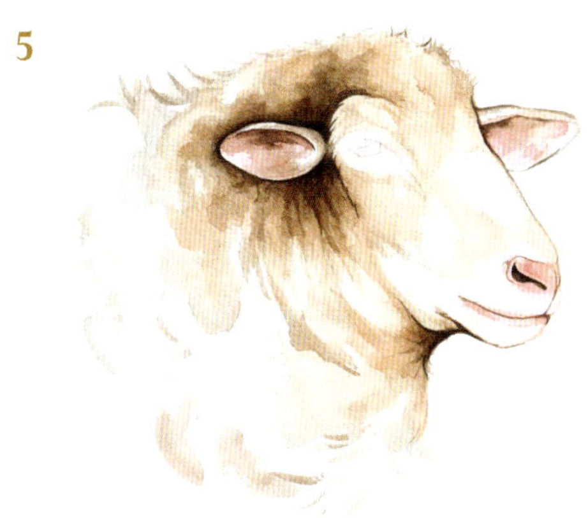

Step 5

Next, add another layer of Rose Doré to the ears and nose to increase the value. After that dries, add details to the ears, nose and mouth of the sheep using a saturated amount of Raw Umber paint and a small round brush. Add a small amount of Payne's Gray around the outside of the ear and below the sheep's jaw to add more contrast.

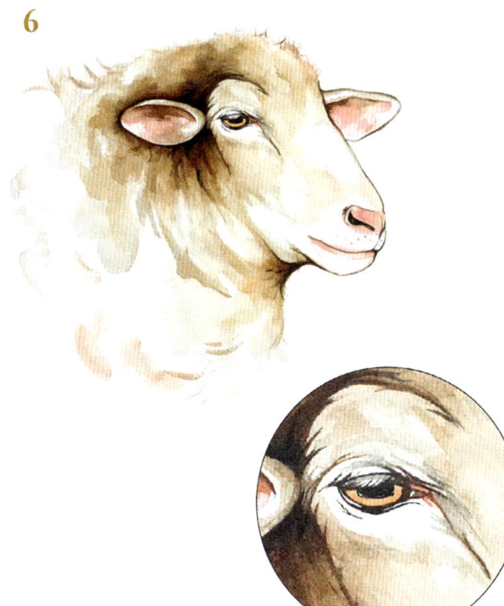

Step 6

For its eye, start with a layer of Yellow Ochre in the iris, and then add a small touch of Rose Doré to the outer corner of the eye. Once dry, outline the eye with a saturated amount of Payne's Gray paint and paint some small hair details around the outside of the eye using Raw Umber. Lastly, paint the pupil using Payne's Gray paint, making sure to leave some white of the paper showing for the sheep's white eyelashes.

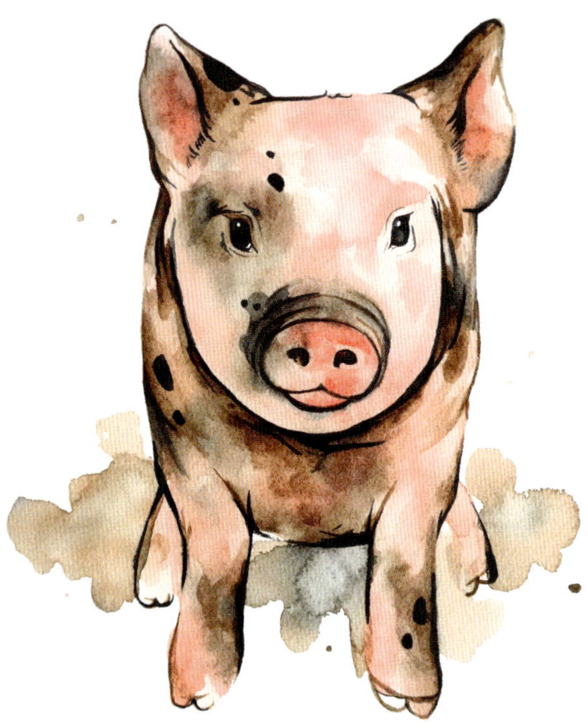

Muddy Piglet

In this tutorial, you will be painting an adorable little piglet covered in mud. Despite their reputation of being dirty, pigs coat themselves in mud to help them keep cool when it is hot out and to protect their skin from the sun.

In this lesson, you will use both wet-on-wet and wet-on-dry techniques to create spots on the piglet. You will also create a simple wash background to help showcase this pig's personality and place it in an environment. For this project, you can get creative and play around with where you want to place spots on your piglet to make it unique.

Lesson
Painting mud on and around
a playful pig

Colors
Rose Doré

Raw Umber

Payne's Gray

Brushes
Medium Round Brush
Small Round Brush

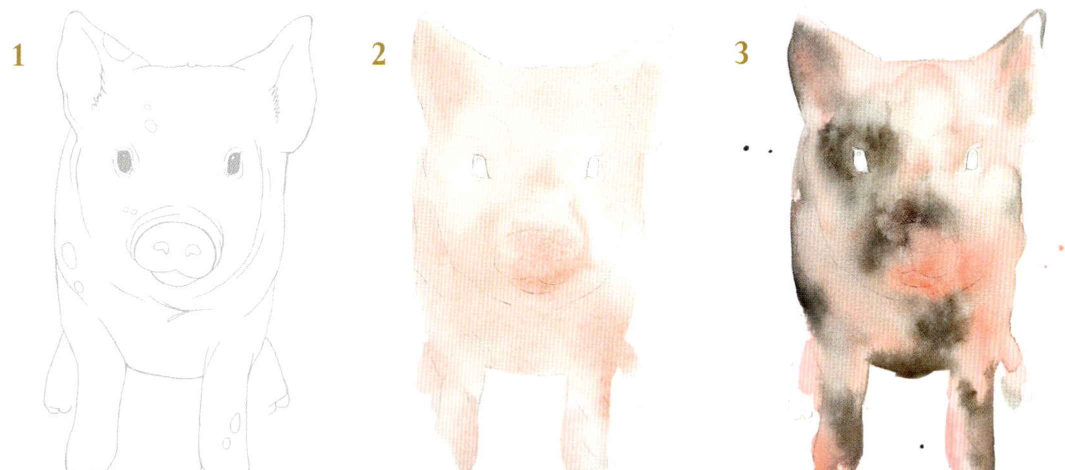

Step 1
Create an outline of the pig's body using the drawing template provided on page 171. Remember to keep your lines light! You will be freehand painting the mud around the pig, so you don't have to sketch that in.

Step 2
Cover the entire body of the pig with a wash of Rose Doré paint. It is okay if your wash is uneven. Don't allow this layer to dry before you move to the next step, since you will be creating a wet-on-wet wash.

Step 3
While the wash of pink is still wet, dab in Raw Umber paint throughout the pig's body to create soft spots. The Raw Umber will represent spots and dirt on the pig, so it doesn't need to look exactly like the image in the book if you want to play around a little. Next, add a little extra Rose Doré paint to the wash, making sure to add some to the nose. While the wash is still damp, splash in some clean water to create texture in the wash. Allow this wash to dry or use a hair dryer to speed up the process.

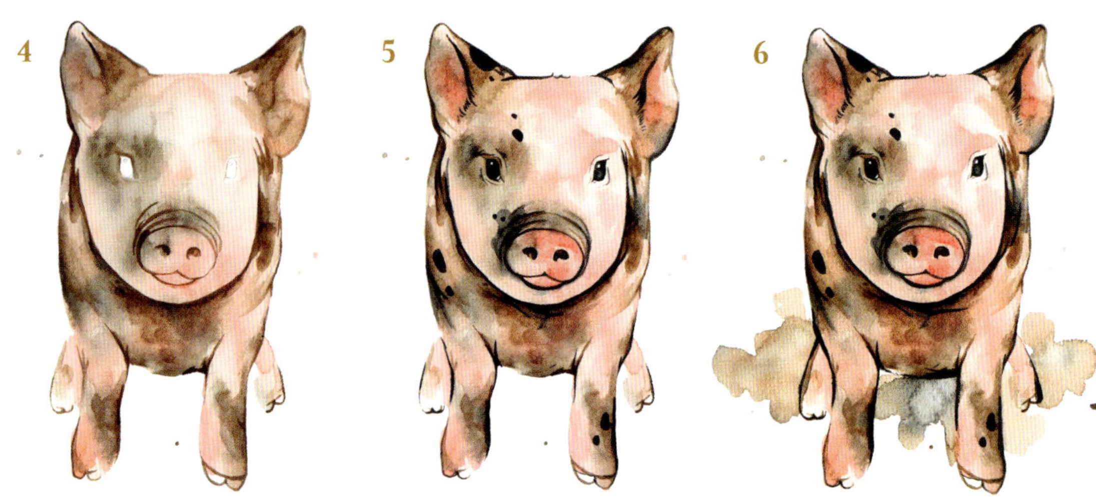

Step 4

Now that you have a great first layer, you will need to define the shapes that make up the pig. Paint over your pencil lines that make up the pig's head and body using Raw Umber paint, making sure your paint is pretty saturated so it appears dark. Add a light wash of Raw Umber with a medium round brush around the pig's head and ears to create shadows. You can also start painting out the mud spots on the pig using this same color.

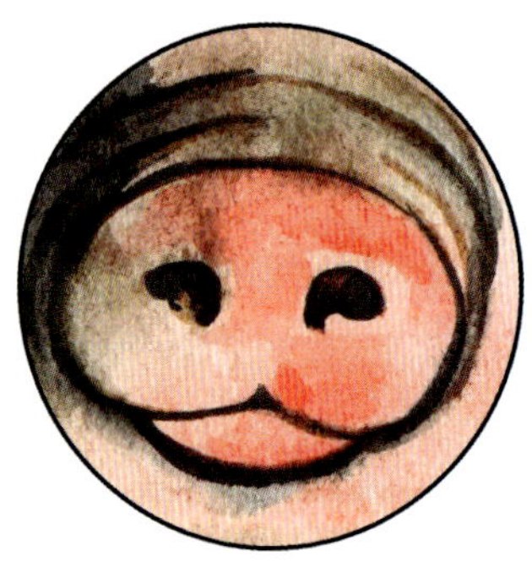

Step 5

Paint the eyes of the pig using a small round brush and a saturated amount of Payne's Gray paint. Next, add a little extra Rose Doré to the pig's nose, ears and the center of its face to increase the value. Lastly, paint out details on the ears and dark spots throughout its body using a saturated amount of Raw Umber paint.

Step 6

This last step is optional. Paint a muddy puddle around the pig using a medium-sized round brush and Raw Umber paint. Start by applying a light, loose wash of Raw Umber paint, and then add in some Payne's Gray under its body to give the appearance of a shadow.

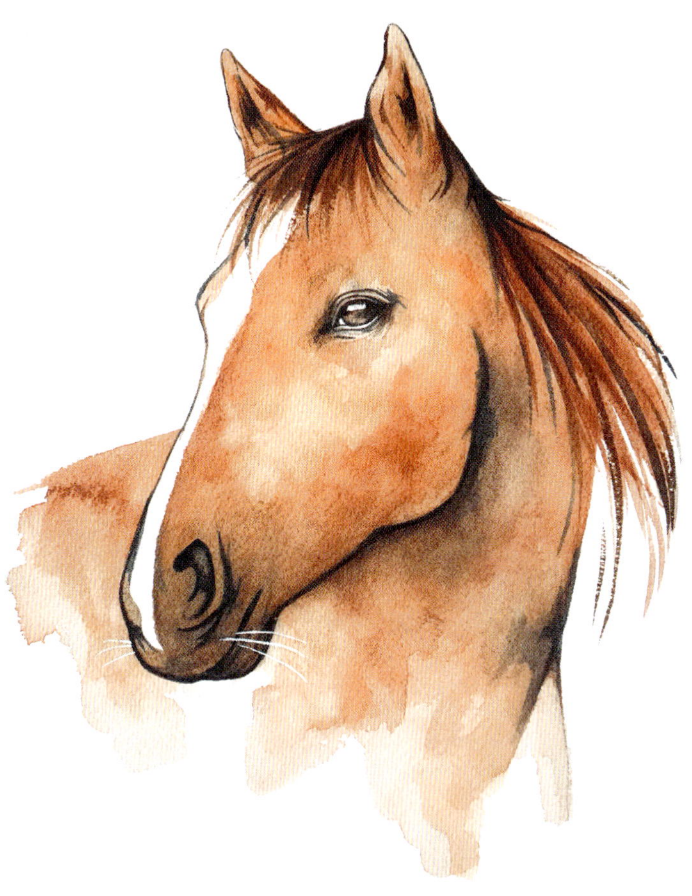

Quarter Horse

Horses are domesticated animals that have helped humans in many ways. They are used for transporting humans and goods, for entertainment and as companions. This is one of the most popular horse breeds in the United States, the Quarter Horse. These horses are named after their ability to outrun other horses in quarter mile races.

In this tutorial, you will be painting a horse portrait and using a dry brush technique to create the horse's mane. You will also be building up multiple layers of light washes to create shadows and dark values.

Lesson

Painting a mane using a dry brush

Colors

Yellow Ochre

Burnt Sienna

Raw Umber

Payne's Gray

Brushes

Medium Round Brush

Small Round Brush

Extra Supplies

White ink or gel pen

Step 1

Create a light sketch of a horse portrait by tracing the drawing template provided on page 173.

Step 2

Using a medium round brush, create a loose wash on the horse using a 50:50 mixture of Yellow Ochre to Burnt Sienna paint. Make sure to leave some white of the paper for the white stripe that goes down the center of the horse's face and for its eye. End the wash of the portrait with an organic edge. It doesn't have to look exactly like the example in the book. Next, paint out the mane of the horse while the wash is still wet.

Step 3

Add a light wash of Raw Umber to the entire head of the horse and end at the bottom of its neck, making sure that the previous wash layer is still showing a little. Allow this layer to air-dry or use a hair dryer to speed up the process. Then add another layer of Raw Umber to the end of its mouth, along its jaw and to its ear to increase the value.

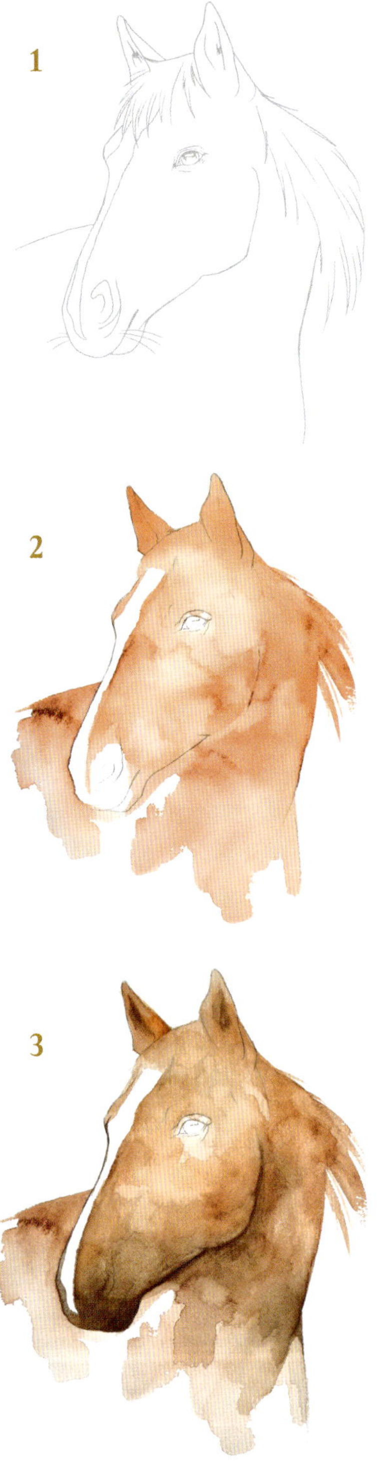

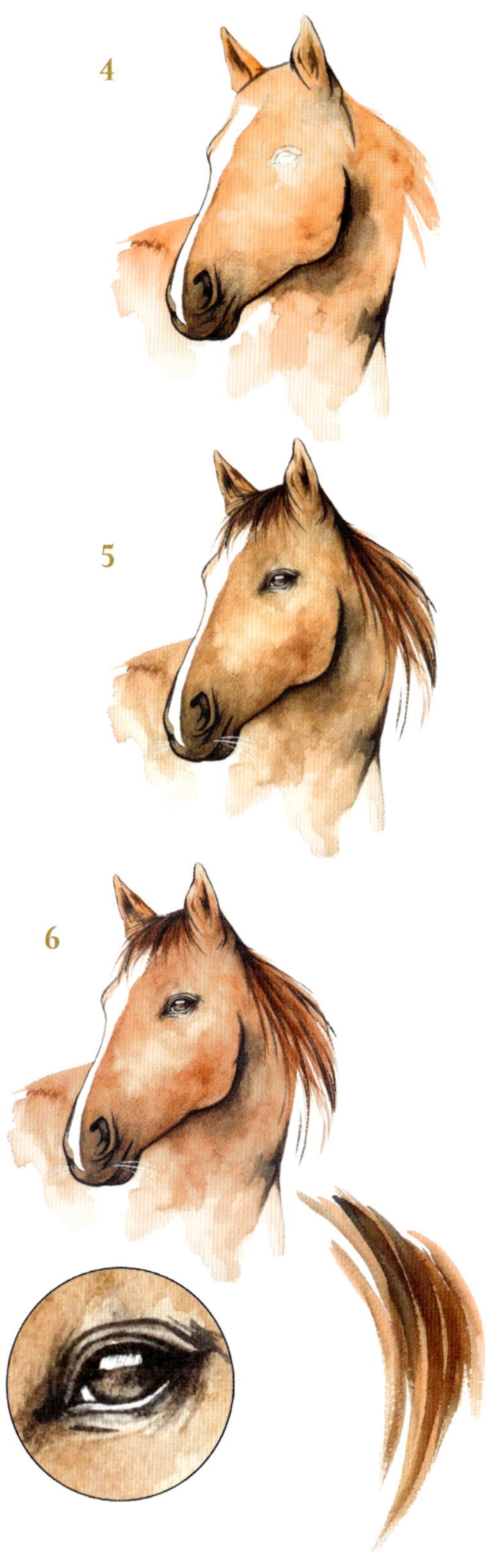

Step 4

You will continue by adding another layer of paint, this time using a 50:50 mixture of Payne's Gray to Raw Umber to further push the dark values. Add this gray and brown paint mixture to the mouth area, neck and ears using a medium-sized round brush. After the layer of paint around the mouth is completely dry, add a saturated amount of Payne's Gray to define the nostril, mouth and darken shadows.

Step 5

For the eye, start with a layer of Raw Umber inside the eye, making sure to leave a highlight at top of the eye. Then paint the rest of the details around the eye using Payne's Gray and Raw Umber. After the layer of Raw Umber on the iris dries, add the pupil using a saturated amount of Payne's Gray paint with a small round brush. You will now need to blend the eye into the rest of the head by adding Raw Umber to the outer eye. Next, paint small whiskers on the horse using white ink or use a gel pen.

Step 6

Add a light wash of Burnt Sienna and Raw Umber to the head and neck of the horse to blend everything together. Use a hair dryer to dry this layer. After that layer is dry, paint the mane using a wet-on-dry technique to create brushstrokes. Create hair marks using Burnt Sienna and then switch to Raw Umber for the topmost hairs.

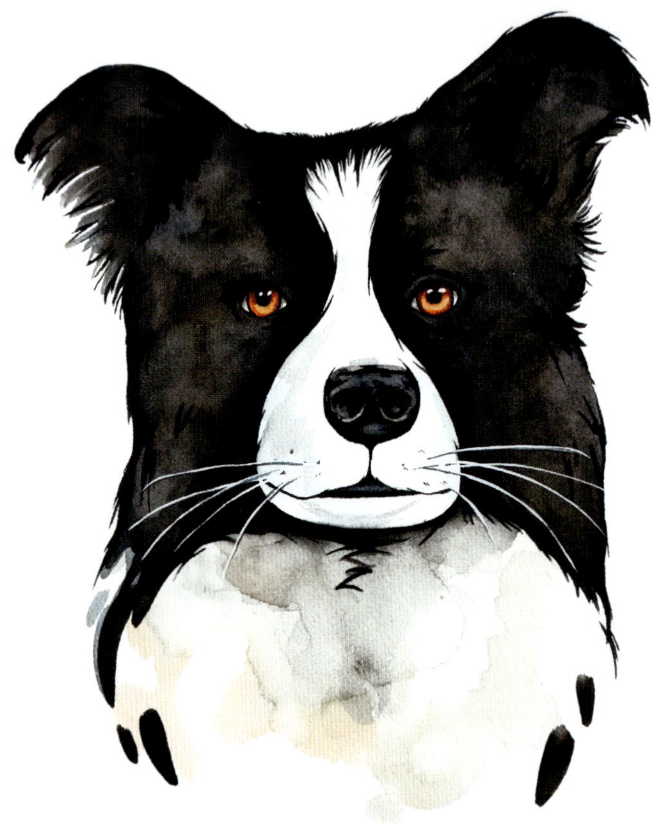

Border Collie

Dogs have lived alongside humans for thousands of years. We first bred them to help us with specific tasks. Border Collies are herding dogs that help keep herds of livestock like sheep safe and move them about the pasture.

In this project, you will be painting an alert Border Collie with black and white fur and bright, amber eyes. The head of the dog is slightly cocked as though it is waiting for its next command. You will start this painting by loosening up and creating multiple loose washes, starting with the light areas first. After the washes dry, you will carefully create the eyes, nose and whiskers.

Lesson

Painting floppy, fluffy ears on a Border Collie

Colors

Yellow Ochre

Raw Umber

Payne's Gray

Burnt Sienna

Brushes

Medium Round Brush

Small Round Brush

Extra Supplies

White ink or gel pen

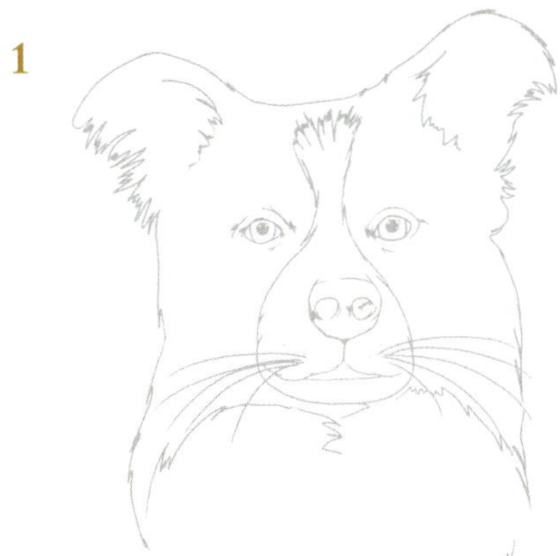

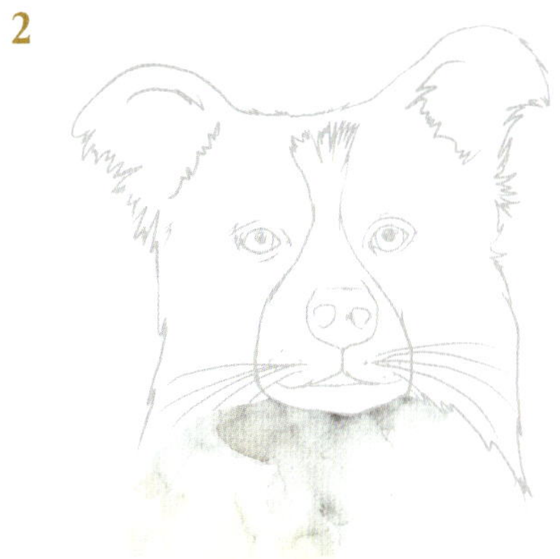

Step 1

Create a drawing of the dog by tracing the drawing template provided on page 175. Keep your lines light by not applying too much pressure.

Step 2

Create a wash on the chest of the dog, starting with a very light wash of Yellow Ochre. While the wash is still wet, use a wet-on-wet technique to add Raw Umber and Payne's Gray below the dog's snout to create a shadow. Add blooms or table salt while the wash is still damp to create texture. If using salt, once the wash is dry, lightly dust it off with your hand.

Step 3

After the last step is dry, fill in the top portion of the dog's head with a large wash of Payne's Gray paint, using a medium round brush. After the majority of the area is filled in, move to a smaller round brush and paint out small hairs on the dog's ears, around the white patch at the center of its face and along the side of its head. To give an impressionistic look to the painting, add a few brushstrokes on top of the light wash using Payne's Gray towards the bottom of the portrait.

Step 4

Now you will be switching to using a wet-on-dry technique, so make sure everything is dry before painting. Start by painting the nose with a medium wash of Payne's Gray paint, and while that layer dries, paint out the mouth of the dog using Payne's Gray as well. After the layer of gray dries on the dog's nose, paint the nostrils with a saturated amount of Payne's Gray. Lastly, use the same color to add a jagged line below the jaw to represent the fur texture there.

Step 5

For the eyes, start by applying Yellow Ochre to the iris and then add Burnt Sienna to the top portion of the iris while things are still wet, making sure to leave highlights in the eye. Using a saturated amount of Payne's Gray paint and a small round brush, paint the pupil and the remaining eye details.

Step 6

Add a very light wash of Payne's Gray to the left side of the dog's muzzle to create a subtle shadow on the white fur. After that dries, switch to a small round brush and add little dots to its snout, and then paint out whiskers using a white gel pen or ink.

4

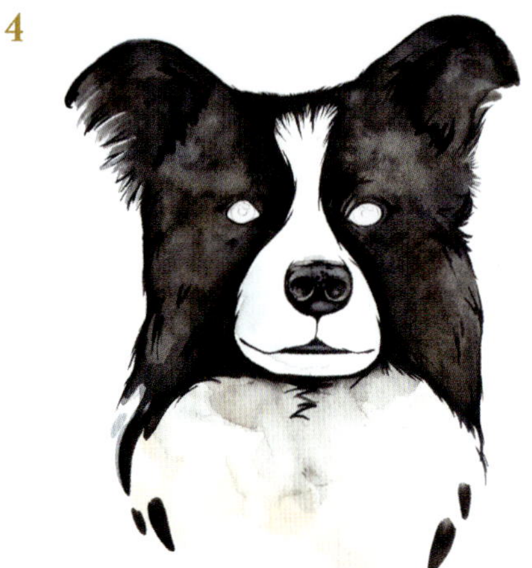

5

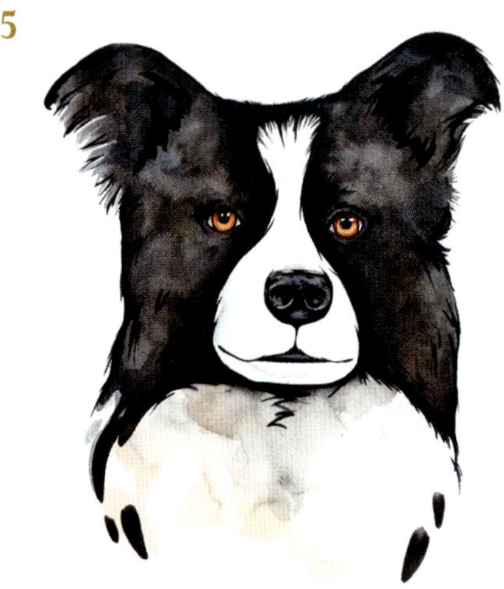

6

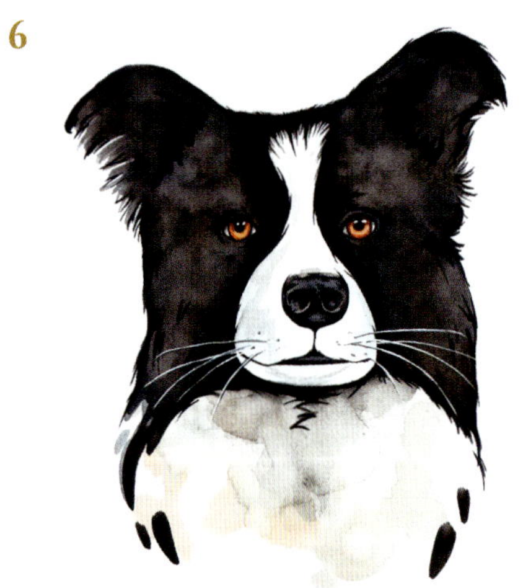

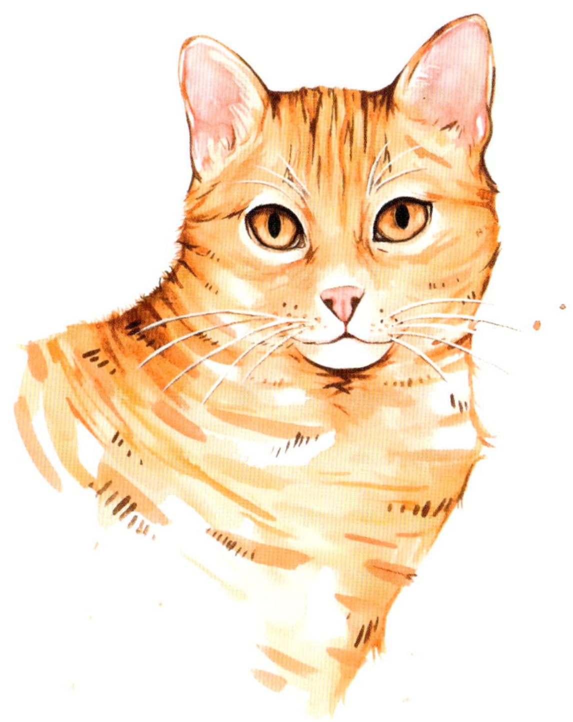

Tabby Cat

These domesticated cats come in many different colors, but they all have a distinctive coat pattern with an M-shaped mark on their heads. Cats are often found on farms alongside other domesticated animals because they help control the mice and rat populations.

The tabby-cat tutorial in this book will be for an orange cat with a layered, stripe pattern. You will start the painting by using a wet-on-wet technique to create soft stripes on the cat. Then you will switch to using a wet-on-dry technique to layer more stripes on top using a variety of orange hues.

Lesson

Combining wet-on-wet and wet-on-dry techniques to create a layered, striped pattern

Colors

Cadmium Yellow Medium Hue

Yellow Ochre

Burnt Sienna

Rose Doré

Payne's Gray

Cadmium Orange Hue

Raw Umber

Brushes

Medium Round Brush

Small Round Brush

Extra Supplies

White ink or gel pen

Step 1

Draw an outline of a tabby cat by tracing the template provided on page 173. You can draw some of the cat's stripes if you would like; otherwise, you can freehand paint the pattern later.

Step 2

The first step of painting this cat is to add a light wash of Cadmium Yellow Medium Hue paint mixed with Yellow Ochre to the portrait of the cat, about a 50:50 mixture. Add this paint to the head and chest of the cat, leaving some white showing through the ears, around its eyes, mouth and on its body.

While the wash is still slightly damp, but not too wet, use a small round brush dipped in Burnt Sienna to paint thin lines, creating a pattern on the cat. Focus the pattern on top of its head and on its back. The lines should be soft but still in a distinctive line shape.

Step 3

Fill in the ears and nose of the cat using Rose Doré paint and a medium round brush. After the first layer of pink dries on the cat's nose, paint some details using a saturated amount of Rose Doré and a small round brush.

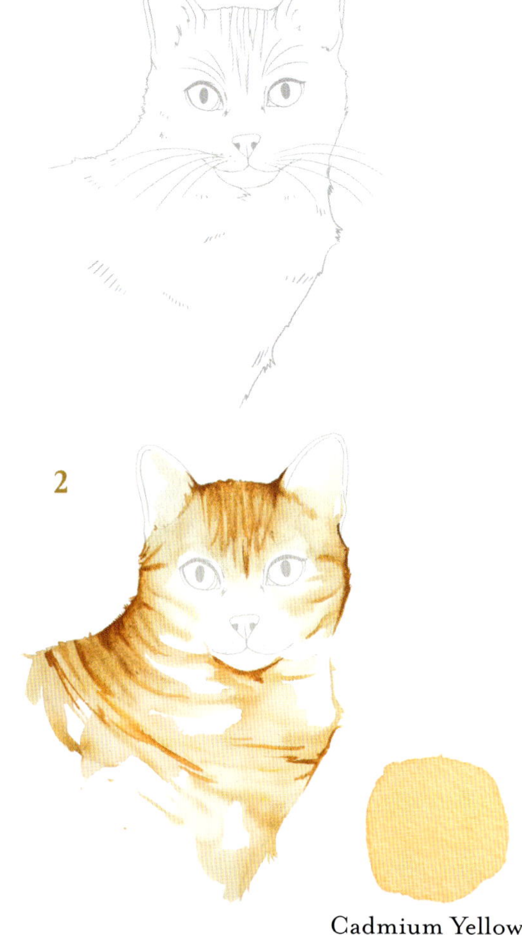

Cadmium Yellow
Medium Hue mixed
with Yellow Ochre

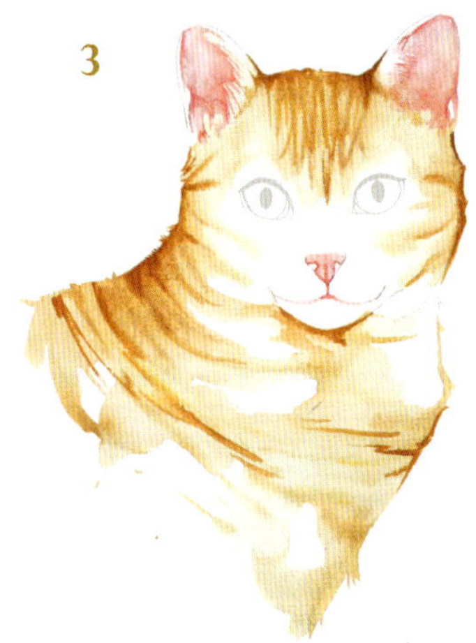

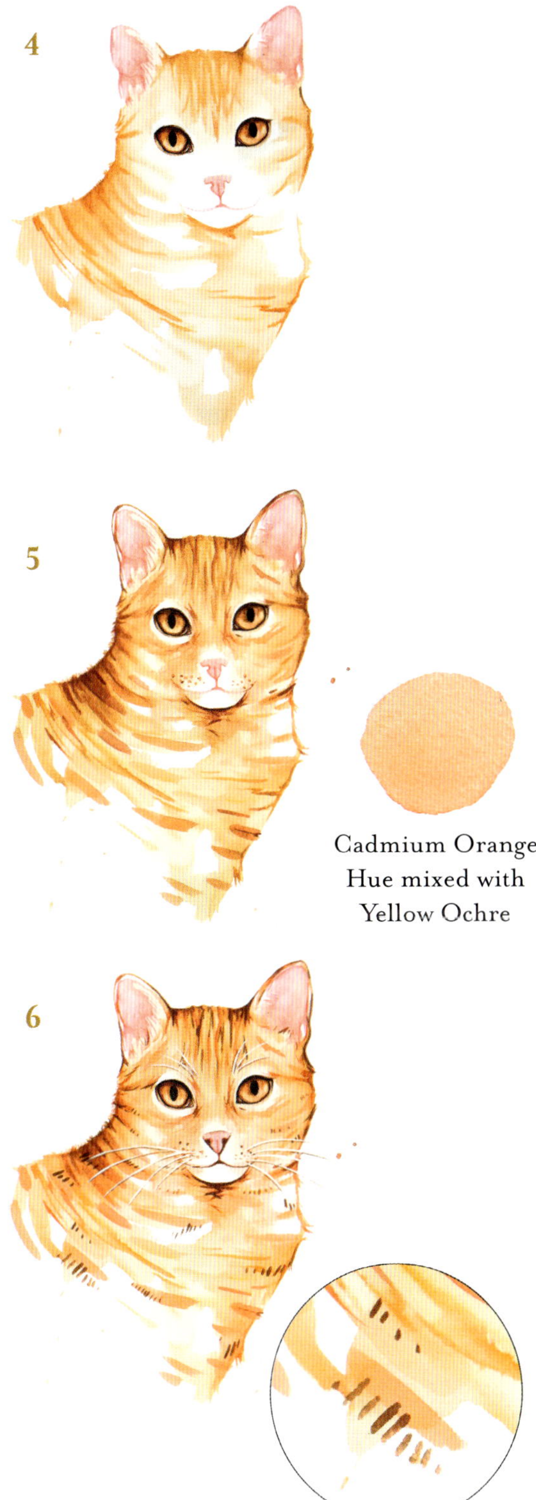

4

5

Cadmium Orange
Hue mixed with
Yellow Ochre

6

Step 4

Next, you will be painting the cat's eyes starting with Yellow Ochre for the base layer. Then add Burnt Sienna to the top portion of the eye. After the first layer of paint in the eyes dries, add a saturated amount of Payne's Gray with a small round brush to the outside of the eye and then paint in a pupil.

Step 5

Mix Yellow Ochre and Cadmium Orange Hue paint together, about a 50:50 mixture. After mixing those two colors, dilute the paint until it appears very light and then add it to the head and body of the cat. Before this wash dries, pull small hairs out on the back of the neck and a few tufts by the chest.

After this light layer of orange is dry, add more stripes to the cat's head using a small round brush and Burnt Sienna paint. For the stripes on the body, use a medium and small round brush to create both thick and thin stripes. Lastly, paint small dots around the cat's mouth with Burnt Sienna.

Step 6

Create small dash lines on the cat's fur with Raw Umber paint using a small round brush. With the same paint and brush, paint out whiskers, more stripes on its forehead and a line under its chin. After that paint dries, add white ink on top of the whiskers to make them pop.

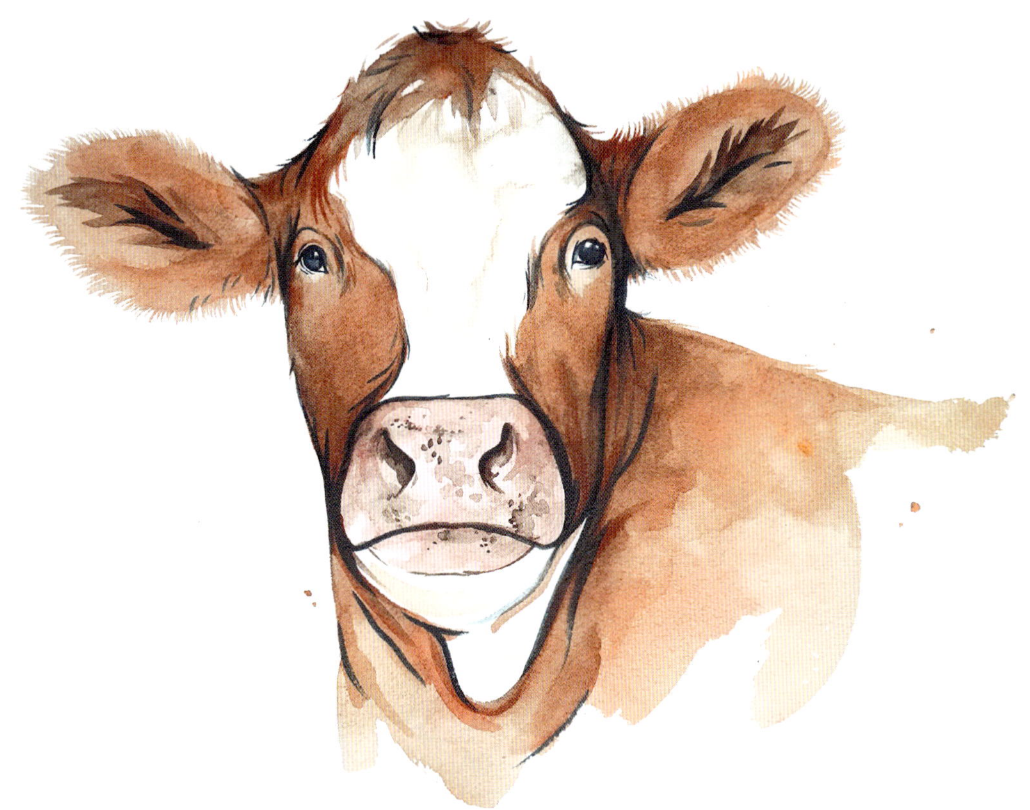

Dairy Cow

The cow you will be painting is a Guernsey, which is a breed of dairy cow. These cows are either a fawn brown or reddish with white marbling or patches. This adorable cow has soft ears and a fluffy patch on the top of its head.

The cow you will be painting in this project will be created using large washes to fill in most of its head and upper body. After creating the large wash, you will paint a detailed, spotted pink nose. Then you will build up shadows around the cow's head to define its shape and lastly add its sweet little eyes.

1

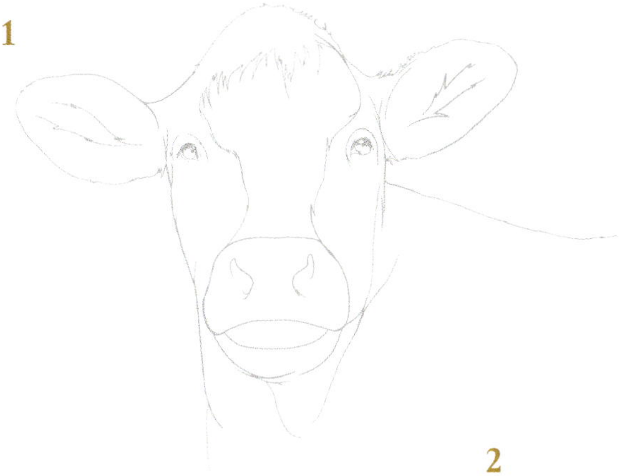

2

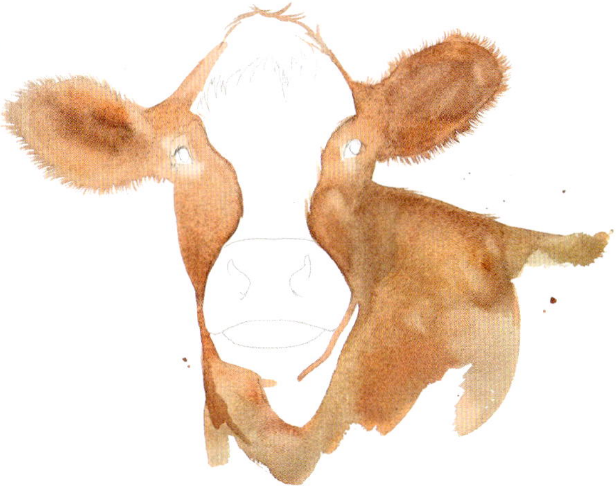

Step 1

Create an outline of a cow using the
template provided on page 175.

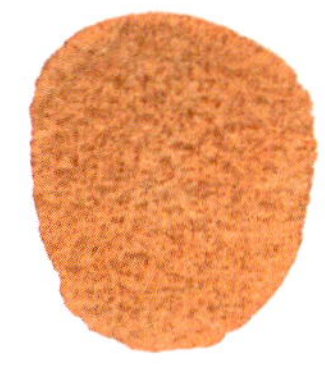

50:50 Yellow Ochre and
Burnt Sienna mixture

Step 2

Mix together a 50:50 mixture of Yellow
Ochre and Burnt Sienna and start applying
paint with a medium round brush, starting
at the cow's head and ending with the loose
wash around its neck and back. While the
wash is still wet, add small hairs around
the cow's ears and on the top of its head
by pulling out each strand.

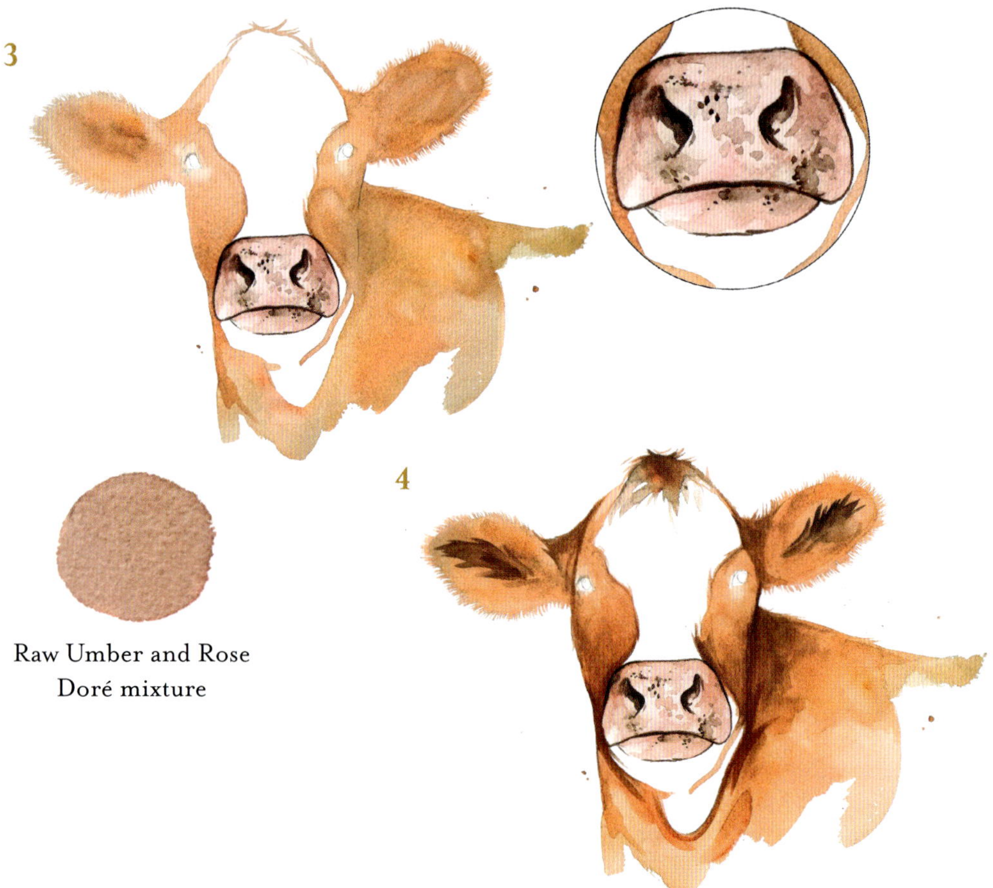

Step 3

Begin by filling the entire nose with a light wash of Rose Doré paint. After that dries, add a light layer of Raw Umber mixed with Rose Doré, about a 50:50 ratio, on top of the first layer, making sure that some of the first layer is peeking through. After things dry, use a small paint brush to outline the nose and mouth with a saturated amount of Raw Umber paint. Lastly, paint the nostrils and some spots on the nose using the same brush and paint.

Step 4

For this step, start by applying a layer of Burnt Sienna to the shadows of the head and neck of the cow. Add some hairs to the top of the cow's head using Raw Umber and a medium-sized round brush, and, while the paint is still wet, dab in a small amount of Burnt Sienna. Lastly, add Raw Umber to the inner ear of the cow using a medium round brush.

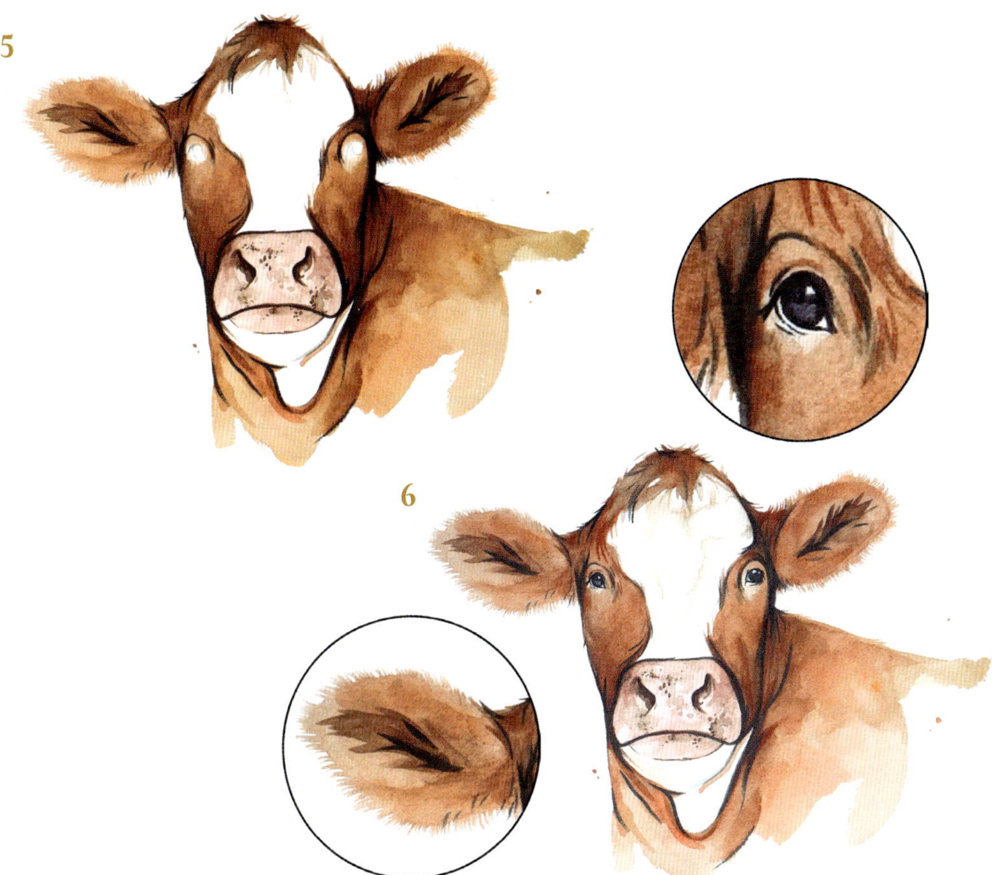

Step 5

In this next step, you will be adding the last layer of shadows to really increase the contrast on the cow. Using Payne's Gray paint, paint around the head of the cow and then add hair marks with Payne's Gray to the top of its head, ears and neck.

Step 6

Next, use Payne's Gray to paint the eyes of the cow, making sure to leave a highlight in them. Add a very light wash of Yellow Ochre to the center of the cow's head. The fur here on the cow is white, but you don't want your painting to appear flat, so adding a light layer of color will help provide more depth to your whites. And now your cow is complete!

Thank You

I remember when I was in elementary school, I would spend hours sitting at the dining table with numerous how-to art books spread across the table, trying to re-create the images (usually without reading any of the instructions because what eight-year-old has time for that?). I would never have imagined that one day I would be writing my own how-to art book for others to follow and gain inspiration from. I want to give a huge thank-you to Page Street Publishing for making this book possible.

Thank you to my parents for always supporting my artistic pursuits, from purchasing art supplies for me when I was young to attending my latest gallery exhibitions. Mom, you have always been my number one fan and would proudly display any of my art, even if it was just a stick figure. Thank you to all of my other family members and friends who have supported me and bought and shared my art throughout my artistic journey. It really means a lot to me.

Lastly, thank you to my husband, Sam, for your consistent enthusiasm and encouragement. It has been a joy to be the partner of a fellow artist and maker. Thank you for building me a beautiful new art studio as I wrote this book so I no longer have to paint on the floor. I promise I will paint you an otter this year.

About the Author

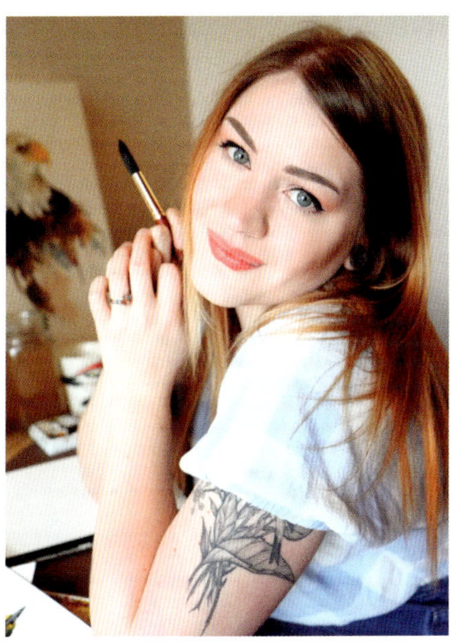

Kiley Busko is a watercolor artist focusing on painting birds and other wildlife. She is from Sioux Falls, South Dakota and currently lives in Minnesota. She has her art displayed at multiple galleries and shops throughout the Midwest. She teaches beginner-to-intermediate-level classes online through the platform Patreon and has a YouTube channel offering free watercolor lessons and insights on what it's like to have a career as an artist.

When she is not painting in her studio, she enjoys spending time out in nature going on hikes, cycling and birdwatching. She is also an award-winning fine woodworker and Windgate Fellow, and she often collaborates with her husband on building mid-century modern-inspired furniture and décor.

For more information about Kiley, you can visit her website at www.paintedwing.com or follow her on social media. Use the hashtag #paintedwingclub to share your paintings created following the lessons found in this book.

◎ Instagram.com/painted_wing

▶ Youtube.com/@PaintedWing

⬤ Patreon.com/Painted_Wing

Index

Striped Chipmunk, 93–95, 161

stripe pattern, 27

stripes technique, 56

supplies, 8–12

T

Tabby Cat, 139–141, 173

techniques, 14–21

  animal features, 22–27

  blooms, 18

  dry brush, 19

  light values and, 14–15

  loose and tight, 21

  mark-making, 19, 20

  salt, 19

simple wing, 25

splatters, 20

stippling, 48, 50

stripes, 27, 56

washes, 16–18

wet-on-dry, 16, 17, 18

wet-on-wet, 16, 17

templates, 12–13, 151–175

template supplies, 12

tight watercolors, 21

towels, 12

tracing images, 13

turtle, 54–57, 155

V

value, 14–15

variegated wash, 17

W

washes, 16–18

water cups, 12

wet-on-dry technique, 16, 17, 18

wet-on-wet technique, 16, 17

white ink/paint, 11

White-Lipped Snail, 48–50, 153

White-Tailed Deer Fawn, 102–104, 163

wings, 25

wren, 63–65, 155

Templates

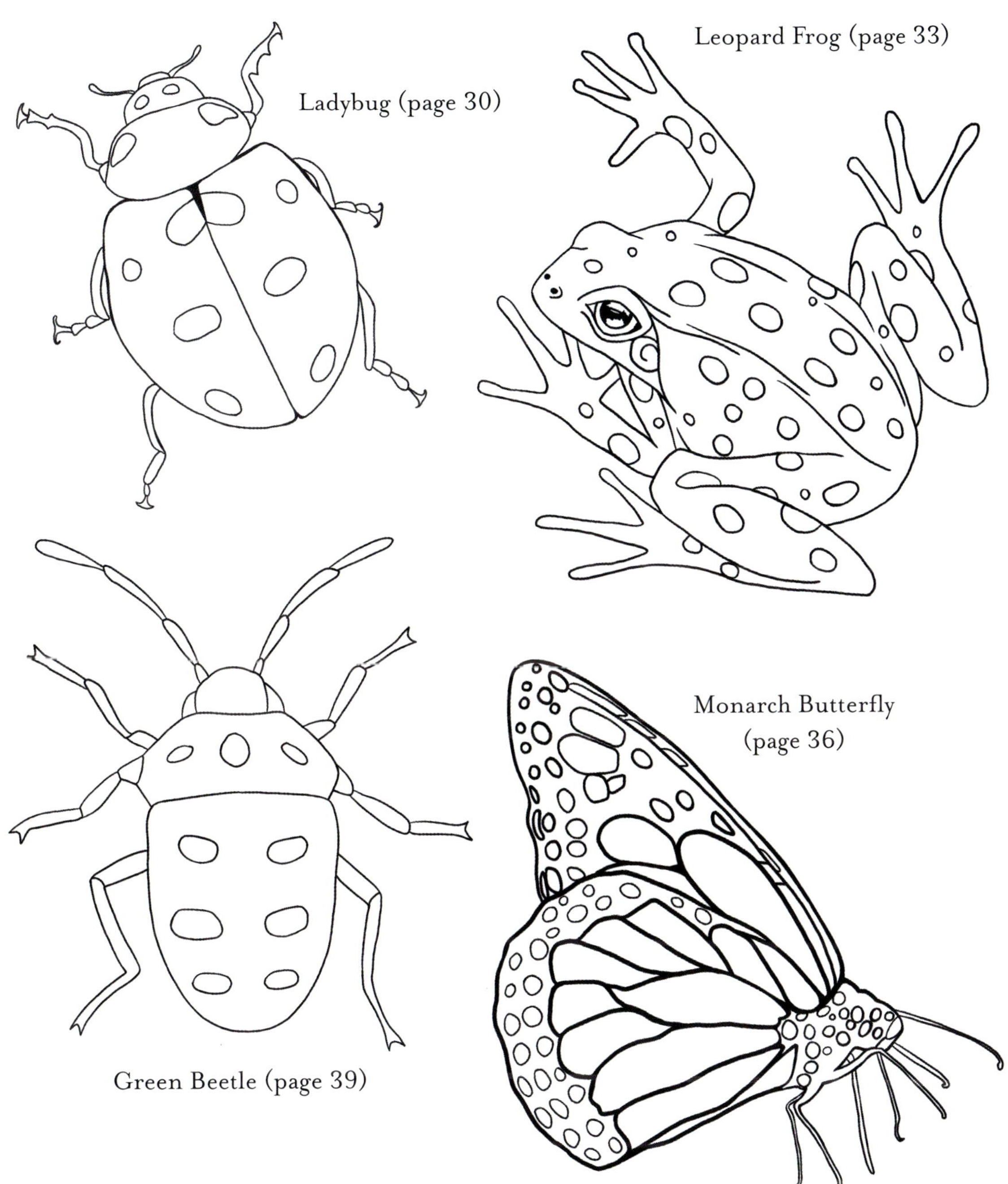

Ladybug (page 30)

Leopard Frog (page 33)

Green Beetle (page 39)

Monarch Butterfly
(page 36)

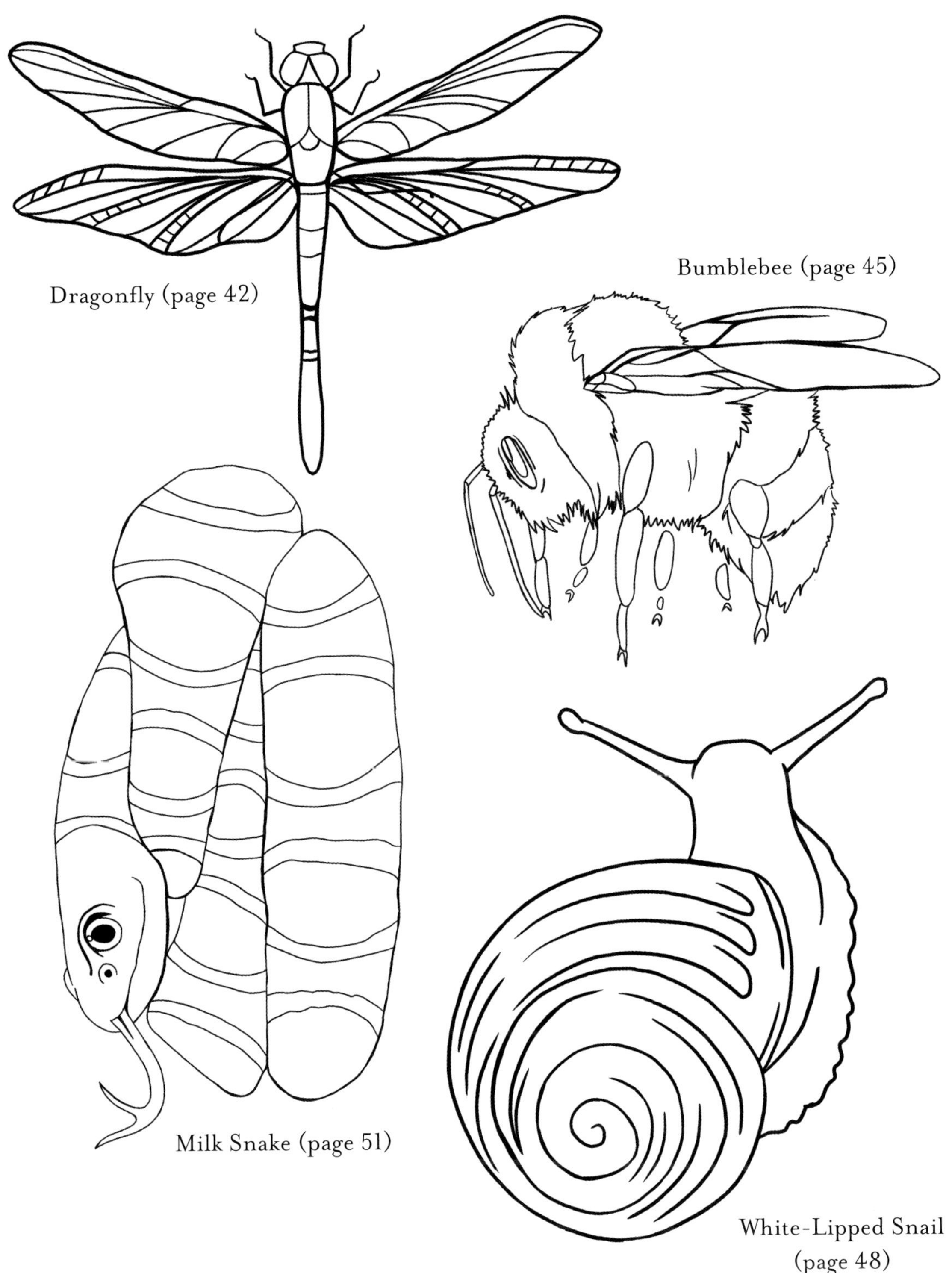

Dragonfly (page 42)

Bumblebee (page 45)

Milk Snake (page 51)

White-Lipped Snail (page 48)

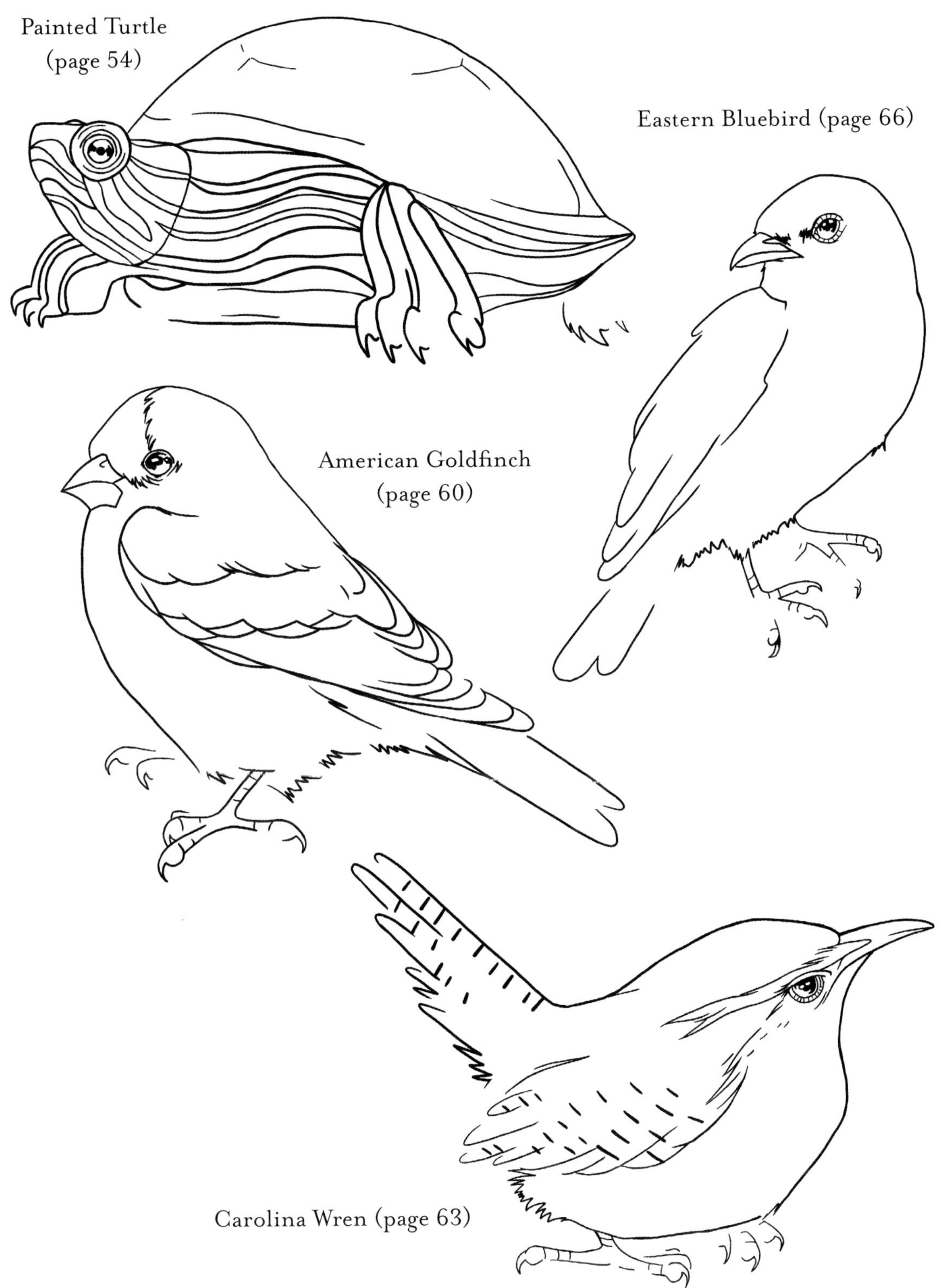

Painted Turtle
(page 54)
Eastern Bluebird (page 66)
American Goldfinch
(page 60)
Carolina Wren (page 63)

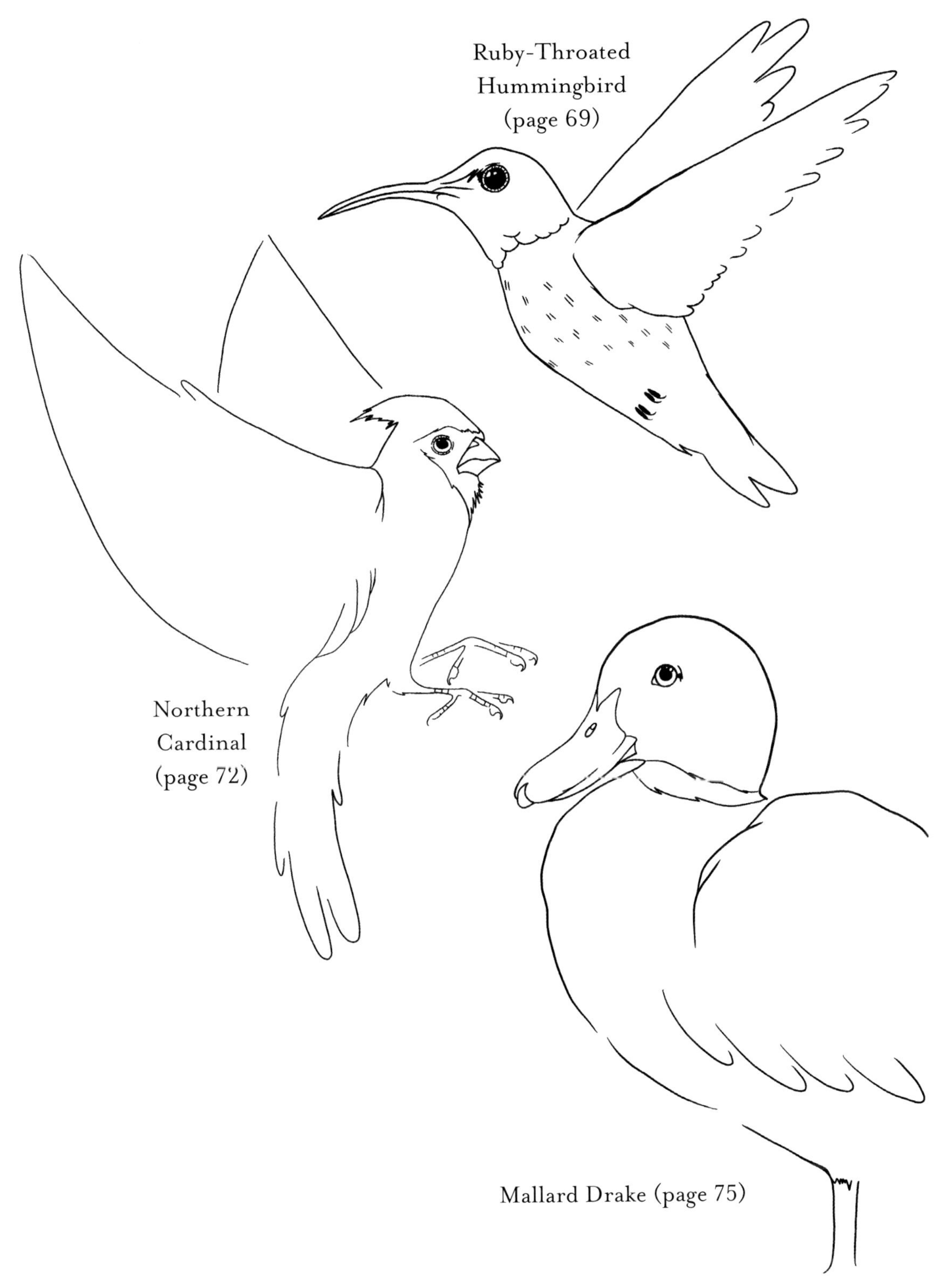

Ruby-Throated
Hummingbird
(page 69)

Northern
Cardinal
(page 72)

Mallard Drake (page 75)

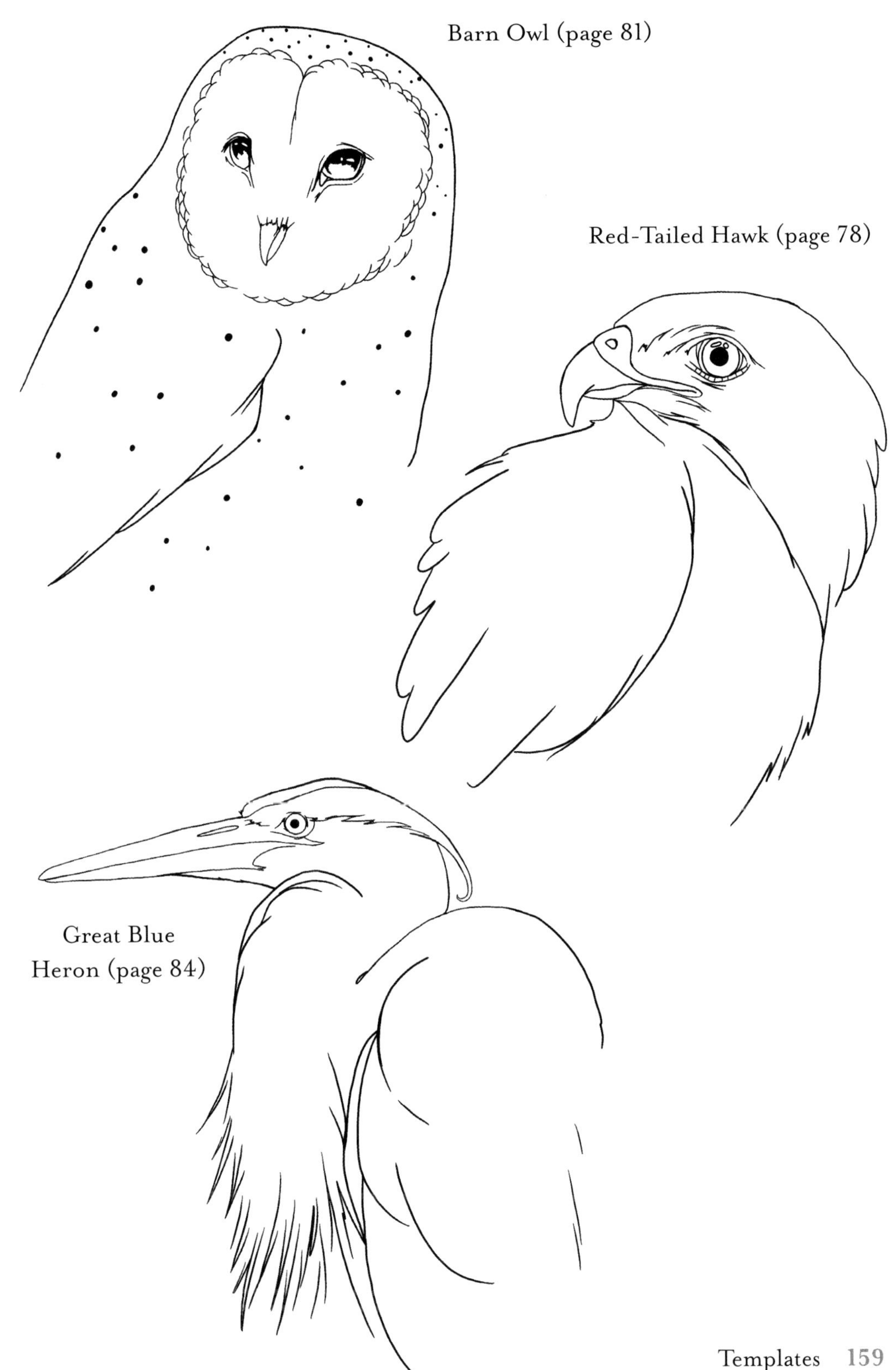

Barn Owl (page 81)
Red-Tailed Hawk (page 78)
Great Blue
Heron (page 84)

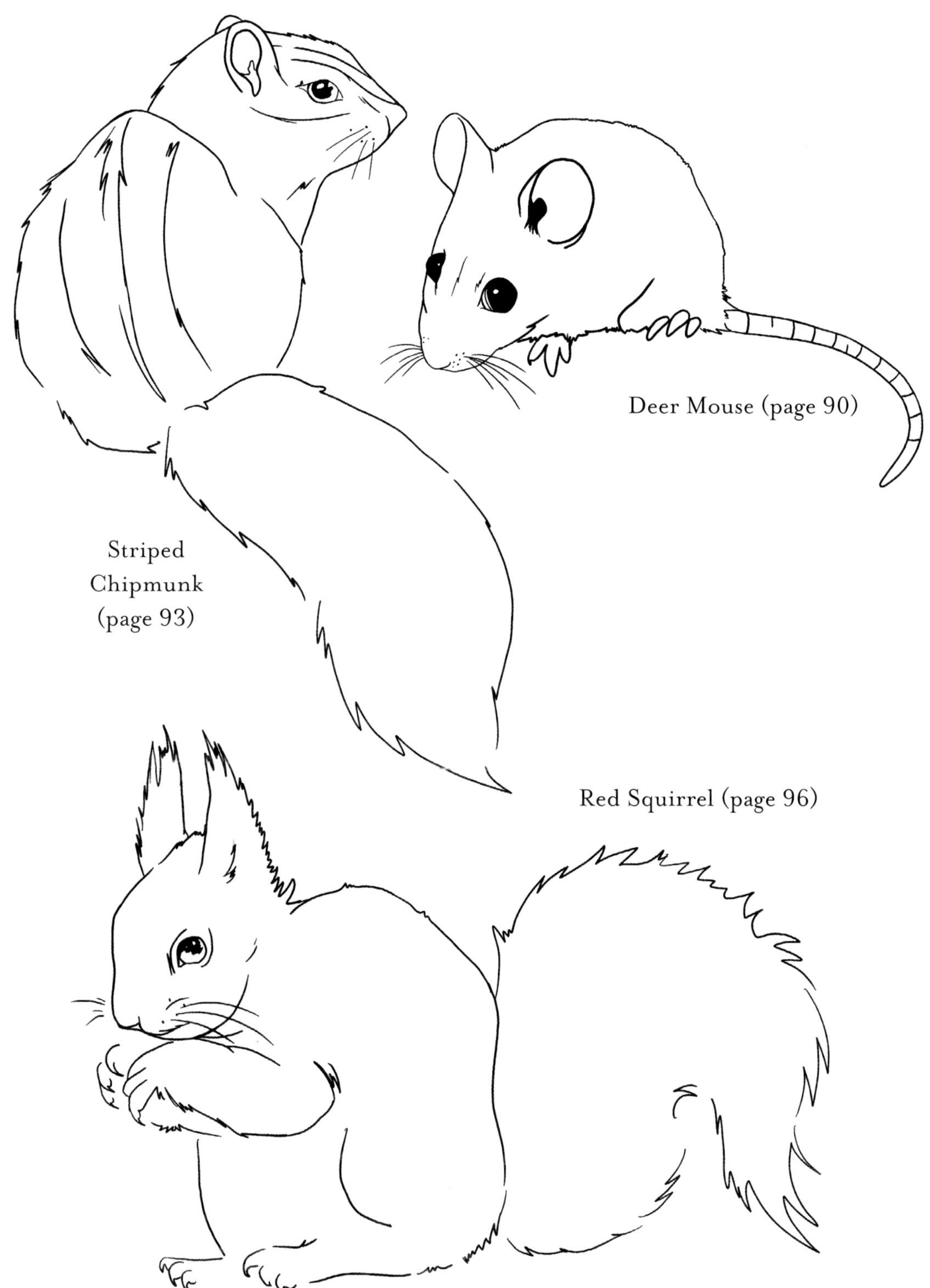

Deer Mouse (page 90)
Striped Chipmunk (page 93)
Red Squirrel (page 96)

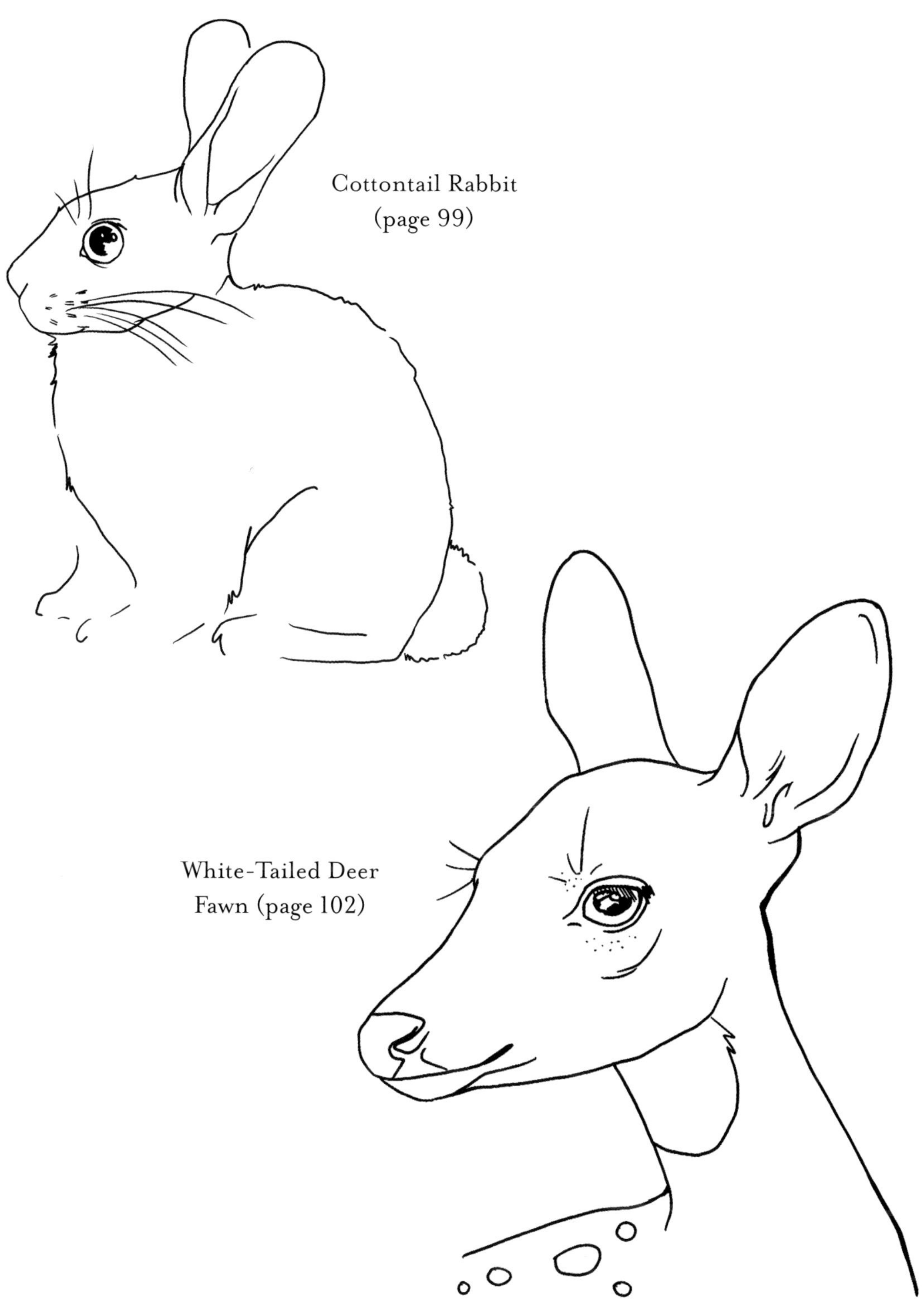

Cottontail Rabbit
(page 99)
White-Tailed Deer
Fawn (page 102)

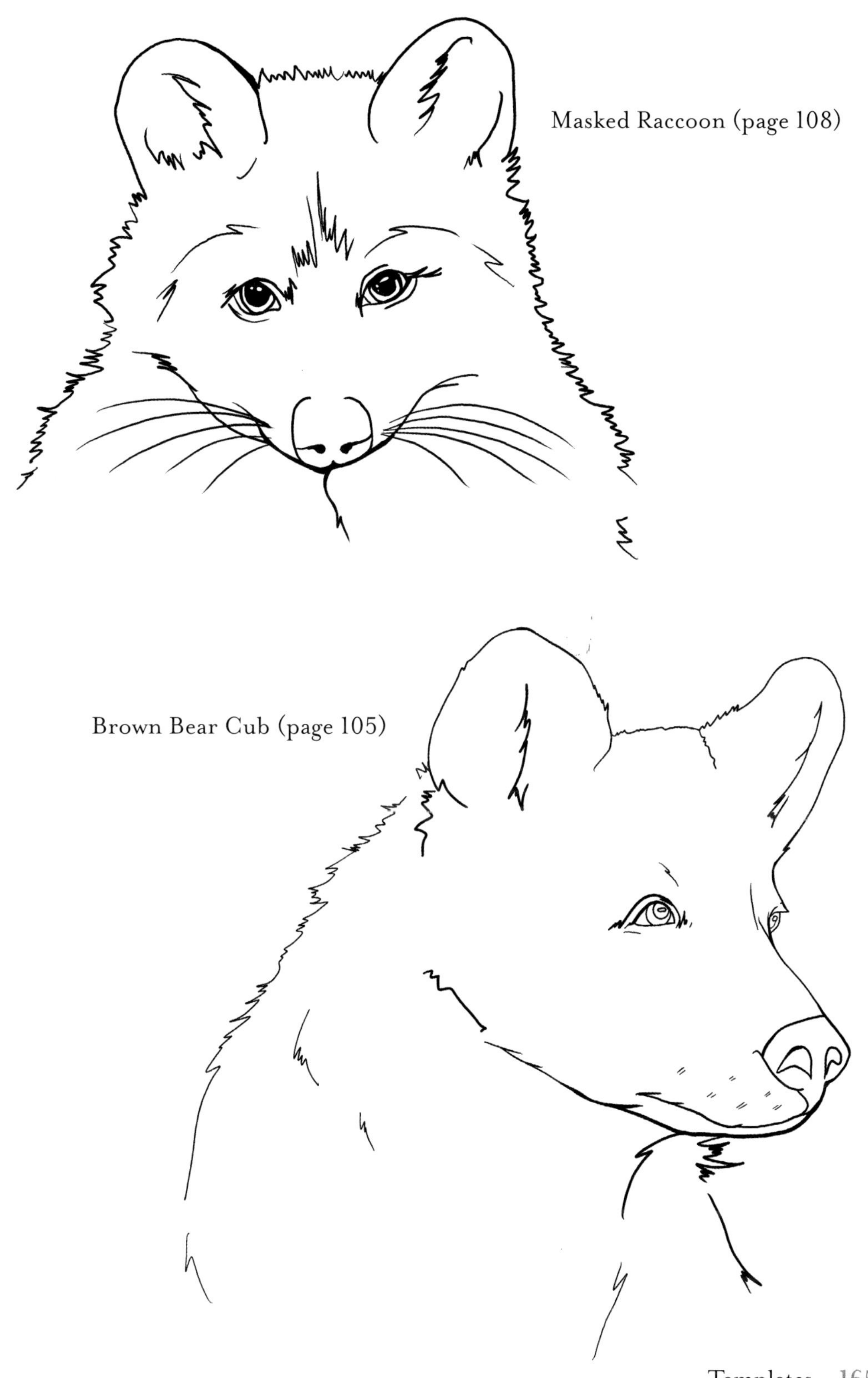

Masked Raccoon (page 108)
Brown Bear Cub (page 105)

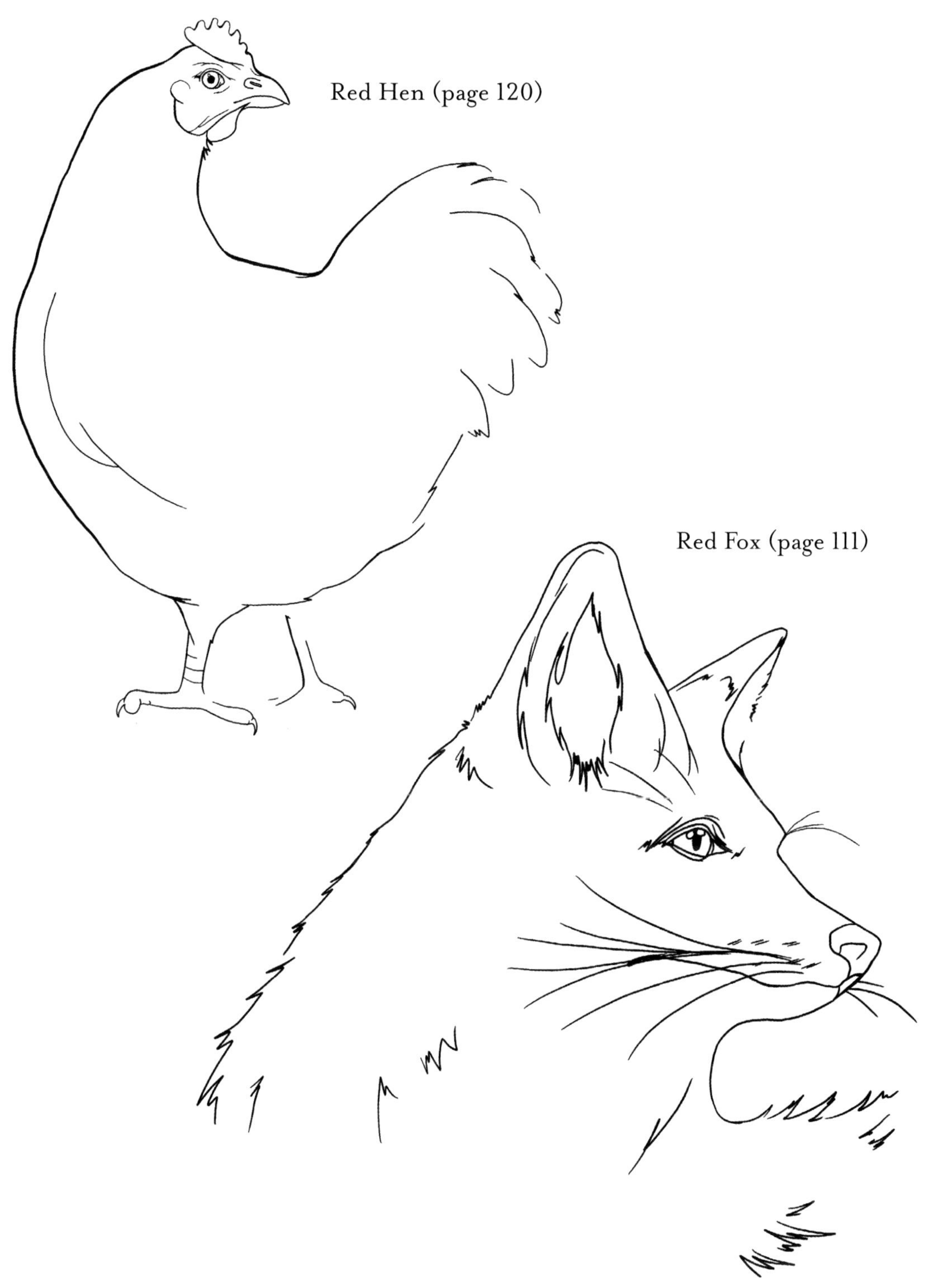

Red Hen (page 120)
Red Fox (page 111)

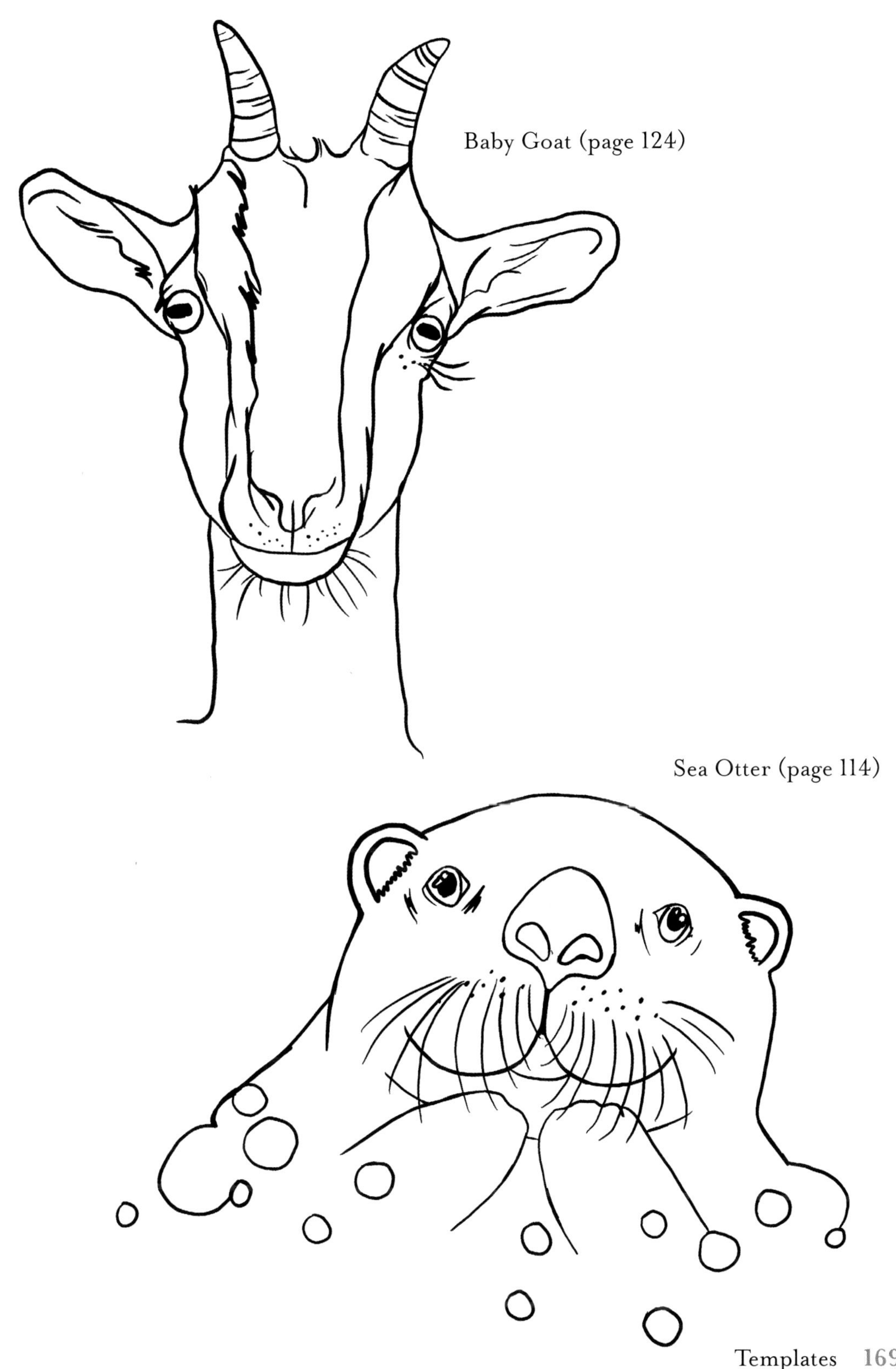

Baby Goat (page 124)
Sea Otter (page 114)

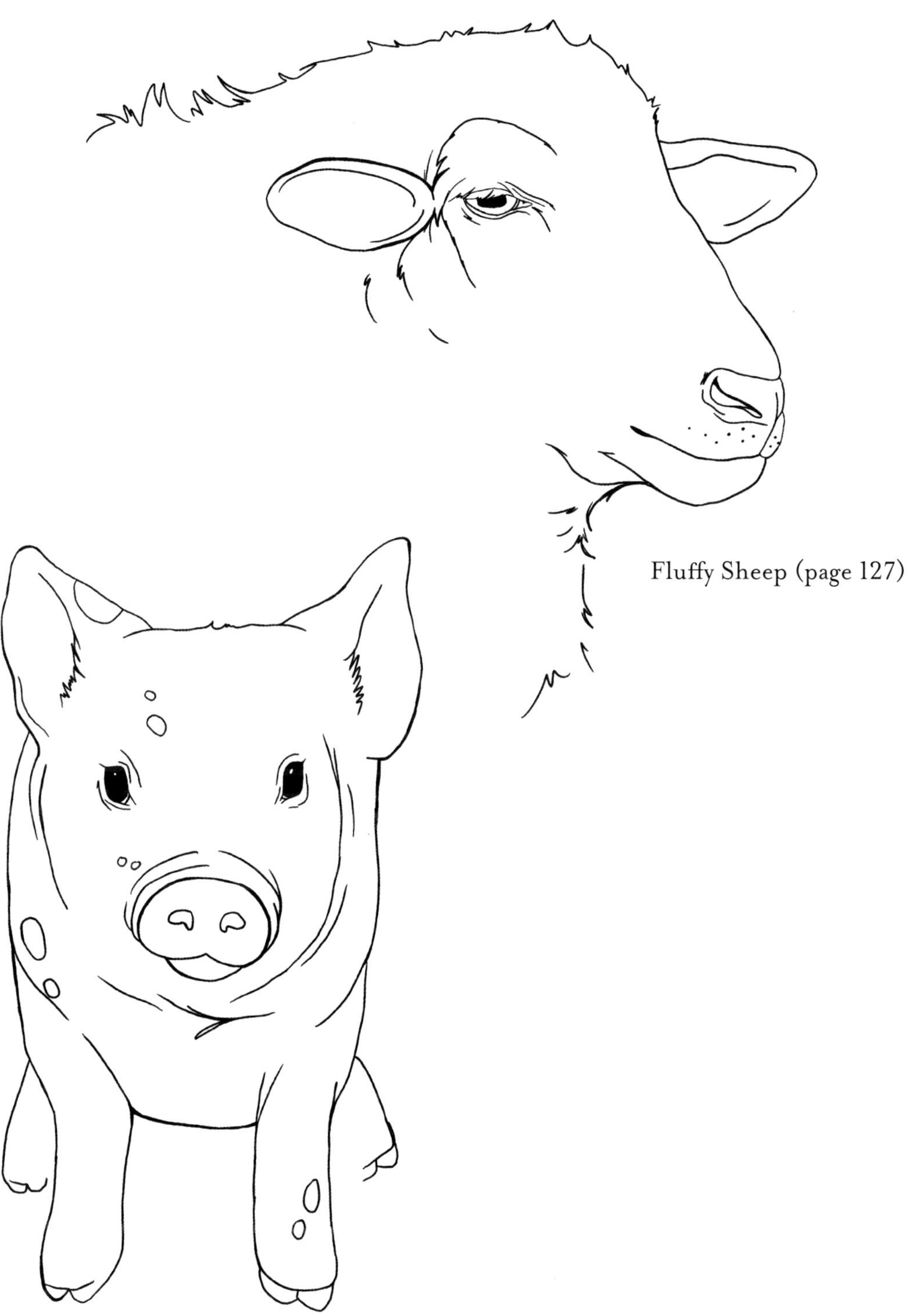

Fluffy Sheep (page 127)

Muddy Piglet (page 130)

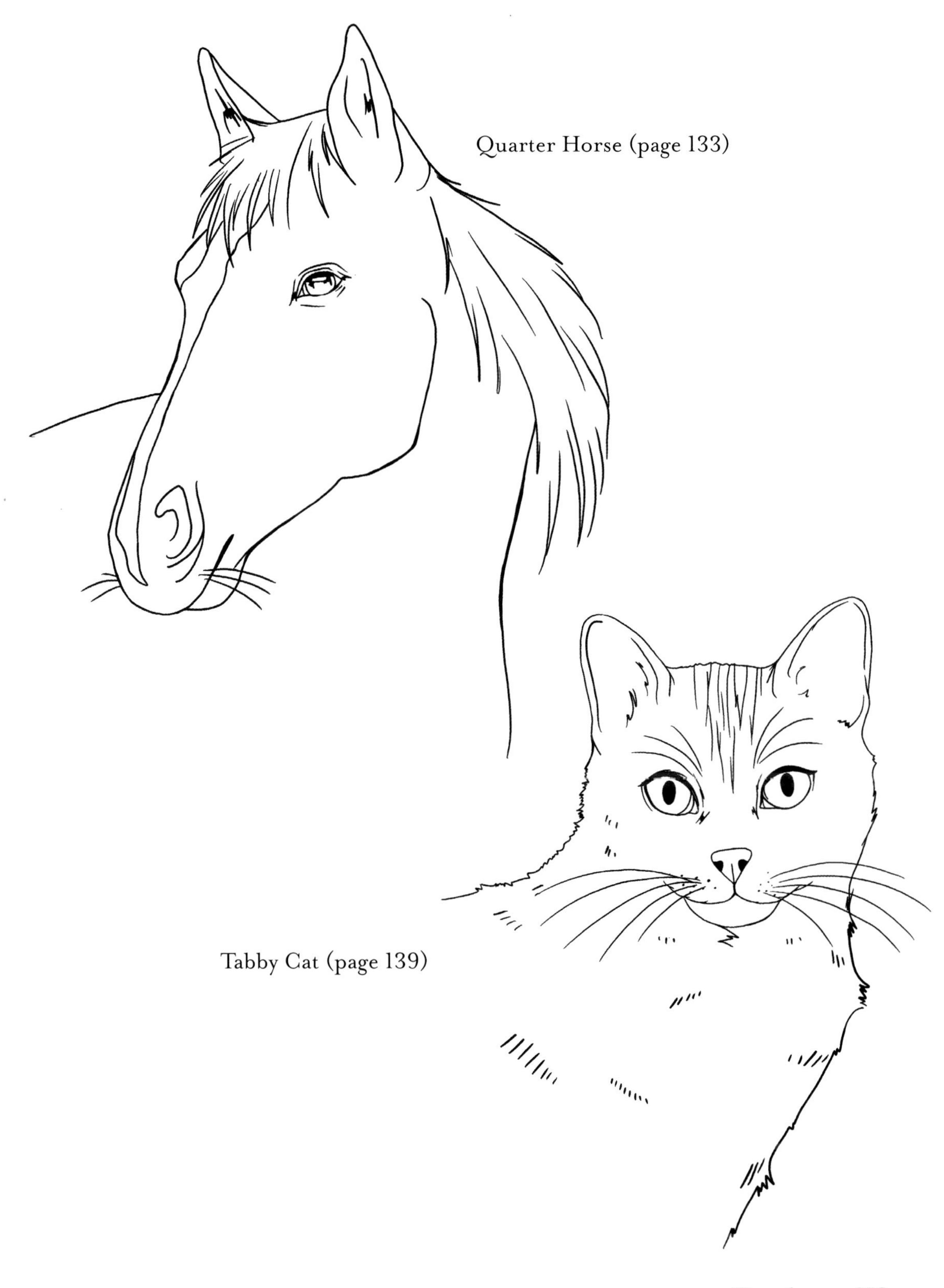

Quarter Horse (page 133)
Tabby Cat (page 139)

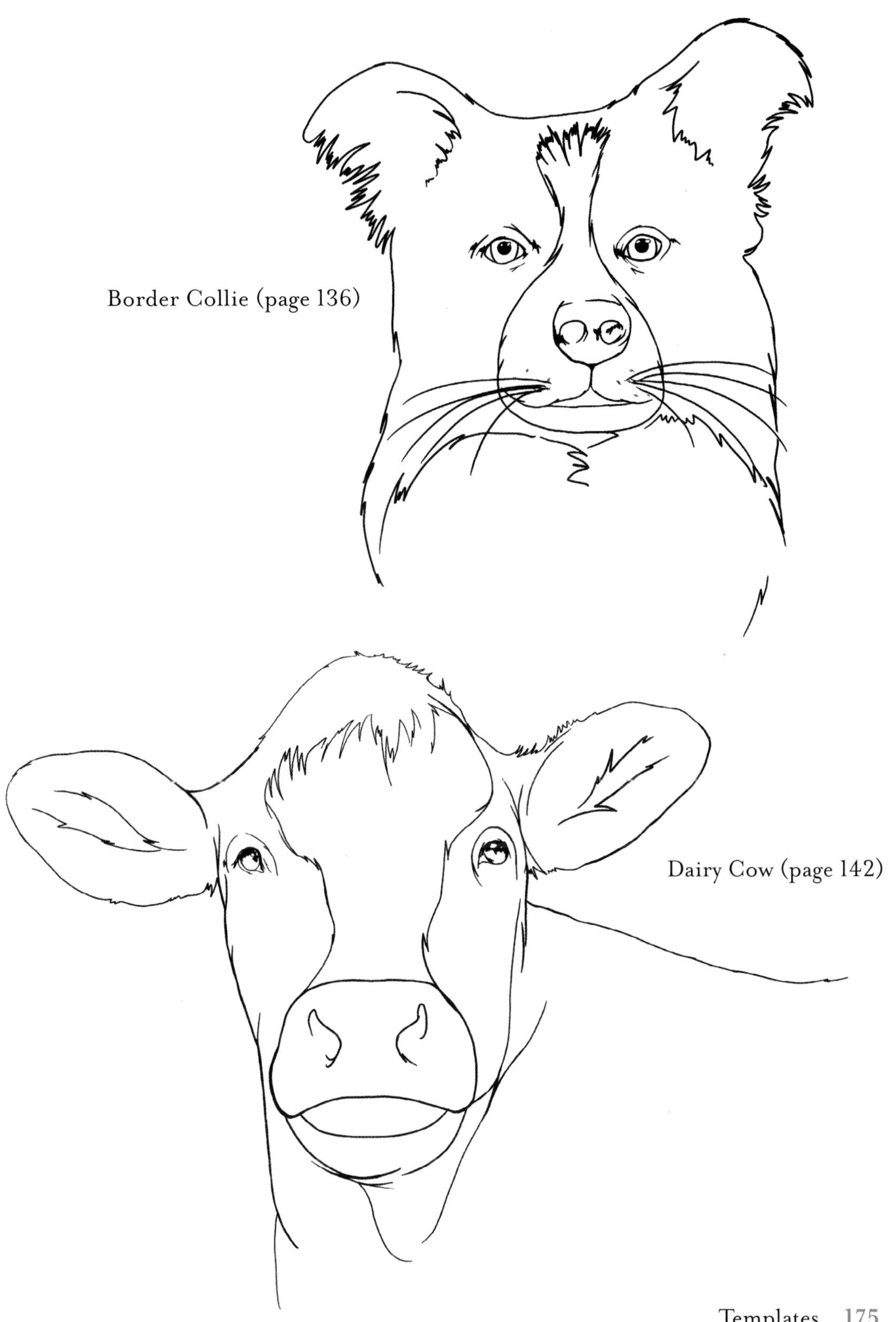

Border Collie (page 136)
Dairy Cow (page 142)